D0838471

KACHINAS
IN THE
PUEBLO
WORLD

*Edited
by Polly
Schaafsma*

KACHINAS IN THE PUEBLO WORLD

University of New Mexico Press

ALBUQUERQUE

Library of Congress Cataloging-in-
Publication Data

Kachinas in the Pueblo world / edited by Polly Schaafsma. —
1st ed.
    p.   cm.
  Includes bibliographical references and index.
  ISBN 0-8263-1472-4
  1. Kachinas.   2. Pueblo Indians—Religion and
mythology.
I. Schaafsma, Polly.
E99.P9K33 1994
299'.784—dc20   93-34920
                                        CIP

CONTENTS

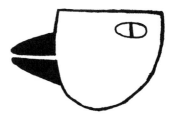

In memory of Fred Eggan

KACHINAS
IN THE
PUEBLO
WORLD

PREFACE

T HIS VOLUME is the outgrowth of a three-day seminar, World View and Ritual: Kachinas in the Pueblo World, that took place at the Museum of Indian Arts and Culture in Santa Fe, New Mexico, in October 1991. The conference was organized for Recursos de Santa Fe by Ellen Bradbury and myself with the competent coordination of Rae Marie Taylor. The seminar was designed to bring together scholars from various subdisciplines in anthropology who had specialized knowledge of the multifaceted aspects of kachinas. It was felt that this meeting would provide the possibility of a dynamic exchange for scholars, who often conduct their research in relative isolation from each other and who have approached the subject from diverse perspectives. Conference papers ranged from those that discuss kachina images in the archaeological record and evidence for kachina origins and development, to the meaning of kachinas for contemporary Pueblo people and how the kachina society and its images have been affected historically by Hispanics and Anglo-Americans. This collection of essays discusses kachinas throughout their geographic distribution, and from their beginnings through the last decade.

The conference was dedicated to the life and work of the distinguished anthropologist Fred Eggan, who had made an enthusiastic commitment to participate in the seminar and submitted a paper during the early planning stages. His classic study of western Pueblo social organization remains the foundation for all subsequent studies on the subject. Fred's unexpected death occurred suddenly before the conference date, and his paper was read by Meridel Rubenstein to initiate the seminar.

Special thanks go to Ellen Bradbury, who suggested a conference on kachinas in the first place, and to Sally Cole of Grand Junction, Colorado, and Kerry David of Polacca, Arizona, whose participation in the conference was much appreciated. I am especially grateful to Stephen Becker, Bruce Bernstein, and Curtis Schaafsma for their support and assistance. Preparation of Fred Eggan's paper for publication was facilitated by Recursos staff and volunteers. I also want to thank an unknown outside reviewer who provided helpful comments on the papers.

Introduction

POLLY SCHAAFSMA

T HE RELIGION of the Pueblo Indians of the
American Southwest is integral to life itself.
The Pueblo lifeway demands the maintenance of
a harmonious relationship and balance between
man and the cosmos, as well as between people.
Instrumental in maintaining harmony and balance are group ritual knowledge and ceremonies.
These ceremonies and rituals are formulistic and
compulsive and include offerings that if properly
performed are effectual in assuring rain, good
crops, and health, and the general well-being of
the people. In addition, religious performances
make visible the invisible, and define and re-
inforce through song, dance, and ritual drama,
Pueblo values and cosmological views. Poetry,
origin myths, and oral histories provide an ex-
planatory framework against which the dramas
are organized and enacted. Prominent in many of
the rituals, dances, and dramas are the kachinas,
masked supernaturals that visit the pueblos and
bridge the worlds of men and gods.

According to one Zuni story, the first kachinas,
the Kokkokshi (see Wright, this volume), had
their origins among the Zuni themselves:

> During their search for the middle the Zunis had to
> ford a stream. The first group of women to cross,
> seeing their children transformed in midstream into
> frogs and water snakes, became frightened and
> dropped them, and they escaped into the water.
> The bereaved mothers mourned for their lost chil-
> dren, so the twin heroes were sent to see what had
> become of them. They found them in a house be-

neath the surface of Whispering Waters. . . . They had been transformed into the katcinas, beautiful with valuable beads and feathers and rich clothing." (Bunzel 1932a:516)

Bunzel subsequently notes, however, that identification of the dead with the kachinas is not complete, as Zunis offer prayer sticks both to the ancients *and to the kachinas.*" The kachinas are said to reside at some distance from each village, sometimes in lakes or on mountain tops, and in general they are, in accordance with the Zuni story, associated with ancestral spirits, clouds, and rain. Accordingly, their visits, in addition to being a source of enjoyment, assure an abundance of crops and good health.

At Zuni the kachinas are known as "raw people who wear masks and dance all the time" (Tedlock 1979:500). They may assume a variety of forms, including that of ducks when they travel to and from Zuni, but here and elsewhere their behavior among themselves is humanlike, and a variety of stories from different pueblos describe how the kachinas themselves, masked and anthropomorphic in form, once visited the pueblos. For various reasons these visits from the real kachinas stopped, but the people were instructed in the making of masks with which to impersonate them. In this way, through the power of the mask, the spirits of the kachinas return via the dancers to bring their blessings to the village and serve as messengers between the Pueblo people and their gods.

The mask is the substance of the kachina, brought to life by the wearer in the context of ritual and ceremony. The mask disguises and is sometimes thought to transform the individual dancer into the spirit represented (see Tedlock, this volume, for further discussion). The mask insures its owner of "powerful supernatural connections" that will determine his status after death. Although kachinas are in general regarded as beneficent, at the same time, the mask, as the embodiment of supernatural power, also possesses

dangerous attributes, and stories of masks sticking to the face and killing the wearer are not uncommon. In terms of dance and ritual drama the use of masks suggests the miraculous. It powerfully creates an aesthetic distance that serves to remove the masked actor from daily life, communicating with great conviction the presence of supernatural powers. Masked kachina impersonators not only impress their audiences with supernatural presence but also at the same time evoke fear, respect, entertain, and amuse as the case may be, and overall facilitate the communication of cosmological belief systems, social values, and influence natural forces.

Masking in itself is a universal practice common to societies all over the world. Today and prehistorically a rich tradition of masking prevailed in Mexico, a tradition that was nevertheless substantially altered by the Spanish conquest (Esser 1988). In the Southwest masks are unevenly represented in the archaeological record. Among the Anasazi they occur only rarely before the thirteenth century: possibly on an occasional Basketmaker anthropomorph, and even more rarely among later Anasazi figures or possibly on figurines. In Mimbres pottery painting, however, a small number of masks are convincingly represented, and in Jornada-style Mogollon rock art sometime after ca. A.D. 1050 masks are found in significant numbers. These southern masks and their stylistic and iconographic context initiate the art tradition we find in the Pueblo world after A.D. 1300, in which kachina masks are an important element.

These essays, as individual papers and as a collected work, also reflect changing concerns of anthropologists regarding kachinas. Unlike many earlier works which are focused primarily on description, from the "field-guide" classificatory approach to books with expanded descriptions that include ritual contexts, the issues explored here include the deeper meaning of the kachina concept, metaphorical symbolism, kachinas as part of a broader Pueblo world-view, the social implications of the kachina organization, and the agents of change. Lack of consensus on various issues often relates to the differing routes of exploration followed by individual scholars. Past major works on kachinas have dealt primarily with the ethnographic aspects of kachinas among the western Pueblos (Anderson 1951, 1960; Bunzel 1932*d;* Fewkes 1897, 1903; Earle and Kennard 1938; Washburn 1980; Wright 1973, 1985), or with Hopi kachina dolls (Colton 1959; Wright 1965, 1977). More recently research has also focused on exploring evidence for the kachina society and its origin and development as evidenced in the archaeological record (Adams 1991; Cole 1989, 1992; Hays 1989; Schaafsma 1992*b;* Schaafsma and Schaafsma 1974). The essays that make up this volume, through their diverse perspectives provide a multifaceted view of the kachina phenomenon. Varied perspectives contribute to a dynamic dialogue on the kachina topic.

General themes that run through various papers include commentary on kachina origins or precedents for the society's development, the social implications inherent in its structure and function within a pueblo village, possible prehistoric ideographic relationships beyond the Pueblo area, and continuity and change in the organization through time and space. The issue of change contributes to problems and potential pitfalls in attempts to identify specific kachinas in their archaeological manifestations. Dynamism and innovation as exemplified through pottery decoration, rock art, kiva murals, and in historic masks and costume changes have characterized kachina iconography from its inception. Kachina imagery presents a shifting suite of mask iconography through time, but one through which can be traced, nevertheless, patterns and symbols consistent with those on modern masks and other elements of costuming.

Fred Eggan, Louis Hieb, and Edmund Ladd address the meaning of kachinas among contemporary western Pueblos. In the opening chapter Eggan presents an overview of the Hopi world.

He establishes the context of the kachinas as mediators, messengers, and bringers of clouds and moisture within the framework of Hopi myth / history, other Hopi supernaturals, social organization, and the natural / sacred landscape of northern Arizona. Eggan's essay thus sets the broader stage for understanding the meaning and function of kachinas within the context of pueblo life. In "The Meaning of *Katsina*" Hieb assembles a variety of Hopi texts and ethnographic "frames" that begin to suggest or construct a cultural definition for these beings. He suggests they be viewed as spirit "persons," a category parallel to those used in discussions of kinship. He explores aspects of *kachina* as seen in the context of the Hopi view of a bipartite world within which reciprocity functions as a cultural dynamic. The Ma'lo and Koyemsi kachinas are examined for their contrasting symbolism, metaphorical of the world-view fundamental to the Hopi perspective. From a native Zuni perspective, Ladd discusses the mask, or Kokko, at Zuni, and how it functions and articulates with Zuni beliefs. His commentary includes the treatment of and attitude toward masks as physical objects.

These papers are followed by discussions that focus on the archaeological evidence for the origin, development, and social significance of the kachina society in Pueblo prehistory, expanding conventional perspectives of the kachina in space and time. Essays by E. Charles Adams, Kelley Hays, Polly Schaafsma and Patricia Vivian present data from the Little Colorado River drainage and the Rio Grande regarding the prehistoric evidence of kachinas, beginning early in the 1300s and possibly earlier. These chapters discuss the iconographic forms in several media that signal the presence of kachina ideology as well as secondary evidence such as changes in settlement pattern, village, layout and configuration that would have been made possible by the integrative nature of the kachina society. More specifically, Adams reviews the iconographic evidence and architectural patterns that signal the presence of kachina ritual from a western Pueblo perspective, and he addresses the integrative functions that the kachina society would have had on Pueblo social organization. P. Schaafsma examines similar evidence from the eastern Pueblo region, with a focus on rock art in which kachina iconography is prolifically represented. Hays discusses kachina imagery on ceramics with an emphasis on the western Pueblo region where kachina masks as pottery decoration are more prevalent and diversified in the fourteenth and fifteenth centuries than in the Rio Grande valley. Functional considerations of these masks on pottery are examined, and Hays also addresses interpretive problems inherent in these early figures.

murals

In addition to rock art and ceramics, kiva murals painted between the 1300s and 1600s were one of the most elaborate and sophisticated Pueblo art forms. These murals sprang from the same stylistic and ideographic sources as did the rock art and representational ceramic designs of the same period, but because of their greater complexity, the kiva murals serve to elucidate further the related simpler images in these other media. The Pottery Mound murals recorded by field schools and research teams during the late 1950s and early 1960s represented the apex of this art form as it is known to date. The anthropomorphic figures of Pottery Mound, some of which are kachinas, are the subject of Patricia Vivian's paper.

The question / recognition of Southwest-Mesoamerican parallels is one that has been addressed intermittently in the anthropological literature over the years. Over the last two decades or so, however, explorations into the subject have lost favor to research focused on in-situ developments, and an almost "isolationist" perspective on the Southwest has prevailed. Nevertheless the observation remains that "masked dances, sophisticated development of sky and earth deities, divine twins, deeply integrated association of colors and directions, organized priesthoods who controlled powerful sanctions—both divine and secular—

against malefactors—all point to a Mesoamerican homeland" (Hedrick et al. 1974:7). Papers by Marc Thompson and M. Jane Young explore iconographic and ideological parallels between the Southwest and Mesoamerica. Both authors stress that relationships between the two areas occurred on the ideological and not a stylistic level, and their papers proceed to examine this issue. As discussed by P. Schaafsma (this volume) and elsewhere (1992*b*), antecedents to the kachina religion and its ideological context are present in the iconography of life forms on Mimbres ceramics. Pictures on Classic Mimbres Black-on-white bowls (A.D. 1000–1150) show animals, human figures and sometimes masked beings with close stylistic relationships to figures in Pueblo art after A.D. 1300. Thompson's paper does not deal with "proto-kachina imagery" on Mimbres pottery as such, which is quite rare, but rather his discussion focuses on parallels between Mimbres, Mesoamerican, and Pueblo iconography. Thompson argues that Mimbres ceramic art is metaphoric and symbolic in character "reflecting a highly structured and multifaceted cosmology," a comment equally applicable to other art forms such as the mural art and rock art that follow in this tradition. Young discusses ideological and iconographic connections between the Western Pueblos and Mesoamerica. Although for purposes of manageability she limits her discussion to the Aztec pantheon of the fifteenth and sixteenth centuries, she correctly notes that this suite of Mexican gods was "subject to . . . pervasive ideologies of earlier cultures." Many of the supernatural and cosmological principles given focus in Mesoamerican gods are also embodied by various kachinas. While the implications of these relationships and the cultural mechanisms that facilitated the spread of Mesoamerican ideas to the Southwest are not addressed here, in drawing attention to these parallels, these papers serve to emphasize the position of the Southwest on the periphery of Mesoamerica, however marginal or intermittent this connection may have been.

This material suggests ways in which Southwest farmers were participants in a broader, ancient, ideological framework, modified to conform to what is recognized as typically Puebloan in style and thought.

Spanish settlement in New Mexico, beginning early in the 1600s, was accompanied by an intensive missionary effort with an aim to convert the Pueblos to Catholicism. Kachinas were viewed as competitors with the Christian saints and evil objects of idolatry, and the kachina society with its masked dances was a high-profile phenomenon, subject to open and often vicious attack. This period of suppression of the cult, to which the Rio Grande Pueblos were particularly subject, was highly disruptive. Ultimately this led to changes, simplifications, and clandestine participation in its activities. The resulting contemporary pattern has often led ethnographers to believe that the kachina society was never as well developed and pervasive in the Rio Grande as it is historically among the western Pueblos, a viewpoint contradicted by the large numbers of kachinas in the prehistoric art. Curtis Schaafsma's paper examines Spanish documents of the late sixteenth and seventeenth centuries that describe the kachina dances of the eastern Pueblos and Spanish efforts to eradicate these ceremonies. These extensive, but under-utilized, documents demonstrate the existence of kachina dances among the eastern Pueblos, notably the Southern Tiwas and Piros along the Rio Grande at the time of early exploration in the 1580s, and describe their revival in the 1660s. The documentary evidence indicates that reconstructions based on ethnographic data alone may be highly suspect, and in many cases simply wrong.

Barton Wright's paper on the changing forms of kachinas considers the agents of change, as he explores mask and costume modifications that have taken place among four groups of kachinas. The difficulties he demonstrates in identifying a detailed mask from Awatovi that resembles several modern ones is instructive and provides an important cautionary note for archaeologists trying to identify prehistoric images on the basis of modern kachina masks. Wright's more conservative view of kachina history and in-situ development, as outlined in the beginning of his essay, contrasts with that of widespread and pan-Pueblo changes advocated by Adams and P. Schaafsma (this volume) and Anderson (1960). Nevertheless all authors recognize that change and innovation are not only characteristic of the cult, but indicative of its dynamic aspects.

J. J. Brody also addresses the issue of change, within the medium of carved dolls as well as renditions painted on paper. His concerns, however, are basically quite different from those of the previous authors who are working within the parameters of Pueblo culture itself. Brody, on the other hand, examines the impact of Euro-American values on the forms that dolls and painted images have taken over the past century. He addresses the transformation of the dolls as symbols of beings from the sacred realm and into secular collectors' items and art, as Euro-Americans divest them of meaning and focus on aesthetics and visual forms. He examines this interaction on several fronts, including how our changing value systems and perceptions of art have in turn modified kachina doll carvings. His discourse provides a thought-provoking consideration of white preconceptions and how the dolls fit into the ideologies of the acquirers.

Following this expedition through ethnological, archaeological, and historical data on kachinas and a foray into the Euro-American world where kachina imagery has made its way out of context, in the final chapter Tedlock brings the reader back to the pueblos themselves, in this case Zuni. He offers a view of their meaning by presenting Zuni stories and texts about the origins and nature of kachinas "away from the role of organizer and interpreter," as he brings these narratives "into a dialogue with historical, archaeological, and ethnological notions about kachinas." In this way Tedlock addresses the issues of

kachina origins (where and how this event occurred), modes of interaction between the living
and the kachinas, and the relationship between
the dancers and the mask. Our discussion thus
comes full circle.

One final introductory note: the word
"kachina" itself and its spelling merits brief comment. As opposed to the spelling of the names
of specific kachinas, which were standardized
throughout the volume to avoid confusion, the
spelling of "kachina" has been left up to the
individual preference of each author. Alternative
spellings include the frequently used "katsina"
and less often "katchina." "Kachina" and other
terms used by various pueblos for these masked
supernaturals are considered at length by Anderson (1951:1066–1070) whose treatise forms the
basis for this brief discussion. There are various
words that refer to these masked dancers, several of which signify clouds, cloud people, or
storm clouds. Kachina / katsina are widely known
terms, however, in standard use at Hopi and
Keres, Jemez, and Tewa pueblos, in addition to
other words signifying clouds. "Kachina" is also
used at Zuni, although "kokko" is more prevalent
among the Zuni themselves. Linguistic data suggest that "kachina" is Keresan in origin, although
the Northern Tiwa *latsi(na)* "may be a variant of
kachina or it may be the matrix term, a point
bearing perhaps importantly upon the history of
the kachina cult" (Parsons 1940:6). Given these
ambiguities, it seems appropriate to allow each
author to follow his or her own inclinations as to
spelling.

2

The Hopi Cosmology
or World-View

FRED EGGAN

PUEBLO cosmology in general emphasizes the earth rather than the heavens, and begins with the emergence of people from the underworld rather than with the creation of the world. The Hopi Indians share this emphasis and their cosmology provides for the evolution of mankind in four worlds, with final emergence of the Hopi (and all other known peoples including the whites) in the Grand Canyon, by way of the *sipapu* or opening from the underworld below. Life in the underworlds was crowded and difficult, and periodically the leaders led their followers through openings in the ceilings of each cave world, leaving behind troublemakers and witches in an attempt to maintain Hopi teachings. With their emergence into the Grand Canyon near the mouth of the Little Colorado River, the Hopi chief thought they had succeeded, but when his child died he knew that at least one witch had emerged with the rest. When the witch was discovered she saved her own life by showing the chief and his followers that his child was alive in the underworld and playing happily with other children. The Hopi believe that their dead return to the underworld, where they live in villages in the manner of the living, and have a continuing role in Hopi life (Quinn 1983; Voth 1905).

The Hopi do provide a brief account of the creation of the physical world in which the Sky

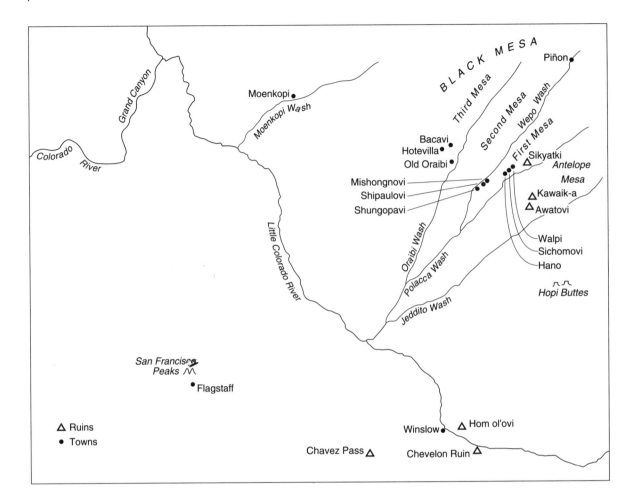

FIGURE 2.1. Map of the Hopi mesas and surrounding geography showing villages and significant landmarks in the Hopi landscape.

God created a beautiful virgin who caused so much rivalry among the other deities that he transformed her into the earth world, her hair becoming the vegetation, her eyes the springs, her secretions the salt, and so on, and he assigned separate regions and powers to the various deities. Thus Muyingwa was placed in the center of the earth to guard the germs of all life; Gnatumsi guards the virgin's heart and fecundates the germs of life; Palölökong, the water serpent, presides over the waters of the earth and nourishes vegetation and animal life; Masau presides over the surface of the earth and is in charge of the dead and the afterworld; Omau is the cloud deity responsible for rain; and Tawa, the sun, is "father" to all (Stephen 1940). This account suggests that

the emergence from the underworld may be interpreted as a "myth of gestation and birth," as
Washington Mathews (1902:738) long ago observed, and makes the conception of the earth as
"mother" to the Hopi intelligible.

In addition to the deities mentioned above, the
Katsinas play an important role in Hopi life as
mediators and messengers of the gods. They come
periodically to the Hopi villages from December
to July as masked dancers to bring gifts to the
children and moisture for bountiful crops for the
villages. Once they came in person but later they
taught the Hopi their songs and dances and now
come to dance in spirit from their homes in the
mountains and springs (Figure 2.2).

FIGURE 2.2. Hemis kachinas, Mishongnovi Pueblo,
Hopi, Arizona. (*Photo courtesy of Museum of New
Mexico, Santa Fe, negative number 82734.*)

The Hopi dead, whose "breath" bodies journey from the grave to the afterworld in the Grand Canyon, are met by sentinels from the Kwan society, who are associated with Masau, and either allowed to proceed or punished in the fire pits for non-Hopi behavior until they are purified. In the villages of the dead they continue Hopi life, existing on the odor or "steam" of food offerings and responding to the prayer offering of the living. Daily they ascend to the San Francisco peaks as Katsinas, and as clouds they provide rain to those Hopis with good hearts who are following the Hopi way of life (Titiev 1944:109–29).

The *pahos,* or prayer sticks, and other prayer offerings are gathered by the sun on his daily travels across the sky and sorted out with Muyingwa on the sun's return journey through the underworld on his way to his eastern house. Muyingwa makes the germs of all living things in the world, the seeds of all vegetation that grows on the surface of the earth and all animals and human beings who walk on it. Muyingwa answers the requests of those Hopis with good hearts by making their crops grow, and discards the requests of witches and those with bad hearts (Fewkes 1894*b*).

In Hopi belief, prayer offerings made with a good heart require the proper return from the deities who are petitioned, but insincere requests can result in drought or windstorms that bring disaster. In this semidesert environment moisture in the form of rain or snow at the proper time is essential for the growth of crops, principally corn plus beans and squash. Hopi prayers are primarily for rain to grow the crops and for good health and long life. The equation of the dead with clouds and rain, by means of the concept of katsinas, provides a system in which the dead maintain their interest in the living and continue to help their relatives by sending rain. In this sytem each individual is responsible for the welfare of the whole community and those who do not conform may be branded as witches. Hence public opinion expressed through gossip is a powerful force for control and until recently was strong enough to obviate the need for policemen.

HOPI SOCIAL organization centers on the matrilineal clan as the basic unit of society (Connelly 1979; Eggan 1950:17–138; Titiev 1944:7–95). Clans were not present in the underworld, but the bilateral groups or bands who emerged via the *sipapu* wandered around for a considerable period during which they took their present names from particular events; the group that became the Bear clan found a dead bear and thus took their name. By emphasizing descent through the female line, the band gradually became a matrilineal clan and established a rule of marrying outside the clan group.

The household likewise became organized in terms of matrilocal residence, with the house belonging to the women and the husbands joining their wife's household, though retaining an important position in their natal households. Marriage became monogamous, but divorce was frequent and remarriage simple. Daughters usually remained in their mother's household, where their husbands joined them. Sons remained until marriage, when they left to join their wives. Each household was therefore composed of a group of women who, with their brothers, formed a clan segment which anthropologists call a lineage group. Men from other clans married into the households, while male members of the lineage married into the other clans and households. Initially clans might be composed of a single lineage but might expand into several households, each of which might become a separate lineage, or alternatively might die out if not enough females were produced.

In Hopi tradition the clan migrations after emergence from the underworld covered much of the Southwest. It was during this period that agriculture reached them from the south, along with potterymaking and cotton weaving. As agriculture became more important and gradually replaced hunting and gathering as the basis for subsistence, the Hopi became sedentary, building pithouse hamlets and later masonry storage structures that gradually evolved into the modern Pueblos. Agricultural land and sources of water became more important and the early Hopi settled on Black Mesa, in the Hopi Buttes, along the Little Colorado River, and in the Grand Canyon.

When the villages on the southern portions of Black Mesa were being established, the Bear clan was the first clan to settle there in Hopi tradition, receiving a block of land from Masau, who owned it. The Bear clan thus became the leading clan and the Bear clan chief became the village chief. Later clan arrivals had to demonstrate their prowess of bringing rain, or as warriors and protectors, before being allowed to settle in the village, where they were given land in exchange for their performance of ceremonies or special ritual services to the Bear clan chief.

The Hopi clans are named after animals or plants or various aspects of nature, and the basic clan system is similar in all Hopi villages. There is an important relationship between the named plant or animal and the clan group, and each clan has a set of names referring to its eponym which are bestowed on its members at birth and at all changes in social status through various initiations. Each clan was likewise given a plot of land by the village chief in exchange for performing a ceremony or ritual essential to the religious system. The Sand clan provides valley sands for the altars, the Tobacco clan provides pipes and native tobacco for ceremonial smoking, in which the smoke is symbolic of clouds, the Badger clan provides the roots to put in water and make the medicines and emetics used in the ceremonies, and a member of one of the water clans provides the water for asperging and other purposes.

With the great drought of the thirteenth century (A.D. 1276–1299), many of the northern Pueblo areas were abandoned, and ancestral Hopis and other Anasazi moved to areas such as Southern Black Mesa where the springs were more

reliable and farming was still possible. In Hopi tradition the initial movements were still earlier. The Pueblo populations in the Grand Canyon left in the first half of the twelfth century, when there was apparently a change in climate, and moved toward the Hopi mesas, some stopping in the Moenkopi area and the others joining relatives on Third Mesa. At about the same time other groups moved from northern Black Mesa to join growing Hopi communities to the south, and groups in the Hopi Buttes to the south moved northward.

Hopi tradition assigns priority to the Second Mesa community of Shungopavi, which was founded by the Bear clan, and the village is considered the "mother" village for all the Hopi. As clans arrived the Bear clan chief, as village chief or *kikmongwi,* tested their contributions and assigned them lands and a place to live. Oraibi was founded by a brother of the Shungopavi chief, named Matcito, and settled initially by his relatives and friends. Later it received an influx from the Moenkopi area and the Grand Canyon. On First Mesa "Old Walpi" was established below the mesa top, and at nearby Antelope Mesa, Awatovi and other villages were gradually settled.

As new clan groups arrived they were fitted into the developing social organization. Clans considered similar in some important respect were grouped into phratries and considered to be kinsmen. Thus the Bear clan, the Spider clan, the Bluebird clan, the Rope clan and others were considered to belong together because of similar or related experiences with the same dead bear that gave its name to the Bear clan. Others, such as the Snake clan, Lizard clan, Cactus clan, and Sand clan were conceptually linked in terms of similarity or habitat. The clans in a phratry support one another and may take over ceremonial or other functions in case of clan extinction, and as such are often rivalrous groups, in competition for higher status. Phratry groups are particularly important in maintaining the ceremonial system but have no control over land. When a clan expands in size, through producing more female members or by aggregation, the lineages may reside in separate households, the "prime" or most important lineage occupying the "clan house" and being in charge of clan lands and ceremonial paraphernalia and providing the chief priests for the ceremonies it controls, with other lineages providing a supporting role and only taking over in case of lineage extinction.

These groupings—lineage, clan, and phratry—are held together by the kinship system, which is a "Crow" type based on matrilineal descent. One's closest relatives are in the lineage and household, and a similar pattern is extended to the clan, so that similarly named clans in different villages are treated as relatives as well. For clans within the same phratry, kinship terms are extended and marriage is restricted, but the obligations are largely limited to hospitality. But the clan *wuya,* or supernaturals, while primarily the responsibility of the particular clan, are shared by all the phratry group.

In Hopi society, the descent is matrilineal, inheritance is through the female line, and women own the houses and the clan fields, though the men, either brothers or husbands, carry out most of the agricultural work. Only the clan has a name, but the lineage and phratry groupings are clearly recognized by the Hopi, and the same kinship terms and exogamic rules are extended to all clans within the phratry.

The villages on each of the three mesas represent independent towns, for the most part, though major villages may have been dependent colonies. We have noted above that Shungopavi is considered the "mother" village in terms of its traditional founding, with Oraibi an early colony. Walpi and other communities at First Mesa and neighboring regions were considered as guardians of the Hopi land base and responsible for its protection. As populations expanded on the Hopi mesas, this pattern was repeated. Thus on Second Mesa, Shungopavi is the "mother" village, and Shipaulovi is a colony established around A.D. 1700 as protection against Spanish reprisals after the reconquest of the region following

the Pueblo Revolt of A.D. 1680. A third village, Mishongnovi, was established earlier as a "guard" village. There is a similar organization on First Mesa, with Walpi as the "mother" village, and Sichomovi as a colony. The refugee Tewas from the Rio Grande, who came around A.D. 1700 and founded Hano or Hopi-Tewa, are the "guard" village. They continue to speak Tewa but are otherwise largely acculturated to Hopi patterns. On Third Mesa, Oraibi was the major village and the largest of all the Hopi villages. An agricultural community had been established at Moenkopi, some forty-five miles to the west of Oraibi, and around the turn of the century became the formal colony of Old Oraibi. With the "split" or division of Old Oraibi in 1906 the conservatives founded Hotevilla and, later, Bakavi a few miles away to escape pressures from the U.S. government. New Oraibi was established at the foot of Oraibi mesa and settled by Christian Hopis and progressives.

There are traditional boundaries between each mesa, as well as within, and the earlier pattern of clan lands is still in operation on First and Second Mesas, but the difficulties that led to the breakup of Old Oraibi on Third Mesa greatly reduced the clan-land system, since it was closely tied to the ceremonial cycle. Between the major communities there is no formal political organization; colonies are tied to the "mother" village by ceremonial bonds as well as by kinship. Within the village the *kikmongwi,* or village chief, has ceremonial authority but little political power, while the tribe as a whole has no formal political organization. As a result of the Indian Reorganization Act of 1934, however, Indian groups were allowed to organize as units and the Hopi voted to accept and established a Tribal Council to represent the whole tribe in 1936. The Tribal Council had difficulty in getting started because of opposition from conservative villages, but was in operation by the 1950s as a spokesman for the majority of villages and has gradually been accepted.

THE RELIGIOUS organization of the Hopi (Parsons 1939; Stephen 1936; Titiev 1944) centers on the katsina cult, mentioned above, and a ceremonial calendar in which "clan owned" ceremonies follow each other throughout the year at roughly monthly intervals. Tradition associates the ceremony with a particular clan, and the controlling clan is responsible for the performance and provides the chief priests as well as some of the participants, but in recent times the ceremonies are carried out by societies whose membership cuts across the clan divisions. Much of the ritual of the ceremonies, including the altar and songs, is secret and is carried out by members who are initiated into the society and represent a cross-section of the community.

At birth an infant is kept in seclusion for twenty days, when the father's mother takes the mother and child to the eastern edge of the mesa and presents the infant to the rising sun, giving it a name from her clan stock of names. On the occasion of a boy or girl joining the katsina cult at the age of eight to ten, a ceremonial father or mother is selected by the parents to look after the novice and help him or her through the initiation. This establishes a kinship relation between the child, and the ceremonial father, and the latter's clan. The ceremonial father inducts a ceremonial son into the various societies that he happens to belong to, including the Antelope society, Snake society, and the Blue and Gray Flute societies. A girl is similarly inducted into the Marau society and possibly, the Oaqol and Lakon societies as well.

At the age of sixteen to eighteen, a young man goes through the Tribal Initiation, joining one of the four major men's societies, Wuwutsim, Tao, Ahl, or Kwan, which collectively initiates new members every few years. At Oraibi most of the young men join the Wuwutsim society, who are councilors and with the Tao, or Singers, associated with fertility. The Ahl, or Horn society, are the watchers or heralds and represent all the horned animals, and are paired with the Kwan society associated with Masau and the underworld of the dead, the most mysterious and feared of the men's societies. Initiation into one of these societies gives a young man a new status. He is now a *taka,* "man," and the four societies together are thought of as "concentric walls of a house" protecting the Hopi against their enemies. Associated with them in this role are the members of the Snake society, who control the deadly powers of the rattlesnake, and the members of the War society, formerly composed of those who had taken scalps from the enemy.

The four societies involved in Tribal Initiation have their own kivas where they perform their particular ceremonies and each group make up a unit in the katsina cult and competes against one another in dances, races and games. When societies without kivas perform their ceremonies they either borrow one of the Wuwutsim kivas or hold the ceremony in the clan house of the controlling clan. In addition there is usually a chief kiva used by the village chief during the Soyal ceremony at the winter solstice. When not in ceremonial use the kiva serves as a men's clubhouse for weaving or other activities. While the kiva is "owned" by the person who takes the initiative in building or repairing it, it can be freely borrowed for any legitimate purpose, and secular meetings often take place in kivas.

In early Hopi history ceremonial activities centered on hunting and gathering and the cure of illness through medicine men or shamans, but as agricultural practices became more important fertility rituals were added to the older hunting rites, and rituals for rain became central in the ceremonial system. In Hopi thinking the growth of the corn paralleled the development of the child, the germs for both being provided by Muyingwa in the underworld. And as we have seen, the dead came to play a role in the bringing of rain and snow, as they ascended as katsinas and clouds and brought moisture to the fields of the deserving.

THE BASIC means of securing rain and good crops is by prayer and offering—*pahos* and other ceremonial gifts to the deities and katsinas, which are placed on altars or shrines or in springs and fields to secure their aid in the growth of crops or other needs. The Hopi make pilgrimages, usually annually, to clan shrines, eagle shrines, ancestral ruins, salt sources, places associated with the katsinas or ceremonies, and places still kept secret. The Hopi have a large number of shrines (Titiev 1944:271), some associated with the emergence of the Hopi from the underworld in the Grand Canyon, some derived from the experiences of various clans in their wanderings, some at earlier sites where they lived for a period, and others in and around their present villages, or in neighboring mountains and springs associated with katsinas. In addition each clan has an allotted section of cliffs along the Little Colorado River and the main Colorado River and in the Hopi Buttes to the south of the villages, where they gather young eagles each spring for ceremonial purposes. The fledglings are brought back to the villages and treated as members of the household, each being given a name and tethered on the roof where it is fed daily until after the Niman ceremony, when it is ritually killed and buried after its feathers have been secured for prayer offerings to the deities.

The most important shrines or sacred areas are in the Grand Canyon where the Little Colorado River flows into the Colorado. Here the sipapu, or place of emergence, is physically present in a large raised pond. Here is their "source," the place of emergence from, and the entrance to, the underworld. Here the deceased Hopi live and respond to the prayers of their descendants. In this area are salt deposits that are periodically visited to gather salt, essential to their diet, with shrines to the Spider Woman, who created the salt, and the Twin War Gods, who are her grandchildren and the protectors of the Hopi and their domain. Here, too, are many of their early villages in which their world-view was shaped, and which are still shrines to their descendants. Only Hopis initiated into Wuwutsim, the Tribal Initiation, could journey to this area, since the trip was physically difficult and involved danger since the spirits of the dead lived in this region and

Masau, the God of Death, had his major home in the cliffs. The Salt journey from Oraibi took several days, and involved stopping at Moenkopi for final preparations and the making of offerings and rituals at a number of shrines along the "salt trail," both going and returning (Talayesva 1942:232–46; Titiev 1937).

Important shrine areas are likewise found in the San Francisco Peaks, the major home of the katsinas. The katsinas are thought to use the entire surface of the peaks to prepare the making of rain and snow, and who manifest themselves daily as clouds above the peaks, as well as appearing from December to July as spirit dancers in the Hopi villages. The peaks are extremely sacred and the shrines on their tops are essential in Hopi ritual, while the high spruce forests furnish symbolically important portions of the katsina costumes, as the katsina join with the men of the village to pray and dance in the kivas and plazas.

Annual expeditions are made to gather spruce boughs for use in the final or Niman home going dance, when the katsinas are sent to their homes in the peaks for the next half year. Other important katsina shrines are on Black Mesa, particularly at Kisiwu, northeast of Piñon, where there is an important spring, from which come the katsinas involved in the Powamu or "Bean Dance" in March and the associated initiation of Hopi children into the katsina cult. The region around Kisiwu is also an important source of spruce for the katsina dances, and parties from different villages regularly visit the spring and make prayer offerings to the resident katsinas before gathering spruce boughs.

Archaeological sites, representing former homes of particular clans, are sacred areas that are visited periodically to make offerings to ancestors, with requests for aid in growing crops. Nearby ruins are visited in connection with particular ceremonies to notify the deceased relatives buried there that the ceremony is in progress and the dead should do their part.

Around the villages are local shrines to particular deities who are impersonated in the ceremonial system and to whom offerings are periodically made. Thus there are shrines to Masau, the deity of the surface of the earth who owns the land and is also the God of Death, near each village, as well as near his "real" home in the Grand Canyon. The Tribal Initiation, itself, dramatizes the emergence from the underworld through the *sipapu,* with each of the constituent societies playing particular roles. On the night of initiation the spirits of the dead are invited to return to the village and Masau is impersonated by the chief of the Kwan society. The novices, who are "little chicken hawks," are apparently "killed" and revived as "men" in the presence of the spirits of the dead, who will thus recognize them when they in turn reach the land of the dead. The Kwan and Ahl societies kindle new fire in the kivas after all the fires in the village are extinguished, in recognition of Masau's ownership of fire, and jointly patrol the village to insure that no intruders enter the village and that the Hopi remain in their houses while the dead are present. The Wuwutsim and Tao societies dance through the village periodically, the Wuwutsim carrying emblems of fertility and taunting the Hopi women, and the Tao singing the songs that were used when the Hopi emerged from the *sipapu.*

When a child dies its spirit or "breath body" does not go to the underworld, but returns to the household of its mother where it resides in the roof and is reborn in the mother's next child. The Wuwutsim initiates go to the general underworld and to the homes of the katsinas in the San Francisco Peaks or the spring at Kisiwu. Deceased Kwan members have a special home at Kwanivi, a small mountain near the Grand Canyon, while Ahl members go to a lake in the San Francisco Peaks known as Alosaka, and the Singers have a home at Dowanasavi, the center of the earth with a shrine south of Oraibi (Titiev 1944:136, n. 48).

Initiation into the man's societies automatically provides for entry into the Soyal ceremony, which occurs at the winter solstice and sets the stage for the new ceremonial year. The kivas are opened by the Soyal katsina, who is impersonated by the village chief and head of the Bear clan, and the main chiefs or priests of the village are involved. The sun is started back on his path toward his summer home by Sotuknangu, the Star or Sky God, impersonated by a Sun clan leader twirling a sun shield, and prayer offerings are made for relatives and friends, for plants and animals, and for known ancestors and placed on shrines nearby. The dead have been invited to come and share the offerings and food. The first katsinas also come at this time and inaugurate the season of katsina dances which continue at intervals until the Niman, or "home going" in July, when other societies take over the task of providing rain for the crops.

Throughout the year offerings may be made to the springs and other sources of water. Springs are sacred, being inhabited by water serpents who are mythical creatures quite separate from the ordinary snakes. The earth is thought to rest on two gigantic water serpents, or palölökong, who may punish the Hopis by turning over and thus causing earthquakes, or by causing floods or other disasters. In tradition a village chief might have to sacrifice a son or daughter to appease them.

The exterior boundaries of the Hopi domain are likewise marked by a series of shrines that the Hopi elders now revisit every year. There are eight major shrines, marked in part by spirals or concentric petroglyphs and buried prayer offerings at locations of importance to the Hopi. In general the eight shrines mark the last staging areas in the final migrations to the Hopi homeland.

Hopi religion is central to their life and for centuries has involved their land. The Hopi have no word for "religion" as such, because for them all aspects of their life have a sacred quality. Relatively isolated on their mesas for centuries, they have integrated their subsistence practices, their land base, their social organization, and their cosmology into one interdependent whole.

As Mischa Titiev has demonstrated in *Old Oraibi* (1944), the underlying concepts of Hopi religion center on the continuity of life after death. The dead are reborn in the underworld where they live in villages like the living and eat the essence of the food offerings the living provide. In return they visit the living in the form of clouds and katsinas and bring rain to those with good hearts. And in ceremonies the dead are notified so that they can participate, which they are thought to do by actual attendance and participation in the most important rituals.

This relation between the living and the dead is reflected in their cosmological beliefs, which include a dual division of time and space. The sun journeys from his eastern "house" to his western "house," and at night travels underground from west to east. Hence day and night are reversed in the upper and lower worlds. Similarly, in the sun's annual cycle, from winter solstice to summer solstice, when it is winter in the upper world, it is summer in the lower world, and the Hopi calendar of six repeated names of the month re-flects this duality. And in the Hopi life cycle, the "breath of life" comes from the underworld and at death returns to it.

The ceremonial calendar reflects the duality of life as well. From the winter solstice to the summer solstice, the spirits of the ancestors are present in the villages in the form of katsinas and clouds, and the rituals performed are preparatory to the agricultural season which follows. Thus beans and corn are planted in basins in the kivas in March during Powamu and the resulting sprouts are brought in procession by the katsinas to every household to demonstrate their powers to the small children and assure the adults that Muyingwa and other deities will aid in the growing of the coming season's crops. As the Hopis say, "Our land, our religion and our life are one, and our leader, with humbleness, understanding and determination, performs his duty to us by keeping them as one and thus insuring prosperity and security for the people" ("Hopi Hearings" 1953:111).

3

The Zuni Ceremonial System: The Kiva

EDMUND J. LADD

IN THE beginning there were no humans in this world. Sun Father came up in the east and traveled across the sky, pausing briefly at high noon overhead, and then descended into the western ocean and it became night. Sun Father traveled all night eastward under the world, to arrive once again in the east to bring a new day. But the days were empty and devoid of joy, singing, dancing, and prayers. Every day as Sun Father traveled across the sky, he could hear the cries of his children deep in the womb of Mother Earth. While he was traveling across the sky he saw a small waterfall below in which two columns of foam were forming. By his power he sent a shaft of light into the foam to create the Twin Gods. He said to them, "Go and bring my children up from the darkness to my light." The twins obeyed and descended to the world of darkness and, after many attempts they succeeded in bringing the people up to this world. Some came up through the springs and lakes to the north and east, others came up in and near a great canyon to the west. All traveled in different and separate directions, moving every four days (actually every four years) throughout the land in search of the Middle-Place. In time they became the Zuni, the Hopi, the Acoma, the San Juan, the Cochiti, the Taos, and all the others who settled this land.

This land, from the four encircling oceans, the mist- and moss-draped mountains, to the sacred springs and peaks, is the sacred dwelling place of the spirit beings and people alike. Above all else, the people who came up from the four worlds below have never lost their faith in the view of their relationship to the universe. They realize the extreme importance of their individual responsibilities and their collective ceremonial and ritual supplication of the spirit beings that help to maintain and operate the universe on an even balance for the good of all people and for the joy of the K/apinna:hoi (spirit beings).

Before the earth became hard, spirits from Kolhuwalaaw'a (spirit village), which is our sacred place, came to Zuni in human form, much like the ancient Greek gods. The gods became humans when they came into this world. They performed the Kokko dances, and the women of our tribe fell in love with the dancers and followed them to Kolhuwalaaw'a. But because they were not dead they could not enter Kolhuwalaaw'a, and it became a great problem. It became such a problem that there were women sitting around the great lake. They couldn't come home, and they couldn't go in because their time on earth had not been concluded yet. And so the wise people of our village, the elders, said to the K/apinna:hoi, you must leave your image with us but disappear forever, never coming again to the village in human form, and that's where the Kokko (mask) began in ancient times. Kokko means the mask, the dancer, and the spirit being, spirits of the afterworld, and the afterworld is a perfect reflection of this world in our belief.

When a person dies its spirit becomes a Kokko, a spirit being, at Kolhuwalaaw'a. And he lives at Kolhuwalaaw'a. When I die the spirit that is in my body now, leaves the body and goes to Kolhuwalaaw'a and that's where it resides. It resides there until it dies four times and then comes back up to this world in the form of any one of the prey animals, depending on what you were in this life—a mountain sheep, rattlesnake, stink bug,

and so on. But there is no reincarnation in human form. There is only reincarnation in animal form. That's why we are reverent to animals, because they are our ancestral spirit beings. They are the K/apinna:hoi—the word is poorly translated in anthropological literature as the "raw people." They are not "raw people," they are spirit beings.

The spirits come to visit in the summer during the rainmaking ceremonies, and in the winter during the winter ceremonies. If you were a person who never attended ceremonies and didn't participate in any of these activities, you would not come as part of a group; have you ever seen a cloud all by itself, the only little cloud . . . that's exactly what spirit you'd be. Alone. Because you didn't participate in ceremonies.

Now, when you are born into Zuni you are born into a clan. Your maternal ties and your paternal ties are the ones that decide on what clan you will be. And in our culture, it's the mother's clan. We trace our descent through the mother, not the father. Like somebody said, everybody knows who their mother is, but the father, maybe. You're a clan member of your mother's clan for life, but in addition to that, to make it a little more confusing you are also a *child* of your father's clan. So we have a dual clan system. First of all you belong to your mother's clan and you are a child of your father's clan. And you cannot marry anyone in your mother's clan. Theoretically, you cannot marry anyone in your father's clan either, but it's done now and again. But the clan is a very, very important function of the Zuni religious system. If you are a female, you have really no problems because there's only a small number of options left as far as a religious position is concerned. If you are an adult and you become ill and you can't be cured by regular medicine, your life is "given" to the curing society. If they cure you of whatever ails you, then you are obligated to become a member of that particular curing society. If you are of the right clan, you might inherit the position of rain priest. But those are about the only options you have as a woman. A male has a number of options. His mother or his father chooses his godfather, the one who is to initiate him into the kiva society. When a boy reaches the age of about eight to twelve, he is initiated into one of the six kiva societies.

There are six kivas to which all the males are divided, and kiva membership cuts across all clan lines. It cuts across medicine society lines, priesthood lines. So if you are a member of a kiva group, you can also be a member of the curing society, and if you are the right clan you can be a Rain priest, if you take an enemy scalp you can be a Bow priest, so as a male you can be in a number of different societies. Women are not completely excluded from kivas. Kivas are inviolate, however, during certain ceremonies in which only men are involved. Otherwise females are allowed to come into the kiva at any time. And as far as women are concerned, however, in my lifetime there were two women that were kiva members. The initiation ceremonies are very stringent and very severe, and although they are not completely excluded, women are not encouraged to be members of the kiva society.

Every adult male kiva member must have a mask made for himself. They don't make it. The kiva society performs that for them. It's a highly religious activity that is quite expensive. It's not something that you do at a whim of an idea. But that mask belongs to you as a person. It's individually owned. That's your passport to Kolhuwalaaw'a. When you die that mask is buried with you or buried at the time you die because when you get into the afterworld, and your spirit comes back to Zuni in the form of rain dances, you have to have your mask to come with. If you don't have a mask, you can't join the rainmaking ceremonies. And so it's very, very important that you acquire a mask when you are a young adult. You can sell your mask to another individual, another Zuni individual, but when you die and you go to Kolhuwalaaw'a, your mask will not be there when you get there if you predecease your purchaser. When the purchaser dies the mask is

buried with him and when he gets to Kolhuwalaaw'a the mask goes to the original owner. So the buyer loses. So it's very, very important to have your own mask, not buy one.

If a person moves away from Zuni the mask stays in the person's home. And the women take care of it. The women take care of it and they feed it. They keep it in the corn storage room with the *a:towa*—the corn.

So you see, the way in which masks are handled and the attitudes about masks are not only mythologically based or based on legends, but these things are put into actual practice even today. I'm not talking about three thousand years ago, I'm not talking about two hundred years ago, I'm talking about now—1994—in which these kinds of practices are still adhered to and still followed by the Zuni people. I'm not going to tell you exactly how the masks are made, or how they are used, or discuss the types or forms of the ceremonials in detail or, why masks are painted the way they are. All I'm going to tell you is that they are owned by individuals who are charged with keeping them in the kiva. They can sell them but it's not condoned. They are not sacred in the sense of the Twin Gods (*ahayu:ta*), which are very sacred to our culture. Ahayu:ta are communally owned—no one has a right to sell, own, or give them away. Masks you can give away or you can sell. During the early collecting days of Cushing and Culin, Hodge and Stevenson and all the rest of the anthropologists, people did sell their masks. But they, the collectors, came to Zuni to buy these things when the Zuni people were absolutely starving. They were hungry, they would sell anything. I read very interestingly, a little comment about how a Zuni man made a corn rock for one of the collectors and said that he must never show it to anybody because it was very sacred. Well, the Zunis learned very early that these guys, collectors, wanted something sacred and they wanted to be told that they were sacred. The Zuni man drew a picture of a corn stalk on a rock and gave it to the collector as a "sacred stone." And he made out. He sold it for fifty cents (which in 1909 was a lot of money.)

Masks are used for different dances and different kinds of masks are made for the purposes of the ceremonial dances. The mask is free to be loaned to anybody, any kiva. Masks are freely borrowed between kivas. A single mask may be used in three or four different dance performances in a year. There are only so many masks of a certain type that are contained in the village. And each kiva has the right to borrow the ceremonial dance mask from another kiva. The mask itself is not used perpetually for one thing. The kiva leader comes to your house and says that a particular kiva is performing a ceremony of so and so next week—we'd love to *illopi,* borrow, your mask. You give it to him, and the kiva leader takes it away and uses the mask. At the conclusion of the dance, the person who used the mask returns it to the home of the owner, cleaned, scraped, and ready for the next performance.

Masks are never kept completely decorated. After each performance they are completely cleaned. All the feathers are taken off, all the paint is removed and the mask is ready for the next performance. If you keep masks decorated, you trap the spirit. The spirit cannot return to Kolhuwalaaw'a and the spirit can do harm to the individual or to the keeper and so it's very important that they be dismantled. You don't keep a mask for an ornament; you don't keep a mask in a completely decorated state as a curatorial or curious object, even replicas of the Kokko. It's not done.

There's not a single thing that I can think of that is used in Zuni ceremonies and religion that should be allowed to be preserved and protected in perpetuity in a museum—masks, prayer sticks—all of these items are made to be disintegrated into the earth. They are gifts to the spiritual beings. We believe that even if an individual sells his own mask and it's in a museum somewhere, that mask will stay there until it disintegrates. It may take ten years, it may take twenty years, it may take a thousand years. But it will eventually go to where it's supposed to go. Zunis say "the mask will eat itself up."

The Koshari Boy Scouts of Colorado were asked to give to Zuni a replica of the Shalako image made from ice-cream cartons and paper towels. Replicas are just as important as the real thing, because how does a child know that this is a replica and not the real thing? You see, what we are trying to protect are the children because if they see this mask unconnected to the body and the spirit being, harm comes to that child. Not to you, not to the owner of the mask or not to the mask, but to the child. So that's the reason that we don't condone or we don't appreciate having masks kept on exhibit—and we had at the Museum of New Mexico eighteen replica masks made during the WPA period that were given back to the Zunis last year. I know that they were buried like real masks in the riverbed to the west of the village.

And the other thing that I wish to point out is the fact that objects that are considered to be sacred, are sacred only in the function of the ceremony. For example, the cloud bowl, the so-called cornmeal bowl or cloud bowl, with the cornmeal in it, when the cornmeal is put in that cloud bowl and it's used in a ceremony, it's a sacred part of the cornmeal and the ceremony. Once that cornmeal is used up and its ceremonial use is over, it's put on the shelf and it's no longer sacred. Or religious, or ceremonial. It becomes a decorative object. So it's the function that makes the difference.

The dolls also have an important function in Zuni, and they are completely out of context when they are presented in this society as collection items. The dolls (the *we ha*—baby) are gifts to girl children from the Kokko. At Hopi also. But the Hopis have commercialized these dolls to the point where it's now all kinds of action kachina dolls, and most are being made for sale. Zunis are still not making them for sale, but they are getting close. The doll is given to the individual child during the ceremonies of the Kokko dances, or during the winter night dances.

A Kokko brings the *we ha* to the child as a gift, and that child plays with that doll but plays with it very carefully because it's a spirit being. It's a Kokko doll and unbeknownst to the child, they don't let her know that the doll, or the *we ha,* is made by her uncle or her brother, or her father. She's told that the female Kokko, in the after-world at Kolhuwalaaw'a, gives birth to that *we ha* and brings it to the child. For the male, it's a little bow and arrow. When the Koyemshi are going by the house, for example, my little sisters would say, "Nana, will you bring me a doll?" And the Koyemshi said, "Okay, we'll tell Kokko that you want a doll." And so, her uncle hears her or her brother hears her and he makes a doll and the Kokko presents it to the child at the plaza dances. At the gathering at the village the child is presented with the doll. It's a big event for the child and for the person that's giving it. So,

there's a world of difference between what you call the "kachina doll" that you saw at the School of American Research and the collections that we have here at the Museum of Indian Arts and Culture that were made for commercial uses. They weren't always. The Hopi dolls were also given for special reasons at a special occasion at Hopi land and still are.

In conclusion: (1) Masks, different types, are privately or individually owned (a male member could possibly own two or three masks). (2) They are freely loaned between kivas. (3) They are not sacred but are highly respected (except for a very special class of masks which are communally owned). (4) Masks are never kept decorated. (5) Women care for the masks and can handle them, but they do not participate in the Kokko dances.

4

The Meaning of Katsina: Toward a Cultural Definition of "Person" in Hopi Religion

LOUIS A. HIEB

I. Of Texts and Frames

The essay that follows is a patchwork, not the ordered patchwork of a quilt but the kind of odd assemblage that sometimes adds life to a child's trousers. The essay consists of texts and frames. The texts are Hopi texts—all statements by Hopi men—recorded by A. M. Stephen on First Mesa in the 1880s and others—again by Hopi men—recorded on Third Mesa in the 1970s. In a sense these texts are not the product of those times but are about a timeless part of Hopi thought. They are, however, both of time and timeless. And there is a gender issue present here. All of the texts have as their source Hopi men. All of those recording these texts were / are men. To be aware is not to have a perspective and so this issue is noted but not addressed.

And then there are the frames, the theoretical perspectives, put forward. For the most part what follows is a kind of literary approach. The *katsina* (*katsiman,* pl.) is regarded as a "text" and the questions asked of it are: *what* does it mean? and *how* does it mean? But what we quickly have—in our effort at crosscultural understanding—are layers of meaning, texts about texts, with this essay and its frame yet another text. One of the frames, my voice, is informed by four seasons of watching and listening to katsinas (1969–71, 1977), by

Communication and meaningful expression are carried on through the use of symbolic elements, words, images, gestures, or sequences of these. When isolated or viewed as "things" in themselves, these elements seem to be merely arbitrary noises, patterns of light, or motions. . . . These elements are meaningful to us only through their associations, which they acquire through being associated with or opposed to one another in all sorts of contexts. Meaning is therefore a function of the ways in which we create and otherwise experience contexts. (Wagner 1975:37) reading various anthropological texts, and by my own sense of the ethics of encounters of this sort. Here and there you will hear Hopi voices speaking *of* and *about* katsinas. Other voices represented here—including my own—have sought to build bridges of understanding but like a bridge in my childhood these have some loose planks and protruding nails. An earlier effort to represent the meaning of *katsina* received beneficial comments from Hopi men at the Hopi Tricentennial Symposium in 1980. I am aware that I have not accounted for all of their concerns, and beyond this I sense they left much unsaid about the meaning of *katsina* to each of them.

II. The Theoretical Frame

Human beings are here conceived of as "meaning-makers" (Crick 1976:3) and as oriented around "symbolizing, conceptualizing, meaning-seeking" (Geertz 1973:140; cf. Shore 1991), and therefore the task of the anthropologist is primarily one of description and translation of these meaningful activities.

In the pages which follow, I will show that the masked face is in part a symbolic means of defining and giving expression to a significant "person" in Hopi moral space, the *katsina*. In using the concept "moral space" attention is purposely drawn to the ethical dimension of a religious world-view: it is not simply a statement of what *is,* it is also a statement of what *ought to be.* The total moral space of the Hopi has many dimensions, each constituted by a system of shared meanings expressed in symbolic form. Like the moral space of most peoples, that of the Hopi consists of systematic conceptions of order (e.g., orientations to space and time), evaluative ideas (e.g., *hopi / qa hopi*—Hopi / un-Hopi), various categories of person (e.g., "kinship," "religious specialists"), theories as to their origin and destiny (e.g. "prophecy"), assumptions about the nature of humans and their relations to one another and their place in the natural order,

etc. This world of meaning has already been partially mapped by several Hopi scholars (cf. Black 1984; Bradfield 1973; Hieb 1979*a;* Loftin 1991; Titiev 1944; Whiteley 1988) and that system of person categories conventionally labeled "kinship" has been the subject of a classic study by Fred Eggan (1950). However, a complete cartography of Hopi moral space would include not just an account of the units and rules of "kinship" but also a characterization of all those culturally defined "persons" who are a part of the Hopi world. For reasons which will become clear, I have placed quotation marks on "kinship" and "persons" as well as other labels, e.g., "religious specialist," "ritual," "mask," and the like, which are convenient for translation and discussion but which require cultural and contextual analyses.

Malcolm Crick (1976:166; cf. Saussure 1966: 110; Culler 1977:20–21) has provided a useful metaphor in suggesting that we think of a system of person categories as structured like a chessboard. In Hopi ritual, the identity *katsina* is just one on a "board" with several other "ritual" persons who are defined and given symbolic expression with different features, including distinctive "faces," and who act within accepted systems of thought and action. The chessboard metaphor makes clear why the *katsina* cannot be regarded as a separate subject of inquiry. To do so is like "someone unfamiliar with the game of chess observing a series of movements and then writing a book on 'bishops.' The point is that the 'bishop' cannot be understood apart from—indeed exists only by virtue of—the whole system of definitions and rules which constitute chess" (Crick 1976:116). Thus, to find the "person" *katsina* meaningful, it is necessary to understand how it is defined and differentiated, how the system of which it is a part is constituted, and how the meanings associated with it and other identities of the ritual system of person categories are given symbolic expression. Finally, it is necessary to recognize that the system of person categories in which the *katsina* is located, intersects with other systems of person categories and various Hopi "belief" systems, some of which are outlined below.

III. *The Hopi Katsina: Some Hopi Texts*

Roy Wagner, in the quote given at the beginning of this paper, states that "Meaning is . . . a function of the ways in which we create and otherwise experience contexts" (1975:37). Hopis often define the *katsina* in ways which assume an understanding of context. This assumption of an understanding of context is evident in the following Hopi statements regarding the *katsina:*

> This is also an aspect of Hopi knowledge that katsinas travel in the form of clouds. . . . And because there is no doubt that they make it rain they come out from places at which water emerges. . . . The Hopi say that a katsina comes here unseen. . . . They also come here in the form of rain because they do not want to show themselves. . . . According to this knowledge they also travel about as clouds. . . . Also according to this knowledge, one becomes a katsina when he dies. . . . For this reason they attach an eagle down feather to someone (i.e., after death), and then he can look down through that. . . . That eagle down becomes a cloud. . . . And then someone (i.e., a dead person) lies on it and watches his relatives here. (Malotki n.d.:25,27)

The text continues with this prayer spoken to the deceased after burial:

> "Alright, don't be lazy to come. . . . Come visit us with rain. . . . If you bring us water and we drink we will be happy, and our plants will grow with it." (Malotki n.d.:28)

The *katsina,* as these texts make clear, can be both visible and invisible, material and immaterial. Because of their beneficence, Hopis call them "our friends" (*itaakwatsim*). As we will see, *katsina* refers to masked and painted impersonation, to the spiritual being impersonated, to the clouds, and to the dead. At the same time, it will be shown that these are but different expressions

or manifestations of one "person," the *katsina.* To fully define the *katsina,* to understand what the *katsina* is, requires that we attend both to texts like these recorded by Ekkehart Malotki and to the contexts which follow.

IV. *The Hopi World and "Religious Specialists"*

The Hopi world-view has been described in several recent essays—all very different, all basically accurate (Black 1984; Eggan 1986; Loftin 1991). One of the basic premises of Hopi life is a conception of a world which is bipartite in structure (see Figure 4.1). Mischa Titiev (1944:173) has written that there is a

> dual division of time and space between an upper world of the living and the lower world of the dead. This is expressed in the description of the sun's journey on its daily rounds. The Hopi believe that the sun has two entrances, variously referred to as houses, homes or kivas, situated at each extremity of its course. In the morning the sun is supposed to emerge from its eastern home, and in the evening it is said to descend into its western home. During the night the sun must travel underground from west to east in order to arise at its accustomed place the next day. Hence day and night are reversed in the upper and lower "worlds."

Life and death, day and night are seen not simply as opposed but as involved in a system of alternation and continuity—indeed (as we will see) a fundamental consubstantiality (i.e., having the same substance). As John Loftin summarizes (1991:11–12):

> The spiritual source of all life and forms issues from the land of the dead, the underworld, where it appears as life-giving water. Indeed, the Hopi petition their own departed ancestors to visit their villages in the form of clouds to bless them with the sacred gift of rain. Thus death is understood by the Hopi as a return to the spiritual realm from which comes more life.

This world and the world of the spirits are transformations of each other and yet are of the same

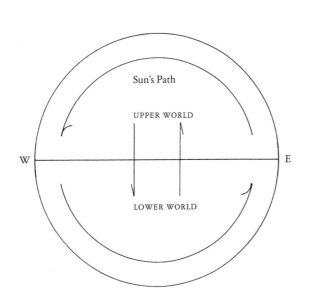

FIGURE 4.1. Bipartite structure of the Hopi world.

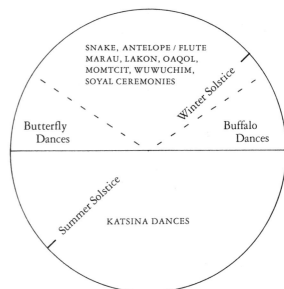

FIGURE 4.2. Hopi ritual calendar.

essential substance. At death a cotton mask, a "white cloud mask" (Stephen 1936:825), is placed on the face of the dead person. At burial it is said, "You are no longer a Hopi, you are changed (*nih'ti,* grown) into a kachina, you are Cloud (O'mauuh)." After death, Stephen writes, "the breath body, *hi'ksi ah'paa,* goes from the grave along the trail to the sipapu in the west" (1936:826). The spirits of the dead return to this world as *katsinas.* All *katsinas* are believed to take on cloud form, to be "cloud people," and their substance is manifested as rainfall. The Hopi do not say, "I am of the same flesh and blood as my parents." Rather, "I am the liquid substance of my fathers." The "spiritual substance" of the *katsina* is, also, the Hopi's "self-substance." Thus, when the *katsinam* (as masked ritual figures) depart, they are petitioned, "When you return to your homes bring this message to them that, without delay, they may have mercy on us with their liquid substance [i.e., the rains] so that all things may grow and life may be bountiful." Everything, in Hopi thought, is dependent on moisture which, when combined with "mother

earth," is the substance of all things (cf. Loftin 1991:10–11). Through this combination and subsequent transformation into corn, the blessings (the gifts) of the *katsinam* (their spiritual substance) becomes the substance of "our" bodies (our substance; as opposed to *qatungwu,* matter without life [Loftin 1991:130, n. 79]).

In the Hopi definition and differentiation of categories of "person" there is, it follows, a major domain of meaning which relates to persons who mediate between the world of the living and the world of the spirits (and/or the dead). How this mediation is accomplished is best understood in the context of the Hopi ritual calendar.

V. *Time and the* Katsina

As noted above, Hopis speak of the *katsinam* as "our friends," and this is an expression commonly used for "masks" as well. Hopis will speak of "those who have friends (masks)" (cf. Geertz and Lomatuwayma 1987:211, n. 65) but rarely use the term *tuviku* (mask; cf. Geertz and Lomatuwayma 1987:235, n. 30; Bradfield 1973:2:49; Stephen 1936:1235). Uninitiated Hopis should not have knowledge of or contact with the "mask." Nonetheless, "masked face" or "mask" will be used here in preference to "face" as it conveys better the sense of the "otherness" and physical difference of this object. At the same time, it should be emphasized that the *tuviku,* the mask, is what defines the *katsina,* is the essence of this "person," as is clear in the emphasis placed on the masked face of *katsina* "dolls" prior to the twentieth century.

"Masks" are only employed in public, "ritual" contexts and it will be useful here to outline the Hopi ritual calendar. As Figure 4.2 indicates, the ritual calendar parallels the dual organization of the world. One half of the year involves "priestly" activities which consist in large part of prayers and prayer offerings (prestations) to the spirit world. Here, for example, the snakes of the well-known "Snake Ceremony" serve as messengers who carry the prayers and prayer offerings of the Snake priests to the lower world through various openings in the surface of this world. It is important to note that none of the "persons" who offer prayers and prayer offerings during the "priestly" half of the ritual calendar wear masks, although most have painted faces (e.g., the "priest" of the Snake and Antelope societies).

For the Hopi, the *katsinam* "are thought to live in the San Francisco Mountains, where they remain during half of the year when there are no masked dances in the village. During the other half of the year they come to the village to dance, sing, bring presents to the children, and above all to bring rain. When they dance they summon their 'cloud fathers,' another form in which the Kachinas appear. It is generally believed that the spirits of the dead go to the west where they become kachinas and return to the village as clouds" (Earle and Kennard 1971:4). The *katsinam* are "messengers of the gods" and according to A. M. Stephen, the literal translation of the word is "a sitter." Thus, "the Katcina is one who comes to sit

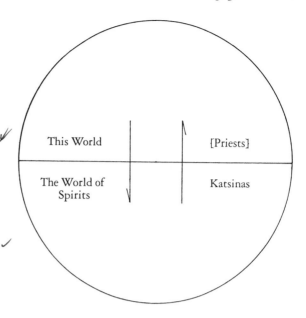

FIGURE 4.3. Reciprocity and Hopi "religious specialists."

and listen to the petitions of the people" (Stephen 1940:103) and bring them assurances that their prayers have been heard. On these ritual occasions, the Hopis "feed" the *katsinam* with prayer offerings and the masked dancers reciprocate with gifts of food. Thus, these two categories of "religious specialist"—"priest" and *katsina*—are opposed in space and time and by virtue of the presence or absence of the "mask." They are, at the same time, however, related through the cycle of reciprocity (see Figure 4.3). Reciprocity involves (according to Lévi-Strauss 1950:xxxvi) the unconscious principle of the obligation to give, the obligation to receive and the obligation to give in return. The counter-gift must be deferred and different (Bourdieu 1977:5). As H. R. Voth noted (1912:55), "it is the supposition that the spirits of the departed come and get the food and the prayer feathers, or rather the *hikwsi* (breath, essence, soul) of these objects." Because the dead "eat only the odor or soul of the food," the dead are not heavy. "And that is the reason why the clouds into which the dead are transformed are not heavy and can float in the air" (Voth 1905:116). While one purpose of ritual in this world involves a contribution to the well-being of the spirit world, the spirit world is obligated to contribute to the well-being of this world by providing rain which is essential to the crops and, hence, to the health of the Hopis (and all living things of this world). Rain is the most common request in Hopi prayer, however the "gift," "blessing," or "benefit" (*na'manqwu;* cf. Voth 1901:146 n. 4) may take other forms as well.

There are perhaps three hundred figures who are *katsinam,* each with a distinctive masked face, identity and role in ritual. In Hopi thought, "there was a time when these supernatural messengers," as Stephen describes them (1940: 103–4),

> actually came direct from the gods, delivering their decrees and returning with the petitions of the people. But at a very early day their visits ceased, though not until they had imparted to certain good men the mysteries of the peculiar rites and ceremonies by which they might acquire the power of communicating with the deities. The different *Katcinas* instructed different priests, who in turn initiated certain of their own people. . . . [The masked ritual dancers] are . . . the initiated who thus represent the original *Katcinas* and are supposed to lose their human identity and to become endowed with his supernatural attributes upon assuming their masks.

VI. The Hopi Tuviku: Masks and Meaning

The katsina "mask" is a ritual object of great importance. Armin Geertz summarizes some basic information in the following (1986:45):

> Every boy who is initiated into the Katsina Cult has the right to own a mask. A mask is made of leather but it is believed to be alive. Therefore it must be kept fed and hidden when stored, just like other animate ritual objects. The term for the mask is *tuviku,* but this term is seldom used, since the

uninitiated children would learn that the Katsinas are not gods but their uncles, fathers and brothers in masks and costumes. Thus the masks are always called *kwaatsi,* "friend."

In this essay, the masked face has been seen as meaningful in the context of Hopi moral space and as the distinctive feature of one "religious specialist." But what of the mask itself? How is it meaningful? In Figure 4.4, two Hopi masks are reproduced: those of the *Ma'lo katsina* and the *Koyemsi Katsina.*

The *Ma'lo katsina* (Colton No. 130; cf. Stephen 1936:215–16; Fewkes 1892*b*:57–59, 1894*a*:Pl. 8, Fig. 21, 1903:103 and Pl. 21) has been a popular *katsina* for impersonation at outdoor "dances" during the spring and early summer and at the Niman or home-going ceremony occurring at the end of the *katsina* period. *Ma'lo katsina* is sometimes called "Stick Kachina" (Wright 1973:176) because of the staff he carries in his left hand. The leather case mask is painted red and blue (or green) with a tubular mouth. At one side of the mask is a squash blossom ("his flower"), "a convention of colored yarns wound around stems radiating from a solid stamen" (Stephen 1936:215), and at the other side two eagle tail feathers with a tuft of red hair. The ruff is of Douglas fir. The body may be painted "any common kachina style" (Colton 1959:50) although Stephen says they are "the cloud colors of the cardinal directions." The red sash over the right shoulder, the kilt, sash and belt around the waist and the usually green moccasins are all common attire. A gourd rattle held in the right hand, a tortoiseshell rattle worn on the right leg and bells worn on the left contribute to the complex rhythms of the *katsina*'s songs. What is significant here is that all the distinct elements of form and content, of shape and color, which comprise the mask are named and in themselves derive their meanings from the Hopi "world-view," a conception that includes a complex system of correspondences that systematically relates direction, color and sequence (see Figure 4.5).

FIGURE 4.4*a*. Ma'lo katsina.

FIGURE 4.4*b*. Koyemsi katsina.

The colors of the *katsina,* yellow, blue, red, and white, are associated with the four directions. The eyebrow is a conventionalized representation of a cloud (indeed it is called *oomaw,* Cloud). Beneath it is the eye (Stephen 1936:215–16):

> The eye of the kachina (any kachina?) is the seed of *all* plants, hence the seed of any plant is its eye (*poosi*), and appropriately the eyebrow becomes a cloud over the seed, in position ready to pour down rain and start germination. The eye is . . . specifically spoken of as seed of cotton, beans, muskmelon. . . .

These seeds are chewed producing a black pigment, the color of the Above. The two black tipped eagle feathers are likewise said to represent the Above, while the cascading feathers on the top of the mask case represent the Below, the region of all color. Of the mouth, Stephen writes (1936:216):

> [It is] an ear of corn, partly perforated and with open slits through which the personator emits his song-prayer. The common convention of a corn ear is nearly a facsimile of the natural object, but in this kachina it is modified in that only its cylindric form is retained to indicate its prototype. Because, Suyuku says, with customary logical iteration, through the mouth come prayers, not only for corn, but for all other essentials, hence the corn ear should not be too specially manifest.

Stephen continues recording similar statements regarding the *Ma'lo katsina*'s staff, its song, and so forth.

The sixfold division of color and space is not simply a matter of cultural convention but has im-

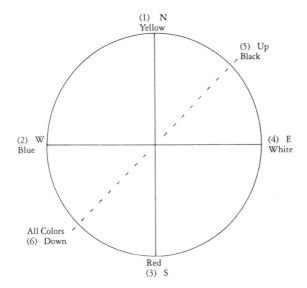

FIGURE 4.5. Direction / Color / Sequence

portant natural basis in the Hopi world as well. According to another early observer of the Hopi, "at least ninety per cent of the vegetable food eaten . . . is made of corn" (Owens 1892:163). More recently, Mary Black has described how the Hopi perception of the life cycle similarities of humans and corn plants forms the basis of comparison for various metaphors. Emergence / birth, taking sustenance, maturation and death are seen as meaningfully related. Of the *Qatungwu / soona* dichotomy, Black writes (1984:280–81):

> When a person dies, it is said that he goes home, *nimangwu,* but that his body is left here as a lifeless, useless thing, *qatungwu,* the corpse, or "that which held life." *Qatungwu* also applies to the corn plant that has been harvested of ears, and so is without life. The lifeless bodies of both are said to be without *soona,* the substance of life (and the complement of *qatungwu* in the sense of form versus substance) or "that which makes life viable." In fact, corn and *soona* are sometimes equated in Hopi, as corn, being the gift that Maasawu promised, is sufficient to sustain the Hopi throughout the path of time.

Hopi corn is yellow, blue, red, white, black and sweet (*katsina* corn). To the Hopi, corn is their "mother" for "they live on and draw life from the corn as the child draws life from its mother" (Voth 1901:149 n. 5; cf. Black 1984). A second basic source of food is beans. According to Stephen, the "old time beans of the Hopi seem to be . . . yellow, blue, red, white, black, speckled" (1936:354). Hopi dependence on corn has decreased since the nineteenth century, but corn remains a meaningful symbol of life, its substance and that which sustains it. Put differently, color is a code (cf. Sahlins 1976) used culturally for the expression of significant distinctions in the Hopi conception or construction of moral space. Or, as Stephen put it in discussing the Hopi use of color in ritual, "this pigmentary manifestation may be called chromatic prayer, as it is definitely regarded as a direct appeal to the clouds at the four directions to hasten with rain to the Hopi land" (1898:265). Although Hopis participate in our world of color, the ritual use of color has not been modified.

The second "mask" in Figure 4.4 is that of the *Koyemsi katsina* or "mudhead" (Colton No. 59; cf. Stephen 1936:174–82; Fewkes 1903:113, Pl. 26). Here Hopis prefer the Zuni name to their own *tatsiqto,* which refers to the balls (*tatsi* = ball) on the mask (Stephen 1936:342, 1149).

A useful point of departure here is the "origin myth" of the *Koyemsi* (Stephen 1936:181–82):

> At the *atkya* (underworld) the Tachukti wore beautiful garments. He wore the same mask he has now, but it was adorned with bright parrot feathers (*kyaarot homasa'at,* parrot wing feathers) set in a large plume just over the brow. He wore the embroidered white cotton blanket and bright woven bandoleer, the colored girdle, and other bright colored belts, fox skin at loins, breech cloth, fine netted shirt (*poronapna*), also netted leggings and blue-green moccasins. *Okiwa, siway tsoova!* Alas! He copulated with his younger sister, and the Kachina chief took all his fine apparel away and doomed him from henceforth to wear a cast off woman's gown.

The account ends with the statement: "He knew well how to bring rain." In the Hopi "myth" of emergence, similar behavior—the violation of the rules of kinship—serves as a metonym for all un-Hopi (*qa hopi*) behavior (Stephen 1929:3):

> In the Underworld all the people were fools [*qa hopi*]. Youths copulated with the wives of elder men, and the elder men deflowered virgins. All was confusion, and the chief was unhappy.

While the *Koyemsi* is a *katsina* and can "bring rain," in his being and behavior he represents the opposite of those meanings associated with the mask and symbolic action of *all* other katsinas. The *Koyemsi katsina* may, and frequently does, accompany other katsinas in "ritual." Thus their presence together underscores not only the physical contrasts but also the meaningful oppositions these "persons" represent.

The masked face and appearance of the *Koyemsi* has been anticipated in the "origin myth." The masks are called *tatsiqtot qoto'at* (knobbed head) and are made of cloth (in contrast to the leather case of all other masks), and have knobs which appear as grotesque inversions of human eyes, ears and mouth. Stephen records that "in the knobs (*tatsi*) of the mask are some of every kind of seed, and the spherical effect is made by stuffing with Hopi cotton" (1936:181). The cloth mask and the body of the impersonator are coated with a wash of clay varying in color from pale pink to brownish red. It is "earth-colored" or better, the absence of those meaningful colors which embellish the mask and attire of other katsinas. The impersonators "put on a old *kwasa*, the woman's dark woolen dress, some wearing it as a skirt with body bare, others wearing it in the ordinary fashion worn by women, over right shoulder and under left arm, blue leggings and bare feet" (Stephen 1936:179), although some wear red-brown moccasins. Until recently, the *Koyemsi* wore a "pouch of entire fawn skin" (Stephen 1936:180; cf. 181, fig. 105) over the right shoulder, flour sacks being used today. Each carries an eagle feather (*kwaa-wiki*—the primary wing feather) in the left hand and a globular or pear-shaped gourd rattle in the right. Sometimes strips of dark blue cloth or yarn are worn around the writsts and below the knees and a rag ruff is tied around the neck.

Singly or in groups, the *Koyemsi katsina* performs a number of subservient roles, for example, wood gathering, announcing the arrival of other katsinas, drumming or singing in chorus with a drummer accompanying dancing *katsinam,* and so on. As "clowns" they dance in a childish, undisciplined manner, frequently tumbling over each other, shouting and laughing and sometimes processing backwards as they sing. On other occasions, as Stephen records, they simply play (1936:176):

> The ball playing of the clowns did not suggest a game—none tried to catch the ball, one merely tried to hit the others with it. When struck, the man fell down and was hauled around by the others till he got to his feet.

As katsinas and as messengers who will bring the blessings of moisture, Hopis make prayer meal offerings to the *Koyemsi.* At the same time, the *Koyemsi* mock this "spiritual" feeding by attempts to consume eatable material, by stuffing eggs and other foods into the mouth orifice. Finally, in contrast to the solemn attentiveness shown toward katsinas like the *Ma'lo,* laughter and occasional physical roughness characterize the relation between Hopis and performing *Koyemsi.*

In Hopi moral space, the *ma'lo katsina* is to the *Koyemsi* as order is to chaos, and within this system of person categories those "beautiful creatures" (as Hopis often refer to the *katsinam*), like the *Ma'lo katsina,* find a significant contrast in the appearance and behavior of the *Koyemsi.*

VII. Rethinking

The history of the social-scientific treatment of "religious specialists" reveals a tendency to isolate the "shaman" or "priest" from the system(s) of person categories and moral space they occupy and to set up contrastive types (shaman / priest, prophet / priest, etc.) which may not exist as ethnographic "fact." In the long run, there is the very strong possibility that this strategy will lessen rather than contribute to crosscultural understanding. The proper context for understanding "religious specialists" should be the native's theory, not ours. David Schneider has convincingly argued that we need to rethink "kinship"; here it is suggested that we need to rethink "religious specialists." One useful point of departure is to ask cultural questions, of which Schneider writes (1972:39–40):

> A cultural question is by definition a question of what units this particular socio-cultural system is constructed, of how those units are defined and articulated, and of how those units form a meaningful whole.

The meaning of *katsina* in its full complexity and richness is beyond the texts and frames of this essay and only fully comprehensible in the lives of Hopi people. As Clifford Geertz once remarked (1983:58):

> to grasp concepts that, for another people, are experience-near, and to do so well enough to place them in illuminating connection with experience-distant concepts theorists have fashioned to capture the general features of social life, is clearly a task at least as delicate, if a bit less magical, as putting oneself in someone else's skin.

In summary, it may be said for the Hopi, as for all Native American peoples, that kinship provides symbols which define and differentiate members of the family and larger social units. These same symbols define and differentiate the kinds of relationships which these persons should have with each other. In a similar manner, Hopi religion provides sets of symbols that define and differentiate categories of person and the relationships between humans and members of the spirit world. These human and spirit "persons" constitute a distinctive "religious" system of person categories which are defined and given symbolic expression with distinctive features such as "faces" (masked or painted) and who act within accepted systems of thought and action (rituals). Thus, in describing the *katsina* as a "person" in Hopi culture, I have also sought to substantiate the need to treat this catagory of person, the "religious specialist," with the same seriousness and respect which anthropologists, like Fred Eggan, have brought to the categories of person which constitute "kinship."

VIII. Some Afterthoughts

The theologian Paul Tillich once remarked that everything is ultimately concerned with meaning *and* power. In considering the intellectual aspects of the Hopi world-view, I have consciously set aside any attempt to describe the emotional force of the *katsina* in its various manifestations. The power of the *katsina* in shaping Hopis' moods and motivations and of the mask in transforming the wearer is suggested in Emory Sekaquaptewa's (1976:39) description of his experience as a participant. Clearly a fuller account of this "person" must take into consideration the affective, creative force which the *katsina* represents (cf. Tonkin 1979).

Second, I noted in my introduction that this paper is a collage of texts which are products of history (cf. Dockstader 1985). While I have not detected any change in Hopi *conceptions* of the *katsina*, I recognize that these ethnographic texts are the products of time, of different villages, of different Hopi voices, of different ethnographic traditions. And if the conceptions of the *katsina* have not changed, there have been and continue to be significant and pervasive changes in Hopi culture more broadly (cf. Loftin 1991). Thus, the experiencial context of Hopi religion and of the *katsina* is very different.

Finally, in reflecting on my experience of *katsina*

dances and the days following, I recalled listening to the songs of the *katsinam* being played back on cassette recorders in Hopi homes I visited. The visual dimension is the most accessible aspect of the *katsina* to those of us who have been guests at dances, but for Hopis much of the meaning of the *katsina* is conveyed through the songs that give shape and direction to their daily lives (cf. Black 1984). Here, too, there is much to understand and appreciate.

5

The Katsina Cult: A Western Pueblo Perspective

E. CHARLES ADAMS

CEREMONIES involving masked dancers, called katsinas, are restricted to the Pueblo people of the southwestern United States. This situation has apparently remained unchanged since before contact because Spanish documents as early as 1582 (Hammond and Rey 1928:79; White 1932a:626) mention the widespread presence of katsina ceremonies and depictions of katsina figures in murals on the walls of rooms. The appearance of katsina-like beings in prehispanic kiva murals in pueblos along the Rio Grande and on the Hopi mesas suggest that rituals involving katsinas are prehistoric. This essay will explore some of the evidence for prehistoric katsina religion among western Pueblo groups and some of the possible explanations for its appearance.

Pueblo design of katsina faces and heads not only distinguish them from one another but also make them distinctive from other Pueblo symbols. Cole (1989) examined specific elements of katsina design and concluded that in archaeological contexts the mask is the only reliable indicator of the presence of katsina ceremonialism. This approach will be used in this discussion.

Eggan (1950:2) noted the natural division between eastern Pueblos on the Rio Grande and western Pueblo groups that live in the canyon and

[handwritten marginal note: but of feathers - not survive ?!?]

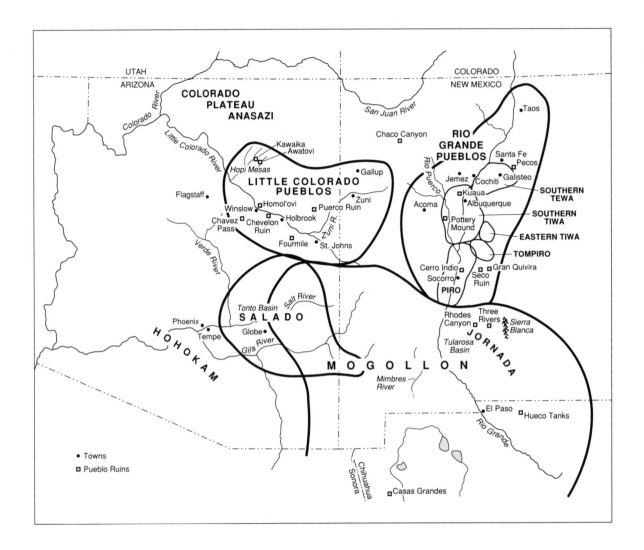

FIGURE 5.1. Map of the Pueblo world and related archaeological areas, showing major towns, contemporary Pueblos, and Pueblo IV sites mentioned.

mesa country to the west. The western Pueblos are quite similar in their social structure, based primarily on lineages and clans crosscut by kiva societies, and consist of Acoma, Laguna, Zuni, and the Hopi villages, along with the Tewa-speaking village of Hano on First Mesa. Among these Acoma, several Zuni villages, and Hopi villages predate Spanish contact and will be considered for this discussion.

Today among the western Pueblos katsinas and katsina ceremonies are highly developed. Membership in the katsina society is universal for all males in western Pueblos and for all females among the Hopi and Acoma and for some females at Zuni (Adams 1991:10). Initiation into the katsina society has age-grading significance and marks a significant step on the ladder to adulthood. After initiation, boys can participate in ceremonies and girls have the insight into their culture's religion to serve as effective counterparts to males. When adult men and women die in western Pueblo society, they have an afterlife in the underworld and come back as clouds or katsinas during katsina ceremonies to bring rain to the crops of their people in answer to their prayers. Katsinas are thus associated with rain, fertility, and curing at Zuni and Acoma. It is quite possible that these distinctive qualities of katsina ceremonialism made it adaptive to the societies that adopted it. Exploration of prehistoric western Pueblo villages may help answer this question.

Villages ancestral to the historic western Pueblos develop the distinctive size, layout, and settlement configuration of their historic counterparts between A.D. 1250–1350. In addition to prehistoric settlements in the vicinity of the modern western Pueblo villages, extensive thirteenth- and fourteenth-century pueblos occurred along the major drainages and the Little Colorado River valley itself (Figure 5.1). It is in these settlements that the data for the origins of katsina ceremonialism, sometimes called the katsina cult (cf. Adams 1991), will be investigated. My use of "western Pueblo" therefore implies cultural continuity with historic western Pueblos as defined by Eggan (1950) in contrast to the more archaeologically derived definition developed by Reed (1948).

In addition to focusing attention on western Pueblo settlements dating 1250–1350 in the Little Colorado River basin, I will briefly explore contemporary developments in other areas that may have been influential.

Previous Research

ICONOGRAPHIC

Past studies of the origin, development, and meaning of katsina ceremonialism have been varied. Parsons (1939) suggested that it was introduced by Mexicans who accompanied the Spanish conquistadors (Adams 1991:21). This purely historic explanation seems unlikely from the weight of evidence of Spanish historical documents of the contact period and numerous lines of archaeological evidence. Brew (1943) challenged Parsons's explanation, based on excavations of numerous kiva murals with apparent katsinas at prehistoric Hopi villages on Antelope Mesa, evoking the possible relationship between katsinas and Tlaloc figures from Mexico.

The evidence for the presence of katsinas invariably lies with iconographic similarities between modern Pueblo katsina iconography and archaeological ones. The earliest to discuss the iconographic evidence was Smith (1952) in his exhaustive study of the kiva murals from Awatovi and Kawaika-a from Antelope Mesa at Hopi. Similar murals at Pottery Mound (Hibben 1975) and Kuaua (Dutton 1963) also saw ties to katsinas and katsina ceremonies. Hibben (1966, 1967) drew close parallels to Mexican origins, a subject not elaborated on by Smith or Dutton. Smith (1952) dates the onset of the elaborated kiva mural iconography to the late 1300s at Hopi. Dutton's (1963) analysis of Kuaua suggests a post-1450 date for the kiva murals. Hibben (1955, 1960, 1975) dates the onset of kiva mural painting at Pottery Mound to about 1350.

Schaafsma (1972) and Schaafsma and Schaafsma (1974) were the first to tie katsinas to rock art, focusing their study in the eastern Pueblos and south into the Jornada and Mimbres areas. The Schaafsmas have also tied katsina origins to the south, most clearly with Tlaloc figures and masks in the Jornada style. Recently, Cole (1989, 1990) has argued for a more indigenous development of katsina religion, noting similarities to

FIGURE 5.2. Selected petroglyphs of katsinas near Homol'ovi II on the Little Colorado River, Arizona. (*Redrawn from Cole 1992: Figs. 5.5a and g; 5.6b.*)

rock art having faces in the Four Corners region. In most cases katsinas in rock art emphasize the head and face often omitting the body altogether. Cole (1990:148–50) assigned dates to the apearance of katsina iconography on rock art in the Little Colorado River basin (Figure 5.2) to 1250–1300 on the basis of association with ceramically dated and radiocarbon-dated pueblos. Schaafsma and Schaafsma (1974) (and see P. Schaafsma, this volume) dated the appearance of katsinas on rock art in the middle Rio Grande to about 1325, also on the basis of association with ceramically dated pueblos.

Katsina-like faces also frequently occur on pottery, in particular in the western Pueblo area. The most frequent occurrences are on Fourmile Polychrome manufactured in the upper Little Colorado River valley dating 1300/1325–1400 (Breternitz 1966; Carlson 1970, 1982*b*). Frequent depictions of katsina faces on pottery also characterizes various Hopi yellow wares dating 1300–1450 (Ferg 1982; Hays 1989; 1991:39 & 41) and various Winslow Orange Wares manufactured at the Homol'ovi pueblos (Hays 1989). The occurrence of katsina-like icons on pottery in the eastern Pueblos is extremely rare prior to 1450 (Adams 1991:146–47). On the basis of ceramic evidence, much of it supported by tree-ring dates, katsina iconography on western Pueblo ceramics apparently becomes widespread between 1300–1350. In contrast, eastern Pueblo pottery katsina iconography is extremely rare until after 1450. Schaafsma and Schaafsma (1974) associated the appearance of katsina icons in rock art, termed the Rio Grande style, with the construction of Classic Period pueblos. The beginning date attributed to this period is about 1325.

NONICONOGRAPHIC

Adams (1991) relates the appearance of katsina icons in pottery and rock art to artifactual and architectural changes occurring in a wide area of the Southwest. The artifacts, which include comals and shoe- or slipper-form pottery vessels, derive from northern Mexico or southern Arizona during the 1200s. (Dixon 1963, 1976; Haury 1945: 109–11). Architectural change includes growth in size and the development of plaza-oriented pueblos. Village size was probably related to consolidation of indigenous and immigrant populations; however, the plaza-oriented layout seems most clearly related to southern origins where adobe plaza-oriented pueblos developed in the international four corners in the early thirteenth century. Adobe architecture is a common feature of western and eastern Pueblo villages of the thirteenth and fourteenth centuries and most plausibly derived from the adobe-dominated architecture to the south.

Finally, "katsina dolls" and their origins must be considered. Haury (1945:198–200) reported a flat katsina doll made of stone dated to the fourteenth century from Double Butte Cave near Tempe, Arizona. This isolated example is probably not a katsina doll, but could be a nonkatsina ritual effigy similar to ones still used by Hopi and other Pueblo groups. Of more interest are sets of carved stone figurines associated with twelfth-century pueblos in the upper drainages of the Little Colorado River. Parts of five sets are now known (Eaton, personal communication) and consist of human figures, animal figures, geomorphic figures, and occasional katsina-like figures. The katsina relation derives from the appearance of the face. The figures are all very similar in having two round to ovate eyes, a prominent triangular nose, and an oval open mouth. The best-preserved set obtained by the Museum of Northern Arizona indicates these figures have detailed heads, necks, geometrically painted bodies, and suggestions of arms and legs held tight against the body (Plate 1). Brody (1991: Fig. 37) illustrates similar human figures from northeastern Arizona.

In many details of body and head form and design, these do look similar to katsina dolls as carved by the Hopi in the late 1800s (Erickson 1977). However, details of the face, including the presence of a nose, the size and form of the eyes, and the size and form of the mouth are inconsistent with facial details of fourteenth century figures depicted in the rock art and on the pottery that are widely associated with the appearance of the katsina cult (Adams 1991; Cole 1989; Ferg 1982; Hays 1989; Schaafsma and Schaafsma 1974). Additionally, their inclusion in groups of figurines in various forms and sizes and their even stronger resemblance to altar figurines suggests that their function was probably as altar pieces, or some other ritual context, and not as katsina dolls, at least in the modern ethnographic context. These figurines could be precursors to a katsina doll form that evolved a century or two later; however, there is no archaeological evidence of this development.

The concentration of these sets of figurines in the upper Little Colorado River drainage provides a geographical tie to early ceramic katsina iconography 150–200 years later and adds circumstantial evidence to an early indigenous development of katsina religion. Together with influence in architecture, food processing, and perhaps iconography from the south on this indigenous ritual

TABLE 5.1. Western Pueblo Ceramics Having Katsina Icons and Their Associated Tree-ring Dates

Type	Breternitz 1966	Smith 1971	Carlson 1970	Carlson*b* 1982*b*	Adams & Hays 1991	Consensus
Awatovi B/y		1300–1375				1300–1375
Chavez Pass Poly				1300–1400	1275–1350	1275–1400
Fourmile Poly	1300–1385		1325–1400	1325–1400		1300–1400
Gila Polychrome	1250–1385			1300–1600		1300–1450
Homol'ovi Poly	1300–1400			1300–1400	1275–1350	1275–1400
Jeddito B/y	1300–1400	1350–1450				1300–1450

system surrounding these figurines it becomes possible to argue for an indigenous development in the western Pueblo area of katsina religion in the early 1300s.

Chronology, Settlement Change and Iconography in the Western Pueblo Area

CHRONOLOGY

The foregoing discussion of iconographic evidence attributed to the beginnings of katsina ceremonialism focus fairly tightly in a 150-year period, A.D. 1250–1400 in the western Pueblo area. Direct dating of any artifacts bearing katsina iconography is virtually nonexistent. The closest example is a Paayu Polychrome (early style of Sikyatki Polychrome) bowl bearing a Sun Katsina face excavated from the floor of a room at Homol'ovi II (Hays 1991:Fig. 3.5*c*). Combined corrected radiocarbon dates from the hearths of adjacent rooms suggest a date of 1349 ± 67 years (Madsen and Hays 1991:Table 2.2). Smith (1952) uses nonstructural, noncutting dates from several beams to suggest a beginning date of the elaborated kiva murals at Awatovi of about 1375.

Easily the most pervasive and most convincing evidence for dating katsina iconography is derived from tree-ring dated ceramic types. Some of these types, such as Fourmile Polychrome, have katsina figures depicted on them, whereas considerable rock art is associated with pueblos whose pottery assemblages can be tree-ring dated.

Pottery types having katsina depictions on them in the western Pueblo area and their tree-ring dated occurrence are presented in Table 5.1. The dates for the six fourteenth-century pottery types having katsina depictions range from 1275 to 1450. None of the ceramics from thirteenth century proveniences at Homol'ovi III or Homol'ovi IV had katsinas, suggesting a post-1300 date. By the same token, the depiction of katsina faces on Homolovi Polychrome and Chavez Polychrome, types that may not have been manufactured after 1350 (Hays 1991), suggests a 1300–1350 date. The presence of katsina faces on Awatovi Black-on-yellow vessels dated 1300–1375 at least dates their appearance before 1375. If Fourmile Polychrome in fact dates after 1325 rather than 1300–1400, it is quite possible that the appearance of katsinas on ceramics in the western Pueblo area began between 1325 and 1350/75. In any case, the close cluster of all these pottery types dates the appearance of katsinas on pottery to the fourteenth century and almost certainly before 1375.

Table 5.2 lists the pueblos with rock art depicting katsinas and the tree-ring dated pottery of associated pueblos. The association of katsinas in rock art with Homol'ovi IV suggested to Cole (1989; 1990:150) that the cult may have started after 1250, but before 1300. This early date is not belied by the published dates for Homol'ovi II, Cottonwood Creek, or Puerco Ruin. However, recent work at Homol'ovi II by the Arizona State Museum, University of Arizona, suggests that

TABLE 5.2. Katsina Rock Art and Tree-ring Dated Pottery Dates for Associated Pueblos

Pueblo	Tree-ring Dated Pottery	Dates	Reference
Homol'ovi II	Awatovi B / y; Jeddito B / y Sikyatki Poly	1300–1400	Adams & Hays 1991
Homol'ovi IV	Jeddito B / o; St. Johns Poly	1250–1300	Adams 1989:178
Cottonwood Creek	Homolovi Poly; Awatovi B / y	1275–1350	Adams 1989:178
Puerco Ruin	Homolovi Poly; Awatovi B / y	1250–1350	Burton 1990:328

Homol'ovi II was not established until after 1300. Because Homol'ovi II has the preponderance of katsina motif rock art among the Homol'ovi pueblos, this suggests that such rock art probably postdates 1300, although a pre-1300 date cannot be dismissed.

Smith (1952) identified a sequence of styles in the development of the kiva murals at Awatovi and Kawaika-a between about 1350 to the establishment of a mission at Awatovi in 1630. The scanty tree-ring dates and the similarity of designs in the murals to those on Sikyatki Polychrome pottery led Smith (1971:601) to conclude that the kiva murals began about 1375 with the depiction of katsina imagery beginning about the same time or by 1400. A kiva excavated by Gordon Pond (1966) at Homol'ovi II in 1962 had murals with dancing figures wearing kilts similar to those on the Hopi Mesas. Although the heads are missing, the figures are suggestive of katsina-like figures in the Awatovi and Kawaika-a murals. The ceramics associated with the Homol'ovi II kiva suggest a date of 1375–1400, adding support to Smith's formulation.

In summary the dating of the appearance of katsina iconography in the archaeological record of the western Pueblo areas is based primarily on tree-ring dated ceramic assemblages. Although these are reliable, a factor of plus or minus twenty-five years should be attributed to ascribed dates. Ceramics and rock art with katsina iconography seem to appear at almost exactly the same time, most likely between 1300 and 1350, although a pre-1300 date cannot be totally dismissed. The appearance of katsinas in kiva murals seems to date between 1375 and 1400 based on highly problematic dating from Awatovi, Kawaika-a, and Homol'ovi II. Given these dates it seems certain that ritual involving katsinas appeared by the first half of the fourteenth century and was well established by the end of that century.

SETTLEMENT CHANGE

As I have noted in detail elsewhere (Adams 1991), the appearance of katsina iconography follows closely on the heels of massive settlement change and population movement. The Four Corners area of the Colorado Plateau is all but abandoned between 1275 and 1300, and settlements associated with these emigrants appear along various areas of the Rio Grande, in the Hopi Mesas area, along several courses of the Little Colorado River, and even below the Mogollon Rim (Adams 1991:124–35). The Anasazi immigrating into these already populated regions undoubtedly faced numerous obstacles, both cultural and environmental. Abandonment sequences in late-thirteenth-century Anasazi pueblos suggest that settlements were abandoned piecemeal over several years and not all at once (cf. Dean 1969). Crosscultural studies suggest that most immigrating populations move to areas with which they are familiar through trade and probably fictive kinship relations. Such trade relationships characterized historic Pueblos and artifactual evidence suggests trade was common prehistorically as well.

What was the stage in the area into which many of these immigrating populations moved? Settlement size in the Little Colorado River basin was typically small in the 1000–1250 period. Settlements were apparently organized around great kiva ceremonial architecture (Bluhm 1957; Martin et al. 1961). If settlements had remained small, as they had been during the 1000–1250 period, new settlers would directly compete with existing small settlements. However, by the mid-1200s larger pueblos developed, also with great kivas as apparent integrative architecture. Smaller ceremonial rooms, perhaps intended for more kinship-based ritual, were incorporated into the pueblo roomblock (Martin and Rinaldo 1960; Martin et al. 1961). The causes of this shift in settlement size and configuration are complex, but environmental degradation in the late 1200s probably precipitated an aggregation response ✓ with settlements focusing on the best lands. Aggregation concentrates people and frees large areas from resident population; however, given traditional Pueblo land-use patterns, ownership of these lands would not have been relinquished.

With the influx of new population into already settled areas in the 1275–1300 period, renewed stress of increased population on fixed resources was applied to indigenous populations. Although instances of violent confrontation between indigenous populations and immigrant populations have been documented (Haury 1958), apparently most were assimilated by indigenous settle-✓ ments. This assimilation process was probably made easier by the nature of the immigrant populations which probably consisted of fairly small kinship groups. Among Hopi oral and historical documentation of land use patterns, new populations were constantly being absorbed into existing villages (Courlander 1971; James 1974; Nagata 1936). The negotiation process involved an understanding of what role the immigrants would play in their new village, including social and ceremonial roles, in exchange for land on which to grow their own corn. The new land was usually at the farthest outskirts of the existing farm areas beyond that used by existing kinship groups in the village.

Evidence of cooperative behavior rather than conflict occurs along three lines: stylistic, artifactual, and village size and layout. Carlson (1970; 1982b:217) noted that Pinedale Polychrome, which is a White Mountain Red Ware manufactured in the upper Little Colorado River drainage beginning between 1275 and 1300, represents a merging of northern Anasazi style and indigenous style signalling a shift in the indigenous tradition. Artifactual evidence is best illustrated in the Homol'ovi pueblos where artifactual and architectural styles suggest the area was settled by immigrants from at least two areas (Adams 1989:185–86). The immigrant populations seem to have settled the area between 1250 and 1300 and lived side by side in small villages for perhaps twenty years before being absorbed into the larger pueblos after 1300.

Between 1275 and 1300 there is a significant and universal shift in village size and layout (Adams 1991:101–3). Increased village size probably continues a trend begun by 1250, but it accelerated after 1275 to 1350. Although the stimulus for aggregation may have been environmental, to adjust to decreasing arable land and water resources precipitated by extended drought in the late 1200s, the accelerated rise in pueblo size was probably fueled by the increasing population in still-occupied regions caused by immigrant populations.

As population and settlement size increased, it would have become difficult to sustain under the traditional Pueblo kinship system based on lineages that probably characterized these prehistoric western Pueblo populations, as they do today (Dean 1969; Eggan 1950; Johnson 1989; Longacre 1964; Steward 1938). What is needed to sustain village size are integrative social or religious systems. During the late 1200s and early 1300s there are indications of the development of at least two systems by western Pueblo groups that were used to integrate larger villages with diverse populations. The first relates to the shift in layout of the settlement itself. Apparently as

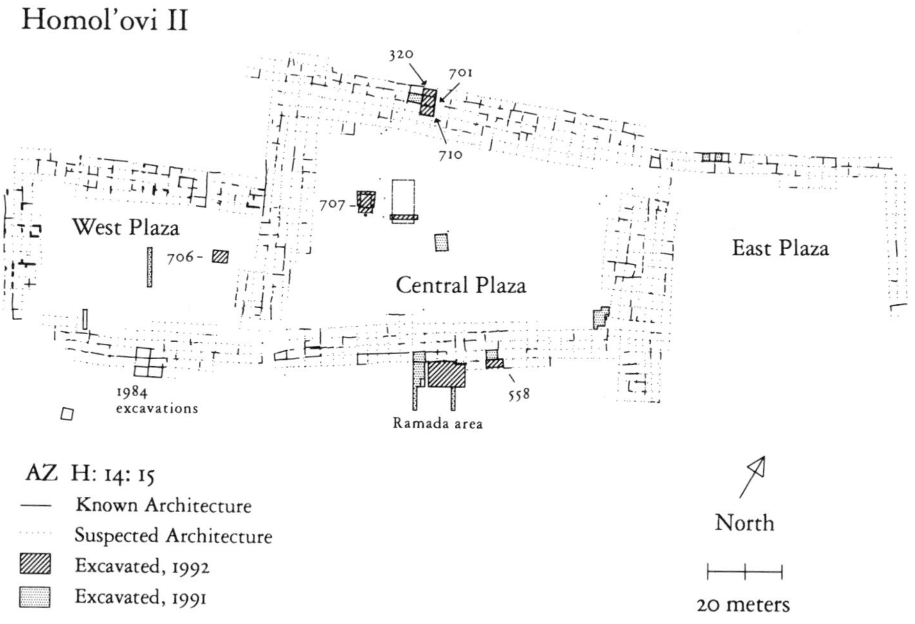

Homol'ovi II

FIGURE 5.3. Site plan of Homol'ovi II (AZ H:14:15) showing room blocks enclosing three plazas.

early as 1250–1275, enclosed plaza layouts for large pueblos began to appear. Enclosed plazas are merely the surrounding of open space with walls or rooms (Adams 1991:101–3) (Figure 5.3). During the 1275–1300 period, this layout became dominant, regular, and characterized all large pueblos in the western Pueblo area, and apparently in eastern Pueblos as well (Wendorf and Reed 1955). Enclosed plazas after 1275 also regularly contain kivas and in the west these are always square or rectangular (Adams 1991:103–10). It is probably not coincidental that at this time great kivas are no longer built.

As I have argued elsewhere (Adams 1991:101–10), it seems that the enclosed plaza replaced the great kiva as the integrative ritual structure for the western Pueblos between 1275 and 1300. Why was this replacement necessary? Because village size had grown so large, a great kiva could no longer involve the entire village or those segments of the village that it needed to provide the integrative cement to hold the society together. The enclosed plaza, on the other hand, was large enough in which to conduct public *plazas*

✓ ceremonies that could involve all necessary members of the village. This analogy of the plaza to the great kiva can be carried farther. The presence of a symbolic sipapu in modern Hopi village plazas would parallel that in the traditional kivas. (Ortiz [1969:20–21] identifies a comparable feature in Tewa pueblo plazas.) The relocation of kivas into the plazas and separate from the roomblocks further conveys a ritual orientation to plaza space. The conduct of public ceremonies in modern plazas certainly parallels probable functions of great kivas. Just as in modern Pueblo kivas, the use of plazas for nonritual activities when ceremonies are not being performed in no way contradicts the plaza's role as integrative ceremonial space. Of course the shift to plaza-oriented villages corresponds with increased village size that was apparently accelerated, if not promoted, by immigrant populations relocating into still-populated areas of the Little Colorado River basin.

Kachina As alluded to in the discussion on plazas, the second development in the integrative repertoire of village leadership was katsina ritual. The universal aspect of village membership in the katsina society among modern western Pueblo communities may have been a feature of their prehistoric counterparts. When prehistoric village leadership was faced with maintaining the village size that was attained in the late 1200s because of environmental degradation and substantial immigrating populations, the solution that was apparently chosen and that continues to work to the present is the katsina cult. Such a conclusion can be drawn from the iconographic evidence of katsina ritual present in the pottery, rock art, and kiva mural art of the fourteenth century associated with most pueblos in the western Pueblo area. As detailed above, this iconography appears between 1300 and 1350, just at the time that the newly aggregated pueblos became established. Whereas aggregation among Anasazi groups had occurred in the past, evidently as a behavioral solution to environmental change and degradation (Dean

et al. 1985), and then dissipated as conditions improved, such was not the case in the 1300s. The several-fold increase in village size obtained in the century between 1250 and 1350 was sustained to Spanish contact in the 1500s and beyond to the present. The most likely reason that increased village size was sustained was the development of ✓ effective, successful social integrative systems. A likely, visible candidate is the katsina cult.

In modern western Pueblo society katsina ceremonies involve the exchange of food from the givers of the ceremony to those in the village who constitute the audience. Katsinas also serve as disciplinarians (in the form of ogres and whippers) and as organizers of communal work parties, for instance, clearing springs. Such community-based activities are designed to integrate and force cooperation among all elements of the Pueblo village (Adams 1991:7). Katsina ritual provides the ultimate cross-kinship integrative system devised by western Pueblo society to counteract the naturally divisive tendencies of communities comprising matrilineally based kinship ties.

As presented in detail elsewhere (Adams 1991), katsina faces in rock art and on pottery bowls are probably the public signalers of the katsina cult's presence, perhaps representing gender (pottery equals female and rock art equals male) differences in its expression (Hays 1992a). In contrast the much more complex kiva mural iconography probably represents the private expression of the ritual, whose knowledge would have been controlled by a relatively few in power.

Sources of Cultural Change

Sources of influence or inspiration for katsina-mask iconography have been generally assigned to northern or central Mexico (Brew 1943; Hibben 1966, 1967; Schaafsma and Schaafsma 1974). It is most frequently associated with Tlaloc, a Mexican rain god, although feathered serpents associated with Quetzalcóatl also appear in iconography related in time and space to katsina-mask icons in rock art (Brew 1943; Schaafsma 1972, 1980). Recently, the focus has shifted to Casas Grandes (Di Peso et al. 1974; Adams 1991) where abstract bird designs, in addition to masked icons, have been related to shifts in ceramic and kiva mural iconography in the western Pueblo area (Adams 1991:96–101). Thus there is almost total consensus that iconographic influence from northern Mexico affected the expression of the katsina cult in the 1300s.

Noniconographic artifactual influence, also apparently from northern Mexico, appears as comals and shoe-form pottery vessels. Development of different and possibly more healthful uses for processing corn would have been cornerstones to sustaining expanded village populations (cf. Snow 1990). Architectural influence from the south, either northern Mexican or Hohokam, is manifest in the plaza-oriented layout of the pueblos and their use of rammed earth adobe architecture. Earthen architecture is known from Acoma, Zuni, Silver Creek (an upper Little Colorado drainage), Homol'ovi, and Hopi Mesa villages dating to the 1300s (Adams 1991:124). (Adobe architecture also prodominates in the Rio Grande area after 1200 [Cordell 1979:143].) Thus influence from the south may have affected noniconographic expressions of village reorganization and the development of the katsina cult in western Pueblos as well.

The uniformity in decorative style, termed Fourmile style (Adams 1991:96), on western Pueblo pottery of the 1325–1400 period that is distinct from styles anywhere else in the Southwest suggests the unity of contact, exchange, and perhaps village organization of the area. The predominance of this style on kiva mural designs suggests that the origin of elaborated kiva murals lies among the western pueblos and was imported into eastern pueblos, such as Pottery Mound, and further suggests its close association with katsina ritual (Smith 1952). The appearance of Fourmile style designs on eastern Pueblo Glaze IV pottery that became stylistically dominant after 1450 also

suggests its association with developing katsina ritual in the east and its later date there than in the west (Adams 1991:136, 142). (See P. Schaafsma, this volume, for an alternative opinion.)

As Cole (1990:150) notes, however, "masking has a long tradition on the Colorado Plateau and among the Anasazi." Whatever influences cultures in northern Mexico and in the southern deserts and transition zone of Arizona had on indigenous people of the Colorado Plateau, they were apparently absorbed into the existing cultural mix. There is no evidence for Mexicans or Hohokam people settling on the Colorado Plateau and directly controlling culture change. The development of katsina religion seems most likely to be the incorporation of economic and ritual ideas into the existing economic and ritual fabric.

Conclusions

This essay has discussed the origin and development of katsina ritual from the perspective of prehistoric western Pueblo culture. The archaeologist's best measure of katsina ritual, its iconography, became visible in several media during the fourteenth century. During this century there is the appearance of increasing formality and complexity in katsina depictions with the generalized depictions on pottery and rock art being supplemented with the elaborate, complex renderings on kiva murals.

Sources of inspiration for katsina icons, in this case the depiction of the mask, were apparently northern Mexican, possibly through a filter of an indigenous masking tradition; evidence for this needs further development (Cole 1990). The figurines dating to the twelfth century in the upper Little Colorado River drainage may reflect this tradition. Nevertheless, once the trajectory of masking was established, it continued on a unique track, quite separate from prehistoric or historic masking traditions in northern Mexico, culminating in katsinas.

A lengthy discussion has been presented concerning the causes of the development of katsina ritual by fourteenth-century western Pueblo occupants of the Colorado Plateau. It has been argued that the appearance of this iconography within a generation or two of the universal adoption of large, plaza-oriented pueblos is unlikely to have been coincidental. The massive dislocation of Pueblo inhabitants of the Four Corners area and archaeological evidence of the relocation of some of these immigrants in areas where masked icons appear is probably also not coincidental. The need to develop social systems capable of integrating newly large and diverse populations seems clearly to be the stimulus for the development of katsina ritual. Although undoubtedly altered by intervening contacts and years, the role of the katsina society in modern western Pueblo ritual and social organization would seem to apply to its prehistoric counterpart. Similarly, the development of enclosed plaza settlement plans makes the most sense if the plaza is viewed as an extension of the great kiva, that is, as a sacred space set aside for public performances of ritual designed to integrate the village populace.

Elsewhere (Adams 1991) I have argued at length about the relative age of the appearance of katsina iconography, and presumably ritual, in the western Pueblo areas versus the east. This has not been a concern of this essay, nor should it be a primary concern for those interested in the origins, development, and ultimate causes of katsina religion among the Pueblo people. It seems clear that most archaeologists who have spent time studying the suddenness and uniqueness of the appearance of katsina iconography can agree that it appeared almost throughout the Pueblo world of the fourteenth century, that stimulus came from northern Mexico (or at least south of the historic Pueblo area), and that its appearance coincides with many other changes in Pueblo culture, namely change in village size and layout, as part of a general reorganization of the Pueblo world following its sudden abandonment of the Four Corners region. I hope that this essay has contributed to the discourse on the subject and that it has taken us away from a focus on the tangible results of the appearance of katsina ritual, namely iconography, to an analysis of the causes of its appearance.

ACKNOWLEDGMENTS

This paper is much revised from the original presented in the October 1991 symposium, "World View and Ritual: Kachinas in the Pueblo World," which was organized by Polly Schaafsma and Ellen Bradbury through Recursos de Santa Fe. Many thanks to Polly and Ellen for organizing the symposium and for inviting me. Polly and an anonymous reviewer have made useful suggestions to the revised manuscript that have been incorporated into this final version. I have also benefited greatly from discussions on kachinas, pueblo ritual, and iconography from Jenny Adams, Sally Cole, Patty Crown, Kelley Ann Hays, Leigh Jenkins, Ed Ladd, Polly Schaafsma, and many other scholars and Pueblo people too numerous to mention. I wish to acknowledge their intellectual stimulation that has resulted in this paper, but I retain full responsibility for any errors in fact or logic.

6

Kachina Depictions On Prehistoric Pueblo Pottery

KELLEY ANN HAYS

Kachinas have been depicted on puebloan pottery for at least seven hundred years. By examining technological and stylistic attributes of a pottery vessel, such as color, paint types, vessel shape, and temper (inclusions in the paste such as sand, rock fragments, and ground potsherds), we can usually tell where and when a pottery vessel was made (Table 6.1). Sourcing and dating vessels with kachina depictions on them tell us that kachina or kachina-like figures were known at particular places and times. Evidence assembled here from published descriptions, examination of museum collections, and excavations at the fourteenth-century Hopi site of Homol'ovi II demonstrate that depictions of masked human-like beings on Pueblo pottery began in the late 1200s and were widespread by the mid-1300s. This spread was apparently so rapid that it is impossible to pin down exactly where the earliest examples of kachina designs are found, but the Upper Little Colorado area seems to be a likely candidate.

A conventional evolutionary model, such as archaeologists often knowingly or unknowingly derive from biology, would predict simple beginnings and diversification over time. That is, one or a few kinds of kachina would appear in one place in the Pueblo culture area, then diversity would

TABLE 6.1. Pottery Types on which Depictions of Kachinas are Found, Organized by Area of Manufacture

Ware / type	Date Range	Sites Where Found	References
UPPER LITTLE COLORADO RIVER			
Cibola White Ware			
(dates from Kintigh 1985)			
Reserve (?) B / w	1000–1125	no prov.	Peckham 1990:77, MNM
Reserve / Tularosa B / w	1100–1350	AZ Q:3:97	ASM collections
Pinedale B / w	1250–1350	no prov.	Hammack 1974, Ferg 1982, Moulard 1984, Adams 1991
White Mountain Red Ware			
(dates based on Breternitz 1966)			
Pinedale Poly	1300–1350	no prov.	Ferg 1982
Cedar Creek Poly	1300–1350	no prov.	Ferg 1982, ASM Collections
Fourmile Poly	1300–1400	Homol'ovi	Adams 1991, Ferg 1982, Hays 1989, Martin and Willis 1940
		Chevelon Ruin	Hays 1989, USNM Collections
CENTRAL ARIZONA			
Roosevelt Red Ware			
Pinto Polychrome	1240–1400	AZ U:8:43(ASU)*	ASU, Rice and Redman 1992
Gila Polychrome	1250–1400+	Beshbagowah	Ferg 1982, Moulard 1984
MIDDLE LITTLE COLORADO RIVER			
Winslow Orange Ware			
(dates from Adams and Hays 1991)			
Tuwiuca B / o	1250–1350	Homol'ovi	Hays 1989
Homol'ovi Poly	1300–1350	Homol'ovi	Hays 1989
HOPI MESAS			
Jeddito Yellow Ware			
(dates from Smith 1971, Adams and Hays 1991)			
Awatovi B / y	1300–1400	Homol'ovi	Adams 1991, Hays 1989
Awatovi / Jeddito B / y	1350–1450	Homol'ovi	Hays 1989
		Mishongnovi	Field Museum collections
Jeddito B / y	1350–1628	Hawikuh	Smith, Woodbury, and Woodbury 1966
		Homol'ovi	Hays 1989
		Rye Creek	ASM Collections
		Roosevelt Lake	ASM Collections
		Chavez Pass	USNM Collections
Jeddito Stippled / Spattered	1350–1628	Tsukuvi	Field Museum collections
Paayu Poly	1350–1450?	Homol'ovi	Adams 1991, Adams and Hays 1991
Sikyatki Poly, early PIV	1375–1450	Homol'ovi	Hays 1989
		Mishongnovi	Field Museum collections
Sikyatki Poly, late PIV	1450–1628	Sikyatki	Adams 1991, Field Museum
		Mishongnovi	Field Museum collections
		Old Walpi	Field Museum collections
		Awatovi	Smith 1952

TABLE 6.1, *continued*

Ware / type	Date Range	Sites Where Found	References
		ZUNI	
Zuni pottery types			
(dates from Kintigh 1985)			
Matsaki Polychrome	1400–1680	Hawikuh	Smith, Woodbury, and Woodbury 1966
Matsaki Brown-on-buff	1400–1680	Hawikuh	Smith, Woodbury, and Woodbury 1966
		RIO GRANDE	
Talpa B / w	1300–1320**	Pot Creek	Wetherington 1968
Galisteo B / w	1300–1400	Las Madres	(Schaafsma slide)
Glaze A Red	1300–1425+	Pecos	Kidder 1936
Glaze A Yellow	1300–1425+	Pecos	Kidder 1936
		LA 70	Snow 1976, Ferg 1982
Glaze C	1450–1500	Los Aguajes	(Schaafsma slide)
	1450–1500	Puaray	(Schaafsma slide)
Glaze D	1490–1550	Tshirege	(Schaafsma slide)
		Pecos	Kidder 1936
Biscuit B	1450–1550	Pecos	Kidder 1936

*median calibrated date for associated radiocarbon sample is A.D. 1280
**date is for this particular vessel only; see Crown 1991
ASM = Arizona State Museum, Tucson
ASU = Arizona State University, Roosevelt Lake Project
MNM = Museum of New Mexico
USNM = United States National Museum, Smithsonian Institution

increase over time, and the images would spread in a regular fashion. Instead, the images of kachinas on prehistoric pottery, like those in rock art and murals (see Adams 1991), suggest that there was a great deal of diversity in the beginning, and that the spread must have been very rapid.

In the present day pueblos, there are many kachinas, and each has a purpose. Together they make up a sort of visual and experiential catalog of all the beings, forces, objects, and ideas that are important in the Pueblo world. These kachinas are organized by a certain logic, what one might call a symbolic grammar, that structures the social and natural worlds. Diversity of kachinas is a core concept of the kachina religion today, and prehistoric images of kachinas suggest that this concept has great time depth. This discussion will present evidence for (1) dating the appearance of kachina depictions through depic-

tions on pottery, (2) defining the distribution of these images, and (3) demonstrating the early diversity of kachina images.

The Ceramic Medium

Most kachinas on prehistoric pottery are not easily identified with specific present-day kachinas. One reason for this is that Pueblo religion is changing and dynamic as well as conservative and traditional. Some kachinas persist unchanged for very long periods of time, but the popularity of others waxes and wanes. Other reasons for this uncertainty derive from the nature of the ceramic medium.

One restriction on identifying kachinas on pottery is that potters were restricted to a narrow range of colors. Color symbolism is very important in Pueblo religion and in identifying

FIGURE 6.1. Sun kachina from Homol'ovi II, AZ J:14:15, Paayu Polychrome (like Jeddito Black-on-yellow but with second color added by diluting brown paint). *(Drawing, reconstruction, by K. Hays.)* Position of line break is conjectural.

FIGURE 6.2. Side dancers on Sikyatki Polychrome bowl with Shalako figure from the "Hopi area," FMNH 21130. *(Drawing by K. Hays.)*

kachinas, and potters must have made changes to accommodate their limited palette. Of about twenty mineral pigments available to mural painters, potters could use only the few that would not burn off in the firing process or wash off later (Shepard 1956). These colors are black, brown, white, orange, red, and sometimes yellow. The range of background colors is similar. No blue firing pigments were available, and greens were restricted to areas using glaze paints, such as Zuni.

Another restriction on painters of pottery is the vessels' two-dimensional surfaces. Human effigy vessels from Casas Grandes and Chaco Canyon have modeled features, but the kachina depictions on the pottery discussed here are two-dimensional. The portrayal of tubular mouths, projecting eyes, and many aspects of costume is restricted. Artists of different cultures use perspective differently. When we see a ruff around the face of a kachina on a two-dimensional surface, it does not necessarily depict something like the feathers around the face of the sun kachina (Figure 6.1)—it could depict a ruff that goes around the neck, or the base of a helmet-like mask. Three horned dancers on a Sikyatki

Polychrome bowl have U-shaped lines on their faces (Figure 6.2). This may be a smile or a two-dimensional straight-on view of a projecting snout. The kind of mouth a kachina has is very important in identifying it, and in this case, it is probably not possible to know what was intended.

We are not only ignorant of the painters' intentions, but we do not know who the painters were. If the past was like the present in certain ways, women probably painted pottery but did not make kachina costumes. We might therefore expect pottery designs to be less accurate, less revealing of details, than actual costumes would be. On the other hand, these designs could have been painted by men who did accurately render costume details.

Another problem with using pottery to learn about religion is that there is no evidence that pots decorated with kachinas were used in ritual contexts. These vessels are found in kivas and burials, and also in houses and in the trash—we have no evidence that they were used any differently than pots with more common geometric designs. Even historic pieces sold to collectors as ceremonial vessels often were not actually used in ritual. In many of the pueblos, pottery used in the most sacred and secret contexts was undecorated. Pots bearing symbols such as clouds, tadpoles, and terraced rims were often used only in the public portions of rituals, to signal the presence of power to uninitiated people. Full initiates did not need pottery that visually signaled the sacredness of the situation (Kenaghy 1986). Therefore, kachina depictions on pottery probably signaled the makers' or users' participation in the public aspects of religion. They are not necessarily accurate portrayals of the most sacred parts of Pueblo religion. Designs on pottery were probably public, not secret information, and there were probably fewer constraints on the potter's free reign of imagination than there would be on the maker of a costume or item of ritual paraphernalia.

In summary, two kinds of factors influence the "accuracy" of kachina portrayals on pottery.

First, the pottery medium limits paintings to two-dimensional design fields and a limited range of colors. Second, due to unfamiliarity with detail, or because this pottery apparently was not used in ritual, we cannot assume that potters replicated the details seen on the performers themselves. Although initiates and other experts may be able to identify early versions of many present day kachinas in the material presented here, this discussion will simply focus on the temporal and spatial extent of kachina depictions generally, and on their inherent diversity.

When Is a Kachina?

The "typical" kachina depiction on prehistoric pottery is a single figure in the center of a bowl, with a relatively simple face shape—a circle, square, or half-circle, a rectangular toothed mouth, elongated eyes, and some kind of headdress. The one in Figure 6.1 was excavated in 1984 from a habitation room at Homol'ovi II, a large pueblo near Winslow (Hays 1991). It dates to the late 1300s, and is easily recognized today as the Sun kachina.

Figures like this probably begin to appear in the late 1200s and are well established by the mid-1300s. Pottery with kachina depictions only partly evolves out of earlier puebloan pottery traditions. To demonstrate their evolution, we have to start with the history of the depiction of humans on pottery, and show how the kachinas differ from other human representations, and where and when the kachinas appear.

PRECURSORS

The first decorated pottery in what most archaeologists call the Anasazi culture area appears around A.D. 600. Most of the designs on early pottery resemble textile and basket designs. A few human figures appear, and these strongly resemble the rock art of the time. They are simple, solid figures, with hair whorls, very simple headdresses such as a single line, perhaps showing a

FIGURE 6.3. Early Anasazi-style human figures, Chapin Black-on-white bowl, after Lister and Lister 1978. *(Drawing by K. Hays.)*

feather. Often there are lines of people holding hands (Figure 6.3, after Lister and Lister 1978). In the Pueblo I period and later, we find occasional fluteplayers and "lizard-men" on pottery, again resembling rock art. Human figures on pottery virtually never have facial features until the late 1200s. There are occasional examples with simple eyes, usually positive or negative dots, but most are solid black. Sally Cole suggests the same is true in rock art (personal communication 1991). This style of depicting humans pervades the Anasazi world, and is shared with much of the Mogollon area.

This early style of depicting humans continues the 1400s in the White Mountains, and at least into the 1500s on the Hopi Mesas (Figure 6.4). When the elaborate mask-like faces appear in the western Pueblos, it is not just a new way of depicting humans. The new style does not replace the old—the masks are a new addition to the repertoire of ceramic decoration. These rock art-like stick and solid figures continue to appear rarely but regularly on pottery up to the end of the pre-

FIGURE 6.4. Human figure from the Pueblo IV period, birth scene, Jeddito Black-on-yellow bowl from the Field Museum of Natural History. (*Drawing by K. Hays.*)

FIGURE 6.5 Mimbres miniature bowl with face or mask, Rock Point Ruin (*Courtesy Laboratory of Anthropology, Santa Fe, MNM 20022 / 11*).

historic period. In contrast, in the Rio Grande region, masked figures and associated iconography for the most part replace older graphic styles.

DISTANT RELATIONS

The exception to this scheme is the Classic Mimbres style, in the Mogollon culture area, dated to about A.D. 1000–1130. The Mimbres Mogollon developed a very complicated style of pottery depiction that includes frequent depiction of humans, asymmetrical layouts and motifs, and narrative style scenes of humans and animals interacting (see for examples Brody 1977a). Some scenes depict the use of masks and other paraphernalia that are later associated with the kachina religion, but for the most part the Mimbres style is very different from the later Western Pueblo depictions of kachinas in terms of color, design layout, and facial details. One Mimbres example

from Rock Point Ruin in the Mimbres Valley (Peckham 1990:42) does bear some resemblance to our "typical" fourteenth-century kachina depiction: an unusually small and shallow bowl depicts a forward facing head with toothed mouth, solid nose, and almond-shaped eyes (Figure 6.5). There are also resemblances between kachina depictions and some human depictions on ceramics from Casas Grandes in Chihuahua (see Di Peso et al. 1974:176, 204, 237, 268–76). Like Mimbres pottery, Jornada Mogollon, and much Rio Grande rock art (Schaafsma 1980), Casas Grandes figures have noses, and the western Pueblo examples virtually never do.

The kachina images discussed here have no antecedents in the Pueblo area and must have either been imported or developed, very rapidly, in situ. There is probably some kind of historical connection between the Mimbres ceramics,

FIGURE 6.6. Reserve Black-on-white jar fragments, from Long H Ruin, AZ Q:3:97 (ASM), near St. Johns. Each face has a diameter of about 10 cm. *(Drawing from slides by K. Hays.)*

Jornada rock art, Casas Grandes ceramics, and the Pueblo kachina depictions because so many formal features are shared. What the nature of this connection might be, however, is not yet clear: were appearances only borrowed and adapted, or does the shared style signal that a whole new system of iconography, perhaps even a new religion, was borrowed? It is possible that the earlier and more distant Mimbres and Casas Grandes images inspired the forms of many Puebloan kachinas, that the general meanings and symbolic associations of some kachinas were borrowed with their forms, or even that an entire complex of religious practice was imported to the Pueblo region and adapted to local needs. Evidence does suggest that this experience was different in the eastern and western Pueblos. Western Pueblos added kachina imagery to an existing art style, and probably added new religious practices that did not replace existing ones, such as medicine and war societies. Western Pueblo Kachina imagery, as described below, differs from Mimbres, Jornada Mogollon, and Casas Grandes imagery. In the Rio Grande, a case can be made for replacement of earlier styles with kachinas and related images, and the resemblance to earlier, southern styles is much stronger. This matter is discussed elsewhere in this volume, and I follow Adams (1991) in arguing that wherever the constituent ideas came from, the social and historical context of kachina imagery seems to have crystallized in the Pueblo area itself in the fourteenth century. What is missing is fine-grained chronological control and further study of the art styles as symbolic systems. Pottery alone cannot meet these challenges, but it provides some important clues.

EARLY KACHINA DEPICTIONS

The earliest examples of faces or masks that might be kachinas appear on large fragments of two black-on-white jars from the St. Johns area, now in the Arizona State Museum (Figure 6.6). The Mogollon Rim country is home to the Reserve / Tularosa style of pottery decoration in the 1100s through the 1200s. This style is characterized by interlocking hatched and solid designs. Except for the faces, these jars are easily classified as a late outgrowth of the Reserve / Tularosa style, and probably date to the late 1200s.

Unfortunately, these sherds were ripped out of context by looters looking for artifacts to sell. The vandals were caught and convicted, but contextual information on the artifacts was destroyed. As a result of this crime, we do not know whether these jars came from a ritual room or from trash. We do not have associated beams to give us exact tree-ring dates, nor even a charcoal sample for a radiocarbon date. All we have of chronological significance is the style and technology of the vessels, and from that, we can say that they certainly date to the mid to late 1200s. They are Cibola White Ware, locally made in the upper Little Colorado area. The designs are typical of this time and place in having repeated units making up an all-over design, and juxtaposed solid and hatched designs. The faces are a unique addition, then, to what is otherwise a typical design for the late 1200s. In their facial features, these are like later kachina faces in having simple elongated eyes and a toothed mouth, and no nose. In contrast, later kachina faces usually appear singly instead of in groups.

A kachina figure also appears on the handle of a Cibola White Ware pitcher depicted by Peckham (1990:77). Peckham types this vessel as Reserve Black-on-white and assigns dates of A.D. 1000–1125. If Peckham's identification is correct, this would be the earliest non-Mimbres kachina figure on pottery, and its date would correlate very well with Mimbres material. The depiction of a nose and the square shape of the eyes are consistent with this time range and affiliation. The poor execution of the slip and design also argue for a early date. However, this vessel would also be admissable to me as an unusually poorly executed Tularosa Black-on-white design due to two features: the even balance of the solid and hatched areas,

and the negative circles inside black triangles. It could therefore date as late as A.D. 1350. Again, tragically, no provenience or other contextual information is available to help us date this vessel, which resides in the Museum of New Mexico.

FOURTEENTH-CENTURY KACHINA DEPICTIONS IN THE UPPER LITTLE COLORADO

Kachinas appear on numerous black-on-white and polychrome pottery types that are native to the upper Little Colorado area. The most common decorative style of this area in the late thirteenth and fourteenth centuries, often called the Pinedale style, has opposed solid and hatched elements, and is an outgrowth of the Reserve / Tularosa style. This style dates to the late 1200s and early 1300s. One black-on-white bird effigy vessel, of unknown provenience, has a kachina face on its "chest" (depicted in Hammack 1974: 32; see also Pinedale Black-on-white vessel on page 35 of the same article, also depicted in Adams 1991 and Moulard 1984). This placement foreshadows the later Fourmile style in placing a single mask as a central focus in the design field, but Ferg (1982) suggests that this vessel may more correctly be typed as Reserve or Tularosa Black-on-white.

Although rare on any kind of pottery, kachinas appear on the late polychrome pottery of the upper Little Colorado (Plate 2) more frequently than on any other ware except Hopi yellow ware. Most examples of kachinas on this White Mountain Red Ware appear on the latest type, Fourmile Polychrome, which was made between about A.D. 1325 and 1400. Fourmile differs from earlier types in having asymmetrical or bilateral layouts as opposed to the earlier rotational or paneled layouts. Instead of isolated units it has a band design that rings the entire exterior wall of bowls. There are full body depictions—a large bowl found at Homol'ovi I (Martin and Willis 1940, frontispiece; also illustrated in Adams 1991:41) is very similar to a Pinedale Black-on-white example of

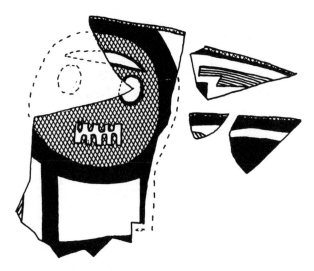

FIGURE 6.7. Kachina face on fragments of Pinto Polychrome bowl from Bass Point Platform Mound, AZ U:8:23 (ASU), near Roosevelt Lake. Associated median calibrated radiocarbon date is A.D. 1280 (Owen Lindauer, personal communication 1992). Crosshatching indicates red paint. Rim of vessel is at top, and associated rimsherds are shown to the right. (*Drawing by K. Hays.*)

unknown provenience (in Moulard 1984; Adams 1991:41). Faces only are most common (see examples in Martin and Willis 1940; Adams 1991; Hays 1989; Ferg 1982). A White Mountain Red Ware bowl with kachinas on it from Hooper Ranch (Martin, Rinaldo, and Longacre 1961:123) and examples on Cedar Creek Polychrome (Ferg 1982) may date as early as 1300.

CENTRAL ARIZONA

Kachinas are very rare on Salado polychrome pottery, which was made in many different areas including the Tonto Basin and the upper Little Colorado area. One example on Pinto Polychrome (Figure 6.7) has recently been found in the Tonto Basin, at the Bass Point Platform Mound near Roosevelt Lake (Rice and Redman 1992:25). The date range for this type is 1240–1400; the associated radiocarbon date for this piece is A.D. 1280

(Owen Lindauer, personal communication). A kachina is depicted on Gila Polychrome, ca. 1300–1400 and probably later, from the grave of a woman at Beshbagowah near Globe, Arizona (Ferg 1982; Moulard 1984). It was excavated in 1937, "disappeared" from the Clara T. Woody museum in Globe, and is rumored to be in a private collection. According to Ferg, the Tonto Basin seems to have received these designs and ideas from the upper Little Colorado area. Most researchers agree that the kachina cult was not actually practiced in the Salado culture area because of a lack of associated architectural features such as enclosed plazas, and scarcity of kachina iconography in this area (Ferg 1982; Adams 1991).

THE MIDDLE LITTLE COLORADO AND THE HOPI MESAS

There can be no doubt that kachinas were well known in the middle Little Colorado area and on the Hopi Mesas in the 1300s. All the examples from the Homol'ovi sites (illustrated in Hays 1989) pre-date the abandonment of these pueblos around A.D. 1400. Kachinas are depicted on locally made Homol'ovi Polychrome and on several types of Jeddito Yellow Ware, which was made on the Hopi Mesas and exported to Homol'ovi. During or just after the late 1200s, on both bichrome and polychrome pottery types from these two areas, bowl designs were laid out in a circular design field, defined by a thin line below the rim. Between the design field and the rim, a broad line was painted. A deliberate break was left in this broad line, and in similar lines that bound decorated bands on jars. This feature is often called the "spirit break." It remains an important feature in some Pueblo pottery today.

Around 1300 potters on the Hopi Mesas began to make large quantities of Jeddito Yellow Ware. This pottery is coal-fired at a high temperature, which accounts for the yellow color and the very hard paste. Large numbers of pots were apparently made for export, perhaps in exchange

FIGURE 6.8. Talpa Black-on-white sherd from Pot Creek Pueblo. *(Drawn by K. Hays, after Wetherington 1968:56.)*

FIGURE 6.9. Galisteo Black-on-white sherd from Las Madres. *(Photo by Polly Schaafsma.)*

for cotton to make textiles, obsidian for stone tools, and ritual items like feathers (Adams 1989). Whatever the exact trade relationships, we find Jeddito Yellow Ware all over the plateau and into the Verde Valley and Phoenix Basin in the 1300s (Adams, Stark, and Dosh 1990). Some of the vessels that were traded out of Hopi have kachinas on them—one example in the Arizona State Museum was found at the present location of the Angler's Inn on Roosevelt Lake.

THE RIO GRANDE

The earliest example of a kachina figure on pottery from the Rio Grande area is a Talpa Black-on-white sherd (Figure 6.8) from Pot Creek Pueblo that almost certainly dates between 1300 and 1320 according to Crown (1991; see Schaafsma, this volume, also Wetherington 1968). It has round eyes with pupils, rectangular toothed mouth and possible tongue, and at least one curv-

ing horn on a round head. It fits very well with the Upper Little Colorado examples, and suggests an appearance of kachinas at about the same time on the Rio Grande as in the Upper Little Colorado. Oddly enough, the site of Pot Creek Pueblo is associated with Taos and Picuris, which do not have the kachina religion today. This sherd is important because it is the only kachina depiction on Rio Grande pottery that clearly dates earlier than A.D. 1320, assuming Crown's analysis of tree-ring dates is correct and Pot Creek was abandoned around 1320 (her case is very convincing), and assuming that this sherd was not deposited in a later use of the site.

Another early Rio Grande kachina depiction, on a sherd of Galisteo Black-on-white from Las Madres, is dated between 1370 and 1390 (Figure 6.9; see Schaafsma, this volume). It has a horizontally divided face and a feather headdress.

Kidder (1936) depicts a kachina on Rio Grande

FIGURE 6.10. Jeddito Spattered sherd from Tsukuvi, FMNH 80076. *(Photo by K. Hays.)*

Glaze A Red (1300–1425+) from Pecos. It has elongated rectangular eyes with pupils, rectangular toothed mouth, triangles appended to the head as a ruff. Kachinas also appear on Glaze A yellow at Pecos, which has the same dates. An example with a half-circle-shaped head like those on Fourmile and Homol'ovi Polychromes and Jeddito Black-on-yellow appears in the Rio Grande on Glaze A Yellow from Pueblo del Encierro (LA 70, Snow 1976; Ferg 1982).

THE FIFTEENTH CENTURY

Sikyatki is one of the Hopi Mesas villages that grew when the Homol'ovis, Chevelon Ruin, Bidahochi, Chavez Pass, Puerco Ruin, and other large fourteenth-century sites were abandoned. Awatovi and Kawaika-a on Antelope Mesa also grew, as did many of the Hopi villages that continue to be occupied. Adams (1991) has shown how the initial appearance and crystallization of kachina iconography, enclosed plazas, and rectangular kivas accompanies the early fourteenth-century aggregation of western Pueblo populations. During this second aggregation period in the late 1400s, elaborate kiva murals with kachinas appeared, pottery designs lost their previous organizational principles, and kachina iconography on pottery became more elaborate.

Sometime after the mid-1400s, the very flamboyant Late Sikyatki style appears. Potters broke away from the earlier geometric tradition with a proliferation of color, bird and feather designs, and other life forms. Spattering, engraving, dry brush, and other techniques increased (Figure 6.10). The practice of laying out a design field with a circular line disappeared and so did the sub-rim banding line. The whole vessel became a field for the design.

In this Late or "Classic" Sikyatki style that flowers before the arrival of the Spaniards, we see kachina depictions that are more detailed than before. The style is less rigid. Instead of just showing a masked face straight on, in a static, "iconic" way, we see figures moving or dancing, often in groups that may depict actual ritual performances. Brody calls this a "narrative" style of depiction, as opposed to an iconic manner of depiction (Brody 1991). Not all of these necessarily represent kachinas. Clowns, Antelope priests, and birth (see Figure 6.4) scenes are also occasional subjects.

Kachinas are also depicted on fifteenth-century pottery from Zuni and the Rio Grande. At Zuni, two Hawikuh bowls show very abstract figures (Smith, Woodbury, and Woodbury 1966), with rectangular bodies, small heads on top, and arms projecting from the upper corners. These resemble figures found in Jornada Mogollon rock art, and even resemble rock art figures in Sinaloa, Mexico (Bently 1987). We do not find figures like these in the Hopi area. This suggests that there are some differences between fifteenth-century Hopi and Zuni iconography, with Zuni partaking in some way of an older Mogollon style that is not found further west. Even so, these vessels were made at a time when there is a great deal of overlap between Hopi and Zuni ceramic styles. The Matsaki style is usually called an imitation of the Late Sikyatki style. Both share a yellow base color, achieved at Zuni with slipped surfaces, asymmetrical design layouts and elements, brown and red figures, flamboyant bird forms, dragonflies, and feather motifs.

By A.D. 1450 kachina depictions on pottery appear regularly in the Rio Grande region, on Glazes C and D and Biscuit B. The Rio Grande examples sometimes have noses, and sometimes have triangular heads—in these features, they resemble the Jornada-style rock art more than they resemble their western Pueblo counterparts. (Examples appear on a bowl exterior, Glaze C from Los Aguajes, 1450–1500, MNM 49560/11; a bowl interior, Glaze D from Tshirege, 1490–1550, MNM 21741/11; for many examples from Pecos, see Kidder 1936). But at the same time, there are some kachina figures here that resemble

western examples in having noseless round or semicircular heads with ruffs, elongated eyes, and toothed mouths (Biscuit B from Pecos, 1450–1550, MNM 42926/11), and the Galisteo Black-on-white sherd noted above. One bowl from Puaray has a round mouth and eyes with sprout-like hooks, possibly depicting a clown (Glaze C 1450–1500, MNM 21154/11).

SUMMARY

The earliest examples of kachina-like depictions appear in the Upper Little Colorado River region in the mid to late 1200s, with no stylistic antecedents in the Pueblo area. Examples that are almost as early occur on pottery types that were made in the Rio Grande, Homol'ovi, and Hopi areas. The appearance of kachinas on pottery is thus widespread by the mid-1300s, and the current state of pottery-based chronology does not offer much help in pinning down the origins and spread of this phenomenon. Table 6.1 shows the types of fourteenth-century pottery that bear kachina depictions, along with their dates and areas of manufacture.

Cultural Context of Kachina Depictions on Pottery

It is no coincidence that kachina images appear around A.D. 1300. The late thirteenth and early fourteenth century was a time of great artistic, architectural, and social changes in the Southwest. Changes in pottery were discussed above. At the same time, people moved from many smaller settlements into fewer, larger pueblos of several hundred rooms, often ten times larger than the norm of only a few decades before. During this aggregation period, social relations must have become far more complicated than ever before because more people were living close together than before. They came together from disparate areas and so must have brought with them different traditions. Forging a common religion that could accommodate these differences

FIGURE 6.11 (above, left). Jeddito Black-on-yellow bowl with Tsakwaina kachina, FMNH 75803. *(Photo by K. Hays.)*

FIGURE 6.12 (above, right). Sikyatki Polychrome bowl with Shalako figure and stars, FMNH 67128. *(Drawing by K. Hays.)*

FIGURE 6.13 (below, right). Possible Shalako figure on Jeddito Black-on-yellow bowl from Chavez Pass (Nuvakwewtaqa), USNM 157546. *(Drawing by K. Hays from photo by Peter Pilles.)*

and promote cooperation would have been important and advantageous to survival. The kachina religion plays such a role today, and probably played this role at its inception (see Adams 1991).

The diversity of kachina images on pottery shows that a wide variety of kachinas were present in the early years of this religion. Faces are usually round or semi-circular, but squares, rectangles, ovals, and triangles are common. Eyes may be elongated, round, spiral, rectangular, or simple dots. Sometimes facial features are omitted altogether. Kachinas wear feathers, face paint, neck ruff, or are simple and plain. A few specific kinds of kachina can be shown to have very ancient roots: Sun kachinas and Tsakwaina-like figures are found as early as the 1300s, and beaked Shalakos appear by the 1400s.

The Sun, called Tawa in the Hopi language, is one of the most important chief kachinas. He is frequently depicted on historic pottery and other objects made by Hopi people today. Figures with round faces radiating lines appear to represent a Sun kachina and are found on pottery dating as early as the 1300s. Today, the Sun has a triangular mouth, showing that he is a smiling, benevolent being. Some of the prehistoric examples (such as Figure 6.1) have the rectangular toothed mouth typical of many early kachina depictions, and this mouth form may also represent a smile. The late style Sikyatki Polychrome canteen in Plate 3 probably also depicts a Sun kachina.

Tsakwaina is a warrior kachina with a toothed mouth, fuzzy hair, and crescent-shaped eyes. Present day examples have a protruding tongue. It is difficult to know if prehistoric depictions of kachinas with toothed mouths and crescentic eyes actually represent the same being, but the formal resemblance is strong (Figure 6.11; see also Adams 1991). Like the sun figures, Tsakwaina-like kachinas appear in the 1300s and continue into the late prehistoric period.

Shalako kachinas were clearly known at Hopi by the late 1400s. Three vessels from the Field Museum collections depict triangular-bodied, beaked and feathered beings that closely resemble Shalako figures. One is illustrated in Figure 6.12 (see also Hays 1992*b*). A possible Shalako (Figure 6.13), very stylized, but with a triangular body and feathered head, appears on a Jeddito Black-on-yellow bowl from the site of Nuvakwewtaqa (Chavez Pass Pueblo), which was abandoned sometime around A.D. 1400.

The fifteenth-century beaked figures from the Hopi bowls bear some resemblance to the Zuni Shalako, which is not a kachina but a god (Edmund Ladd, personal communication). The fifteenth-century Hopi versions lack the horns worn by the Zuni figures. They have the beaked mask of the present day Zuni Shalako and the feathered body of the Hopi Shalako, which lacks a beak. Two of the vessels show a small, dark human figure inside the feathered body—this is the puppeteer who holds the head up on a stick and works the beak with a string. The form depicted on these vessels is probably ancestral to the Hopi Shalako, which somehow traded in its beak for a rainbow chin and tablita. These two features probably came from the Rio Grande pueblos sometime between the manufacture of these vessels and the 1880s, when Stephen described the Hopi Shalako (Stephen 1936:422). The rainbow chin and cloud terrace shape of the tablita are often depicted in Rio Grande rock art of the Pueblo IV period, and also in the earlier Jornada Mogollon rock art style of the El Paso region (Schaafsma 1980).

Conclusions

Although human figures appear on the earliest decorated pottery, figures recognizable as kachinas appear on pottery around A.D. 1300 in the Upper and Middle Little Colorado areas, the Hopi Mesas, and the Northern Rio Grande. A few categories of kachinas that would be recognizable to modern Pueblo people can be identified on prehistoric pottery, and remarkable continuity of traditions exists. Many kachinas on prehistoric pottery have no close modern counterparts, and inter-regional and intraregional diversity is the rule. Changes over time show that Pueblo religion is vital and dynamic, not stagnant.

Kachinas are always a small part of the ceramic ✓ design repertoire, that is, pots with kachinas on them are rare in any given time and place, but kachinas appeared regularly throughout the late prehistoric period (1300 to Spanish contact). During the Spanish period, potters stopped depicting kachinas on pottery, possibly due to religious persecution. In the 1880s, potters at Hopi again began to put kachinas on pottery, and they also appear on historic Rio Grande vessels. Kachinas continue to be an important part of pottery decoration, especially in the new Hopi carved styles made for the fine arts market.

ACKNOWLEDGMENTS

Special thanks to the Arizona Archaeological and Historical Society and the Museum of Northern Arizona for supporting my research on this topic, and to all those who gave me access to collections: Christine Gross at the Field Museum of Natural History, Mike Jacobs and Art Vokes at the Arizona State Museum, and Owen Lindauer at Arizona State University's Roosevelt field lab. Peter Pilles and Polly Schaafsma generously provided slides. Thanks also to all those who shared their thoughts and criticisms of this presentation at the symposium "World View and Ritual: Kachinas in the Pueblo World," especially Chuck Adams and Polly Schaafsma, and to Recursos of Santa Fe for bringing everyone together. Any errors remaining are my own.

7

The Prehistoric Kachina Cult and Its Origins as Suggested by Southwestern Rock Art

POLLY SCHAAFSMA

KACHINA images appear in the archaeological remains of the Pueblo world of northern Arizona and New Mexico by the fourteenth century. At this time masks become a distinctive feature of petroglyphs and rock paintings associated with early plaza pueblos (Adams 1991; Cole 1989; Schaafsma 1980, 1992*b;* Schaafsma and Schaafsma 1974). In New Mexico from the fourteenth century on, pueblo rock art sites between Socorro and Santa Fe are dominated by kachina imagery where thousands of masks display a complex, well-developed formal iconography, or visual system of conventionalized symbols.

Kachinas also occur on pottery and in other media that can sometimes be more precisely dated. In the Rio Grande valley, masks are painted on black-on-white and glaze wares. One of the earliest well-dated ceramic examples is a horned mask with round eyes and a small toothed mouth on a Talpa Black-on-white sherd from Pot Creek Pueblo in Taos County (Hays, this volume: Figure 6.8). It is likely that this sherd dates from before A.D. 1320–1325 when the site was abandoned, and late thirteenth century dates are also possible (Crown 1990:72). A mask on a Galisteo Black-on-white sherd (Hays, this volume, Figure 6.10) from the Galisteo Basin is dated between A.D. 1370 and 1390 (Schaafsma 1992b). Kachina faces on Cieneguilla Glaze-on-yellow and Agua Fria Glaze-on-Red (Ferg 1982: Fig. 1,d; Kidder 1936: Figs. 21, 51a; and collections, Museum of Indian Arts and Culture, Santa Fe) are dated between A.D. 1340 and 1425 (Sundt 1987:136, Table 2). Star kachinas on clay pipes at Pecos first appear in the fourteenth or early fifteenth century as well (Kidder 1932: Figs. 138e, 139, and pp. 181–82). In the western Pueblo region in the Little Colorado River drainage, kachina imagery is more prevalent as ceramic decoration from the fourteenth century on, with slightly earlier dates being possible (see Hays, this volume). In general, however, kachinas on pottery are still relatively rare. Kachinas with small toothed mouths, a feature characteristic of the kachinas faces on pottery cited above, were painted as well on sandstone slabs, a form of altar paraphernalia found in fourteenth- and fifteenth-century contexts in eastern Arizona sites. For a summary discussion of these slabs see Di Peso (1950). Kachinas also appear in Pueblo IV kiva murals at Pottery Mound and on the Hopi Mesas, probably by the end of the 1300s (Crotty 1985; Smith 1952; and see Vivian, this volume). A consensus of opinion on the dates of these murals has not been reached, however, and therefore they are not currently particularly useful for exploring kachina origins.

As discussed here and elsewhere (see Adams, this volume), the development of large, aggregated, plaza-oriented pueblos concomitant with the appearance of kachina iconography in several media may reflect the socially integrative features of the kachina organization. Patterns of occurrence of prehistoric kachina imagery along with concurrent archaeological data, however, have led to differing conclusions regarding the origin and development of the kachina religion (Adams 1991; Schaafsma 1980 and 1992b).

In brief, Adams has proposed that the Pueblo kachina cult originated in the Little Colorado, probably under stimulus from the Mimbres region. He stresses that the dry climatic conditions that prevailed provoked the in-situ development of an ideology and ritual to cope with problems of dry farming, following the abandonment of the San Juan and the influx of people in the Little Colorado region. Adams postulates that kachina ritual, which he associates with western square kivas, once it had developed in the Little Colorado and at Hopi, spread eastward to the Rio Grande valley in the late 1300s, where after A.D. 1450 it was amplified by additions from the Jornada Mogollon (Adams 1991: 132–33).

This paper offers an alternative reconstruction of the origin and spread of kachinas based on data in the rock art. I maintain that although kachina iconography appears widespread throughout the Pueblo world in the fourteenth century, the Rio Grande Pueblos, in communication with the Jornada Mogollon at that time, were a central focus for the early development and spread of pueblo kachinas, as opposed to being recipients of kachina ideology as it diffused from the Little Colorado region. The large numbers of masks present in the rock art of Cerro Indio, a fourteenth-century Piro site north of Socorro (Figure 7.1) and the diversity that these figures exhibit, indicate that kachina ideology is more complex and well developed early in the Rio Grande than it appears in Little Colorado sites. Cerro Indio and other masks along the Rio Grande contrast significantly with the much simpler and limited number of figures found in Little Colorado sites from the same period. Furthermore, Rio Grande masks show well-established typological relationships to those in Jornada Mogollon rock art (A.D. ca. 1050–1400), bordering the Pueblo area to the south. In the Mogollon, masks seem to have been significant for possibly as long as two centuries before they appear in the Pueblo iconography in meaningful numbers.

It should be pointed out here that Adams

(1991:139–40) redefines the Jornada and Rio Grande rock art styles. The following discussion is based on these styles as previously defined that adhere to important iconographic distinctions and that conform to specific cultural / geographic boundaries (Schaafsma 1980).

Antecedents

As discussed elsewhere (Hays, this volume; Schaafsma and Schaafsma 1974), precursors of kachinas and their associated iconography are not found in the rock art of the Colorado Plateau, but in the pottery paintings on Mimbres ceramics, in an occasional mask on late thirteenth-century ceramics from southern New Mexico and Arizona, as well as in the rock art of the Mimbres and Jornada Mogollon. Although Colorado Plateau Anasazi rock art may include the depiction of elements of ceremonial attire or artifacts that have persisted in the Anasazi-Pueblo sequence for at least two thousand years (Cole 1991), these do not provide the specific link to the kachina cult and other Puebloan supernaturals that are evident in the Mimbres–Jornada–Rio Grande continuum. Pueblo IV masks occur with ceremonial figures, animals, horned serpents, cloud designs, and so forth that are similar to those in the Jornada style. Such a significant change from Anasazi rock art styles that prevailed prior to A.D. 1300 indicates that we are viewing a major ideological shift in the fourteenth-century Pueblos.

Representational figures on Mimbres pottery and similar elements in Jornada-style rock art (A.D. 1000–1450) (Schaafsma 1980:199–242) stand in contrast to those in other southwestern art styles and are believed to reflect a distinctive ideological tradition. Mimbres pottery art and Jornada rock art display large life forms, often drawn in outline with fully developed heads and facial features. Human figures may be depicted with naturalistic contours. Legs are defined with fully developed calves and large feet with well-defined heels, stylistic features that are charac-

FIGURE 7.1. Jornada-style Tlaloc-like rain god, north of El Paso, Texas, A.D. 1050–1400. The large eyes, trapezoidal shape and stepped cloud elements are typical. Similar personages occur in most Jornada style sites. (*Photo by Polly Schaafsma.*)

teristic of this style and prominent in the later rock and kiva art of the Pueblo Rio Grande. The iconography includes elements related to the later Pueblo kachina cult and other aspects of Pueblo IV religion after ca. A.D. 1300 such as horned serpents, corn, and clouds (Carlson 1982a), as well as masks (Brody 1977a, Fig. 141); Dedrick 1958, Pls. IX, Figs. 3, 4, XIX, LII, Fig. 2); Peckham 1990:42, Fig. 23). A continuity of mask/face iconography between that on Mimbres ceramics and that in Jornada-style and Pueblo rock art is easily demonstrable. Although the demise of the Mimbres culture and its distinctive animals and human figures on funerary ceramics occurred around A.D. 1130–50, it is apparent via the rock art of the region that Mimbres religious ideology and its associated art forms survived in other media.

An additional element present in nearly every Jornada-style rock art site, including those of supposed Mimbres origin, is a large rectangular or trapezoidal figure with huge eyes and with a torso frequently decorated with stepped motifs (see Figure 7.1). These elongated stepped cloud designs are typical of those found on several southwestern pottery types after ca. A.D. 1050. This large-eyed figure shares distinguishing characteristics—notably the overall shape, the eyes, and cloud decoration—with the Mexican rain god Tlaloc (Schaafsma 1980:203–8). Small wooden effigies of similar personages (proto-kachina dolls?) have been found in caves in Hidalgo and Lincoln Counties (Dillingham et al. 1989:Fig. 40). Parallels between the rain-bringing Tlaloc cult and the kachina society of southwestern Pueblo farmers has been noted by various scholars in the past (Beals 1943; Brew 1943; Parsons 1933). In addition to the association with rain, clouds, and mountains common to both the Tlaloc complex and kachina belief system, Parsons points out parallels between the two in associated curing practices. The presence of this rain-god figure as well as the various types of masks themselves, plus the related ele-

ments of corn, rain clouds, and horned serpents, all contribute a larger picture that suggests that ideological antecedents to the kachinas, if not the organization itself as a formalized institution, were present in the desert Mogollon area two hundred years before the appearance of kachina iconography in the northern pueblos.

Mesoamerican parallels between ideas expressed in Mimbres art and Pueblo cosmological concepts (see Thompson and Young, this volume) have been explored previously apart from the kachina issue (Brody 1977a, 1977b; Ellis 1989; Ellis and Hammack 1968; Moulard 1981; Parsons 1939; Taube 1986; Young 1989, 1991). Along with Tlaloc-like rain gods in Jornada-style rock art, these broader cosmological similarities further support the idea of southern relationships for the concepts underlying Pueblo kachina ideology. The idea that kachinas were largely derived out of a local Colorado Plateau Anasazi base in response to environmental pressures is challenged by these archaeological data.

Masks are a frequent element in Jornada-style rock art. They may be round or square in shape or have rounded lower contours with flat tops, and facial features are well developed. Eyes tend to be oval; eyebrows are commonly shown. Noses are large, sometimes broadly trapezoidal or triangular and usually located in the center of the face, although some extend from the top line above the eyes (Figures 7.2–7.4). Horizontal banding, rainbow mouths, facial streaks, and clouds are important iconographic elements. Painted masks often display the complex use of negative designs found in Mimbres ceramic decoration. Facial patterning may also be asymmetrical.

These masks, many of which are associated with Mimbres-type human and animal figures, may both predate or have been made contemporaneously with early Pueblo IV work. Brody (1991:75–76) notes the stylistic relationships between Mimbres art and the Pueblo IV Rio Grande style, although he proposes that Jornada-style rock art is found only in the vicinity of late Jor-

FIGURE 7.2. Jornada-style mask with cloud terrace on head. Note the rainbow in the base of the terrace. Almond-shaped eyes and eyebrows are typical of many Jornada style masks. The nose is hourglass-shaped and the mouth a rectangle. Three Rivers, New Mexico, A.D. 1050–1400. *(Photo by Curtis Schaafsma.)*

FIGURE 7.3. Jornada-style mask with teeth, Three Rivers, New Mexico (A.D. 1050–1400). The image is pecked over an angle in the rock, denoted by the vertical line.

nada Mogollon (post thirteenth-century) sites. An examination of site records, however, shows that Mogollon habitation sites located in proximity to Jornada-style rock art, often span the entire time frame between A.D. 1000 and 1400–1450 (Schaafsma 1992b). There are no superimpositions or other indications to suggest that the masks in the context of Jornada-style rock art were made later than the rest of the figures.

Particularly noteworthy as well is that a terminal date of A.D. 1300 is suggested for Jornada occupation in Rhodes Canyon in the San Andres Mountains (Wiseman 1983:134) where Jornada-style painted masks are essentially the same as those from Hueco Tanks (Figure 7.4).

Rio Grande–style Pueblo masks in the southern pueblo districts closest to the Jornada region display the greatest similarities in shape

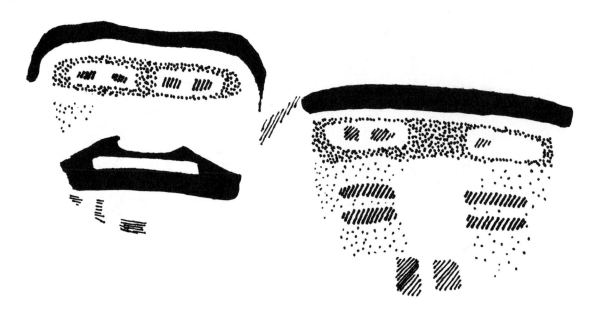

FIGURE 7.4. Jornada-style painted masks from Rhodes Canyon, San Andres Mountains, New Mexico (prior to A.D. 1300). Solid and hatched areas indicate dark red and yellow ochre respectively. Dots show dark and light orange. The horizontal marks indicate green paint.

and decoration to Jornada-style masks. The association of these masks with fourteenth-century Pueblo sites in the Piro region, along with masks in other media, argues for their early appearance in the Pueblo regime. It should be pointed out in this regard that the apparent absence of kiva murals and kachina iconography on ceramics at the well-studied fourteenth-century sites of Pindi and Arroyo Hondo pueblos near Santa Fe (Stubbs and Stallings 1953; Habicht Mauche, personal communication 1991) suggests that the kachina ritual may not have been universal among pueblos at this time. Particularly noteworthy is the absence of Rio Grande–style elements among the numerous life forms on Pindi ceramics. On the other hand, in the vicinities of these sites, no rock art is known, the major medium in which kachina iconography occurs in the Rio Grande.

Special consideration is merited by the mask characterized by a small rectangular toothed mouth mentioned at the beginning of this paper. In several fourteenth-century examples on pottery, kachinas are shown with such mouths (Ferg 1982; Hays, this volume). The small toothed mouth has antecedents in Mimbres toothed personages before A.D. 1150 (Peckham 1990, fig.

23; Dedrick 1958, Pl. XIX), and it is found occasionally on late thirteenth-century ceramics from south central Arizona and New Mexico. Very rarely toothed faces or masks are represented on Reserve/Tularosa Black-on-white, and other western Pueblo Anasazi pottery contemporary with or following the Mimbres period (Hays, this volume; Peckham 1990:77; Collections of the Edge of the Cedars Museum, Blanding, Utah). The image on the unprovenienced Black-on-white pitcher with published estimated dates between A.D. 1000 and 1125 (Peckham 1990) or possibly as late as 1175 (Peckham, personal communication 1991) is very similar to masks with broad noses from the Jornada-style assemblage at Three Rivers (Figure 7.3). The latter could easily date from the same time period.

Masks with small toothed mouths are also occasional motifs on Escondida, Villa Ahumada, and Ramos Polychrome from Casas Grandes (DiPeso et al. 1974: vol. 6, pp. 237, 268, 274, 285, 310) for which dates range between A.D. 1200 and ca. 1450 (Ravesloot 1988:5). A brief reconnaissance of the rock art in the vicinity of Casas Grandes indicates that this region is an integral part of this ideological interaction sphere, a factor supported by the presence of trade pottery and so forth (Di Peso et al. 1974, vol. 8:142). Petroglyphs in the Casas Grandes region are stylistically the same as Jornada-style rock art in New Mexico (Withers 1976; Schaafsma and Wiseman 1992). Shared elements include apparently masked human figures, profile faces, horned serpents and certain abstract designs.

Significant to this discussion is a mask with a small toothed mouth painted in a rock shelter near Gran Quivira, New Mexico, along with a rectilinear horned serpent similar to those depicted at a site near Casas Grandes (Figure 7.5). The painting is well dated between A.D. 1250 and 1300 by its association with the nearby Seco Ruin, an early plaza pueblo (Caperton 1981:8).

This ancient type of mask has persisted for hundreds of years and is current in the kachina

FIGURE 7.5. Square mask with small toothed mouth and hourglass nose, a Jornada style feature, from the Seco Site near Gran Quivira, New Mexico, A.D. 1250–1300. Solid areas are red, and dotted areas are yellow-orange.

mask repertoire today. The figure on the Pot Creek sherd (Hays, this volume, Figure 6.8) resembles the contemporary Hopi Tsakwaina or the similar He'e'e Warrior, as well as the masks of Horo Mana (Cold Bringing Woman) (Wright 1977:54–55) and Soyoko Ogre kachinas (Figure 7.6).

In summary the data currently available do not point to a Little Colorado origin for this image (Adams 1991:52) which occurs widely and sporadically in the Mogollon and Anasazi areas after A.D. 1000 and at Casas Grandes probably by A.D. 1200. Ceramic designs show that small toothed mouths continued to be a recurrent feature of kachinas on Pueblo ceramics in the 1300s, and similar masks are also present in the rock art of the Jornada–Rio Grande Pueblo border zone between A.D. 1250 and 1300.

Pueblo IV

Pecked and painted in profusion, rock art of the Rio Grande Pueblos between A.D. 1325 and

FIGURE 7.6. Hahai-i Wuhti, Nataska, Soyok' Mana, Walpi, 1897. The mask style of Soyok' Mana is centuries old (compare Figure 6.8 on page 57). *(Photo by James Mooney. Courtesy of Museum of New Mexico, Negative number 49494.)*

1600–1680 contains more kachina imagery than is to be found in any other Pueblo region. If the mask image is the key for determining the presence of the kachina cult archaeologically (Adams 1991:15–16), then the many and elaborate masks in the Rio Grande style from the fourteenth century on are a statement not only of its presence, but of its strength and complex development in this area. Rio Grande–style rock art is found throughout north-central New Mexico in association with the ruins of large Pueblo IV towns and villages, on prominent topographic features, and in secluded small overhangs and rock shelters. Figures in this style make up the overwhelming bulk of the rock art of the region, with individual elements numbering into the thousands at some sites. The style is notable for its variety of subject matter and the unending creativity in the form of each figure (Plates 4,5; Figures 7.7– 7.13). Although no two elements are alike, this rock art displays a conventionalized symbol system that contains and expresses Pueblo worldview and cosmology.

This proliferation of imagery suggests that rock art itself took on new and dynamic social dimensions and possibly even new ritual roles among the Pueblos beginning in the fourteenth century. Its public function from the fourteenth to the seventeenth centuries must have assumed major importance among the Rio Grande Pueblos. Imagery in public places, in the vicinity of villages, on conspicuous land forms, as well as in numerous isolated shrine locations, would have functioned to affirm the presence of religious ideas. Today this rock art reflects the strength of the various components of the ideographic system, including kachina ritual.

KACHINAS IN RIO GRANDE ROCK ART

The Rio Grande regions with the most strongly developed Pueblo IV kachina iconography are those in the south and east just north of the Jornada Mogollon, embracing the Piro, Tompiro, Southern and Eastern Tiwa and Southern Tewa

FIG. 7.9

FIG. 7.7

FIG. 7.8

FIGURE 7.7 (above, right). A selection of masks from Cerro Indio (A.D. 1300–1400) showing the diverse use of terraced elements as mask iconography as well as rain, rainbows, and a bird (mouth of figure, lower left). Asymmetry is also a characteristic of several of these figures.

FIGURE 7.8 (left). Cerro Indio masks displaying asymmetry (top and bottom, left.) The bottom three masks have specific analogs in masks portrayed on Mimbres ceramics (Brody 1977a: Figs. 175, 141). *(Profile figures, lower right after Marshall and Walt 1984: Fig. 9.20.)*

FIGURE 7.9 (above, left). Petroglyph masks, Southern Tiwa district, ca. A.D. 1325–1450. *(Photo by Curtis Schaafsma.)*

FIG. 7.10

FIG. 7.13

FIGURE 7.10 (above). Petroglyph panel from the
Galisteo Basin, Southern Tewa district with several
Shalako-like personages, masks, a complex animal,
and birds, ca. A.D. 1325–1520.

FIGURE 7.11 (opposite, top). Shalako, shield with
stars, and other petroglyphs, Galisteo Basin,
Southern Tewa district, New Mexico, A.D. 1325–
ca. 1520. *(Photo by Polly Schaafsma.)*

FIGURE 7.12 (opposite, bottom). Horned serpent,
star, and various masks and masked personages,
Galisteo Basin, Southern Tewa, A.D. 1325–ca. 1520.
(Photo by Polly Schaafsma.)

FIGURE 7.13 (left). Masked dancer, West Mesa,
Albuquerque, Southern Tiwa district,
A.D. 1325–1680.

FIG. 7.11

FIG. 7.12

linguistic provinces (see Figure 11.1, this volume). Interregional Pueblo divisions are based on historic linguistic lines that seem to mirror older and minor differences in ideological emphases and development as revealed through the rock art. As noted previously, due to their location contiguous with the Jornada Mogollon, it is not surprising that Piro and Tompiro masks show the strongest affinities to those of the Jornada (Plates 4,5; Figure 7.7).

Continuities between the Jornada and southern Pueblo sites are seen in the flat-topped masks with rounded lower contours, horizontal decorative banding, oval eyes, or eyes centrally divided with a vertical line, rainbow chin markings and downturned mouths. Stripes, rainbows, and terrace elements, or clouds, may create asymmetrical facial patterns in southern Pueblo masks, a precedent that seems to have originated with the Jornada Mogollon (see Tedlock, this volume, for a discussion of audial and visual asymmetry as it relates to kachina masks and songs and the Zuni concept of tso'ya, or beautiful). Masks pecked on rock angles occur in both areas. On the other hand, specific differences in eyes, noses, and headgear are displayed between the masks of the two areas. Among the Pueblo masks, feathers are often depicted across the top of the head, horns as headgear are more prevalent, and star-faced beings are introduced. Facial features tend to be simpler in the Pueblo work.

For the purpose of the current discussion of the development of the kachina cult, the rock art at the Piro site of Cerro Indio merits special consideration. On the basis of ceramics, this 115-room plaza pueblo is dated between A.D. 1300 and 1400 (Marshall and Walt 1984). Its small size and defensive position on a mesa top are aspects of the site typical of this period. Although sherds dating from a later historic component (1500–1680) were collected at Cerro Indio, these are of minor significance and are believed to relate to the historic-colonial occupation of LA 286 below the mesa and to the west. The voluminous and stylis-

tically consistant rock art is related to the original fourteenth century occupation.

Several hundred kachina masks dominate the inventory of figures. Over two hundred were counted in a partial survey of two concentrations of petroglyphs and painted overhangs, and many more were documented during a subsequent visit to the site. A total of between three hundred and four hundred masks is a conservative estimate of the total number. Cerro Indio masks display a well-developed and diversified iconography.

Masks are square, round, and bowl-shaped, flat on top with a curving lower contour (Figures 7.7, 7.8). Facial decoration is common. Many of the Cerro Indio masks are embellished with rain and rain-related elements such as clouds, rainbows, and lightning. Vertical stripes, horizontal stripes or bands dividing the face are common as are paired short lines used vertically or horizontally, triangular cheek markings, and dots. Specific and less frequent elements consist of feathers from the eye, a bird mouth, and a single handprint taking up the entire face. As mentioned previously, asymmetrical facial designs were popular, and asymmetry was also achieved by making each eye different. Another decorative technique is the use of solidly pecked areas to create negative patterns. Masks pecked over the angle of rock corners are also present. Headdresses when shown consist of feathers, and more rarely horns and a stocking cap-like element. Masks with beaks and a face-wide mouth with teeth at Cerro Indio (Figure 7.8, lower) are similar to masked figures on Mimbres ceramics (Brody 1977a:141, 175).

Birds, animals, and complete ceremonially attired anthropomorphs are represented as well. Animal tracks, especially those of deer, and less often mountain lion and bear, are found in association with the masks.

Most rock art sites in the Rio Grande valley are either found in proximity to pueblos with a much longer occupation, or are less specifically associated with a datable habitation site. Rock art found in these contexts could date from a span of several hundred years. Most Rio Grande–style rock art is believed to have been made between A.D. 1325 and 1600, after which time, Spanish oppression of the native religion and the kachinas in particular, along with a vigorous program of Catholic conversion, was instigated (see C. Schaafsma, this volume). It is likely that less rock art was made after that point, especially in the immediate vicinities of the villages themselves. Eastern Southern Tiwa painted masks and some carved masks are similar to those in Piro sites (Figure 7.9). Petroglyph masks in Southern Tiwa and Tewa sites such as the West Mesa outside of Albuquerque and in the Galisteo Basin respectively (figures 7.10, 7.11) are complex and innovative, but show fewer Jornada-style relationships as one moves north and further from the Jornada region (Eastvold 1986; Schaafsma 1980, 1992*a*, 1992*b*). These sites contain a rich associated iconography that includes horned serpents, complete ceremonial figures, shield bearers and other warriors, and birds and animals with significant ritual associations (Figures 7.12, 7.13).

Many of the design elements present on prehistoric masks are similar to those on Pueblo masks in the twentieth century. A crooked mouth, for example, occurs on a number of rock art representations and is characteristic of the contemporary Hehea kachina at Hopi, a clown, and Heruta, the head kachina at Cochiti. Rainbow and striped chin markings are found in both Rio Grande and Jornada-style masks and characterize the masks of the Hopi Shalako and Butterfly Girl. Most kachinas, however, are subject to innovation and change (see Wright, this volume), and the specific identification of most masks in the rock art is impossible. Under these circumstances, it is surprising that quite a number of kachinas pictured in Rio Grande rock art prehistorically appear to have modern analogs in the western pueblos of Zuni and Hopi. These kachinas, in addition to the large number of unidentifiable figures, help confirm the complexity of the cult prehistorically in the east, as well as

its widely shared list of personae. While this is not the place to go into a lengthy discourse on kachina identities per se, and with all due respect for Wright's cautionary treatise (this volume) a few examples may be cited. Deities and chief kachinas are more stable in the forms that they manifest. The continuity in mask form between the image on the Talpa Black-on-white sherd, parallel figures in the rock art, and certain Hopi masks was mentioned earlier. Specific kachinas and other supernaturals can be tentatively identified at Cerro Indio on the basis of facial designs and / or headgear. Among these are Sotuknangu, the Heart of the Sky God (Schaafsma 1992*b*: Fig. 126), and Kököle, a chief kachina, impersonated today at Hopi. Shalako-type figures with triangular (sometimes feathered) bodies and beaked masks are well represented in Southern Tiwa and Galisteo Basin sites (Schaafsma 1992*a*) before A.D. 1525 (see Hays, this volume, Plate 3, for comparable figure on a fifteenth-century Sikyatki Polychrome bowl). The mask with a large central handprint may represent one of several kachinas, including Anahoho (Zuni) and Matia (Hopi). A kachina, known as the Bloody Hand kachina, was formerly important at Cochiti but has been dropped, being considered dangerous (Lange 1990:460–62).

In addition Rio Grande rock art figures two-horned ogres, Hilili and other one-horned guard kachinas, mudheads, and various clowns. Tsakwaina, Ahulani (or Kerwan), Shulawitsi, Paiyatamu, or the flute kachina, and Somaikoli are other suggested identities of various pecked and painted Rio Grande masks (Cole 1984; Eastvold 1986; Schaafsma 1980; Sims 1963). Certain round faces with circular features situated close to ground level in cracks and low overhangs may represent Masau, the god of the Underworld, Earth Surface, and Fire among contemporary Hopis (Schaafsma 1990).

Because of the inability to date rock art precisely, at the moment there is little or no evidence to indicate that these kachinas, most of which are associated today with the western Pueblos, occur earlier in western Pueblo archaeological contexts than in eastern ones. Kachinas that have been identified in Homol'ovi II rock art and on fourteenth-century western Pueblo ceramics include Masau, Tawa, Giant Ogre kachina, Mudhead, the Sio Shalako, and Tsakwaina and possibly a few other warrior kachinas (Adams 1991: 62–63; Hays 1992b, this volume).

THE WESTERN PUEBLOS

In contrast with the Rio Grande, kachina rock art imagery associated with prehistoric Pueblo sites in the western, or Little Colorado River region, is relatively scarce, and kachina images that do occur are much simpler. Homol'ovi II, a seven-hundred-room village near Winslow, is a good comparative example with the much smaller contemporary pueblo, Cerro Indio, on the Rio Grande. In contrast to the several hundred masks present at the latter site, a complete study at Homol'ovi II brought to light sixty-seven masks. Most are circular or rectangular in shape. Dots mark the eyes and some have bared teeth and headgear (Cole 1989:327, Figs. 6, 7; Pilles 1975: Figs. 20–22). Overall these masks lack the endless variety of elaborations found in the Rio Grande masks. Some of the Homol'ovi masks may have been added later by Hopis who continued to visit shrines in the vicinity into the historic period (Cole 1989:313; Fewkes 1898).

Elsewhere, a few circles at Chavez Pass, a fourteenth-century site south of Homol'ovi, may or may not denote kachina faces. In a survey of Little Colorado River rock art sites between Holbrook and Winslow, Pilles (1975) discusses only those at Homol'ovi II. Kachinas occur among the petroglyphs at the Puerco Ruin, initially occupied between A.D. 1250 and 1350. Adams (1991) suggests, however, that some of these may have been added during a later occupation. Notably absent in all of these sites is the complex matrix of related imagery that is associated with masks in Rio Grande– and Jornada-style sites.

Similarly, the Rio Grande style is represented in the Zuni region by a few scattered elements, but the full complement of iconography is missing. Many of the rock art kachina masks around Zuni appear to be historic or made even during the last hundred years or so. Masks carved in detail with metal tools account for a large number of these representations, which are recognizable as specific kachinas, and one site has a suite of over twenty elaborate painted masks that were produced at different times during this century (Young 1988:188–89). Older, and presumably prehistoric examples are relatively simple in concept (Young 1988: Fig. 26, c). Certain shield figures, deeply gouged into the sandstone, look like oversized masks and resemble similar designs from the Jemez region associated with sites that date approximately between A.D. 1300 and 1600. It is difficult, however, to equate these with kachina representations with any degree of certainly. Rock art below Atsinna east of Zuni (A.D. 1250–1350) consists of a few Rio Grande-style birds and animals along with Pueblo III Anasazi work, but masks seem to be lacking. Very little is known about the rock art in the vicinity of Acoma.

In summary, the western rock art sites are restricted in subject matter, in size, and in the numbers, diversity, and complexity of kachina figures that they display. In the Zuni region relatively few of the kachinas in the rock art can be ascribed to the fourteenth or fifteenth centuries. These observations do not support the contention that the kachina cult developed at Hopi and other sites on the Little Colorado during the 1300s and henceforth spread eastward to the Rio Grande along with the glazed pottery tradition (Adams 1991:133, 146). Nor is this contention supported by ceramic data. In contrast with the rock art, where kachina imagery is prominently displayed in eastern Pueblo sites with figures numbering into the thousands, kachina iconography appears to have been somewhat more prevalent prehistorically on ceramics in the west than it was in the east. These differences in media in which kachinas are portrayed may relate in part to regional differences in the function and communication with respect to these images. This is a topic that is beyond the scope of this essay but well worth exploring. Kachina imagery is not found, however, (and by implication was extremely rare if existent at all) on western glazes, and it is rare on the early glazes in the Rio Grande (Ferg 1982; Fig. 1, d; Kidder 1936:Fig. 51). Although the earliest kachina elements that show up on ceramics in the Rio Grande resemble those on Little Colorado ceramics, I suggest that they are a part of a more widespread iconography and do not imply a simple diffusion of these motifs from the west.

In this context a final observation can be made regarding kachina portrayals from Pottery Mound on the Rio Grande and at Awatovi and Kawaika-a on the Hopi mesas (Hibben 1975; Smith 1952: Figs. 27, 28). As all but one of the five or six clearly recognizable masked figures represented in the Hopi murals appear to have been painted between the 1400s and early 1600s, they are not particularly useful for exploring kachina origins as such. One possible figure at Awatovi (Smith 1952: Fig. 27, *c*) could have been painted in the late 1300s, although an early fifteenth-century date is equally possible. Pottery Mound dates between A.D. 1325 and 1450/90 (Voll 1961). Brody (1991:112) maintains that the murals all date after 1400, but reasons for this assumption are not substantiated, and the subject of chronology here is better left alone, until more work has been done. For the moment it will suffice to point out that on the basis of the published material, between fifteen and twenty masked figures can be identified at Pottery Mound, and in addition, there are numerous star-faced beings that can be linked to the kachina complex. While the masked beings portrayed at Awatovi are all anthropomorphic faces, the Pottery Mound masks exhibit much greater diversity and include animal, bird and insect forms in addition to anthropomorphic masks. Whereas the paintings from

both these sites are equally complex and stylistically similar, the greater diversity of masks at Pottery Mound is consistent with observations made in the rock art.

THE LARGER ARCHAEOLOGICAL CONTEXT

The artistic florescence, exemplified by new and innovative approaches to ceramic decoration, the development of sophisticated wall murals and the Rio Grande style, indicates changes in the Pueblo world on several fronts. All of these art forms include kachina imagery and other supernaturals implying that a new ideology was operative. This ideological shift may have been facilitated by cultural changes and crises signified by, and as a result of, the abandonment of the San Juan drainage by the Anasazi at the end of the 1200s. The new art was accompanied by a changing archaeological context. Demographic shifts and population aggregation into plaza pueblos in the Little Colorado River region beginning in the late 1200s is described by Adams (1991) and Kintigh (1984). At the same time similar changes were taking place along the Rio Grande and its tributaries (Cordell 1979:145–46; Habicht Mauche 1988). By A.D. 1400 the Rio Grande valley and related regions were the focus of the Pueblo world, and at the time of the Spanish entrada in the sixteenth century, it was the most densely populated Pueblo region.

Population increased substantially in the Rio Grande early in the late thirteenth and early fourteenth century as the result of demographic shifts and influx from the San Juan drainage (Wendorf and Reed 1955) and probably elsewhere. Beginning around A.D. 1300, movement of agriculturalists out of the northern Tularosa Basin (Sebastien and Levine 1989:94–95) and the Sierra Blanca region (Kelley 1984) may account for population increases to the north and east. Earlier central New Mexican–Jornada ties are noted by Stuart and Gauthier (1981:321). The Jornada Mogollon and southern Pueblo provinces were not only contiguous in distribution (see

Figure 5.1, this volume), but a temporal overlap would have fostered an exchange of ideas between these desert farmers. As described previously, these relationships are well substantiated in the rock art of the southern Pueblo region in the Rio Grande and eastern provinces where a strong continuity with Jornada-style art, including the masks, exists.

This period of population aggregation and coalescence is characterized by multistoried, terraced pueblos arranged around one or more large plazas, many with between four hundred and two thousand ground-floor rooms. These sites have been recorded throughout the Rio Grande Pueblo region (Baldwin n.d.; Barnett 1969; Caperton 1981; Creamer and Haas 1988; Crown 1991; Dutton 1963; Elliott 1982; Haas and Creamer 1992; Hayes et al. 1981; Hibben 1955; Kidder 1936; Lambert 1954; Marshall 1987; Marshall and Walt 1984, 1985; Mera 1934, 1940; Nelson 1914; C. Schaafsma 1987; Schwartz and Lang 1973; Snow and Warren 1976; Stubbs and Stallings 1953; Wetherington 1986; Vierra 1987). Population aggregation is accompanied by the presence of increased and diversified farming techniques, water conservation systems, and ditch irrigation (Boyer et al., n.d.). At the same time, economic benefits resulting from trade with the Plains (Habicht Mauche 1988) contributed to the growth of eastern Pueblo towns.

As mentioned at the beginning of this essay, changes in settlement pattern toward aggregation and village planning around one or more enclosed plazas would have been facilitated by the presence of the kachina society (see Adams, this volume). The kachina organization draws its membership from the entire village, crosscutting kin-based ties and thus serves as an important mechanism for socially integrating a Pueblo community. In addition, kachina ritual and dances involve social and economic reciprocity that further bond the village. Ceremonies take place in the village plazas where everyone meets to participate and become involved in a ritual exchange of gifts. Functioning in this manner, the kachina organization would have been a major factor in promoting the development and integration of large pueblos. This religious organization, manifested archaeologically as kachina images, and large sites arrive as a package in the archaeological record.

Conclusions

That the kachina religion was present in the Pueblo world from the Rio Grande to the Little Colorado early in the 1300s is suggested by kachina imagery on ceramics and in the rock art from both region. Following a time of demographic shifts at the end of the 1200s that reflected environmental and cultural crises, Pueblo receptivity to new ideas from the Mogollon contributed to a dynamic Pueblo religious development and accompanying artistic florescence beginning early in the fourteenth century.

I propose, however, that the "Rio Grande hypothesis" is geographically a much more efficient reconstruction of the prehistory of the kachina cult than is the "Little Colorado hypothesis." Examination of Rio Grande and Little Colorado rock art on a comparative basis indicates that, unless rock art was an unimportant medium of communication and affirmation of religious ideology in the 1300s and 1400s among the western pueblos, we are viewing the graphic expression of a much more restricted religious ideology and kachina complex than occurs on the Rio Grande during the same period. Furthermore, Jornada-style rock art indicates that antecedents of kachina ritual were present in the Mogollon area immediately adjacent to the southern Pueblos. It would appear that the contiguous distribution between the southern Rio Grande Pueblos and the Jornada Mogollons and their temporal overlap for around a hundred years between A.D. 1300 and 1400 is particularly significant, accounting for the strength and complexity of kachina iconography in the adjacent Pueblo region, as opposed to its simpler expression in western Pueblo sites. The abundance of kachina masks on the cliffs below the pueblo of Cerro Indio and their strong stylistic affiliations with those in the Jornada style, contradict Adams's postulation (1991:139) that Jornada influence is not evident in the Rio Grande until after A.D. 1450.

Ultimately, certain of the ideological concepts embodied by the kachina cult may be traceable to Mexico. Tlaloc-like rain gods, conceptually related to rainmaking kachinas, as well as masks themselves, are prominent features of Jornada-style rock art made by desert farmers dependent on rainfall for their crops. Adams's ecological argument that it is likely that the kachina ritual was developed as an adaptive strategy in the arid plateaus of the Little Colorado River country, can equally well be argued for the earlier Mogollon farmers of southern New Mexico, who were engaged in an Ak Chin agriculture and dependent on summer rainfall for the successful cultivation of alluvial fans and river valleys (Creel 1989). Early stylistic relationships with the adjacent Mogollon and the scarcity of early kachina imagery in intervening areas between the Rio Grande and Little Colorado River pueblos are further evidence that the kachina complex did not reach the Rio Grande from the west.

Along with these distributional factors, the preponderance of Pueblo population in the Rio Grande drainage during early Pueblo IV, where village size and numbers exceeded those in the Little Colorado River region, is consistent with the proposal that the Rio Grande pueblos were a major force in the development and spread of this religious institution. The very large number of masks in Rio Grande rock art substantiates the suggestion that the Rio Grande was a high-energy center in itself during the fourteenth through the sixteenth centuries and not a passive recipient of influences from the Little Colorado. Kachinas traditionally regarded as of Hopi or Zuni origin are well represented early in the rock art of the Rio Grande. The data indicate that these same personages once essentially pervaded Pueblo thought and that their contemporary distribution is essentially a "relic population" of a once grander phenomenon. Religious pressure from Hispanics after A.D. 1600 led to the near-demise of kachina ritual in the Rio Grande valley, although it continued to flourish in the western pueblos of Zuni and Hopi further from Spanish control.

ACKNOWLEDGMENTS

Conversations with Curt Schaafsma, Kelley Hays, Chuck Adams, Marc Thompson, Jane Young, and Dennis Tedlock have contributed in many ways to the final version of this paper, and I would like to express my thanks. Any errors in facts or ideas are my responsibility.

8

Anthropomorphic Figures in the Pottery Mound Murals

PATRICIA VIVIAN

THE LARGEST and most complex series of prehistoric wall paintings ever found in North America occurs in underground religious chambers, or kivas, at the Pueblo IV site known as Pottery Mound, located forty-five miles southwest of present-day Albuquerque, New Mexico (Vivian 1961). Thus far, only three other Pueblo sites in the Southwest have presented comparable material. These are the prehistoric Hopi ruins at Awatovi and Kawaika-a in the Jeddito area of northeastern Arizona, and the site of Kuaua, New Mexico, some eighteen miles north of Albuquerque in the Rio Grande Valley.

It is my purpose to review Pueblo concepts of animism and anthropomorphism, and to discuss how these culture traits were manifested formally in the frescoes which played a vital role in Pueblo religious practices. I have chosen to use material from the prehistoric Hopi sites to supplement my discussion of Pottery Mound since there are many similarities, not only in painting styles, but also in personages possibly portrayed. Some of the anthropomorphic figures in these murals may be representations of kachinas, and many are certainly ritualistic. I will also attempt a few possible identifications of some of the anthropomorphized beings portrayed on the walls and their functions in ceremonialism. Toward that

end I have depended on certain correlative material from the Hopi Jeddito sites, as well as the
underlying religious background. Archaeological
material is supplemented wherever possible with
ethnological evidence. In addition, rock art analyses and other studies in the eastern (Vivian 1961;
Schaafsma and Schaafsma 1974; Schaafsma 1992*b*)
and western (Adams 1991; Cole 1992) regions
have contributed to our knowledge of Pueblo art
forms and related ideology during the period of
Pueblo history from the mid to late fourteenth to
the mid-fifteenth centuries—the age of the great
mural painters.

Moreover, kiva mural art of the American
Southwest must be studied within the context of
the physical environment. There can be no understanding of the wall paintings apart from the
natural forms of the rock, sand, plants, and animals around them. Pottery Mound lies in the Rio
Puerco valley, a major western tributary of the
Rio Grande. It is set at an elevation of about five
thousand feet, and the location is included in the
Upper Sonoran life zone. This is the place where
land and sky meet, a universe of space and sun,
vast expanses broken only by low-lying mountains and mesas on the horizons. Rainfall is light
in this country, and although piñon and juniper
grow in the foothills, the sparse amount of plant
life existing on the plains is small and scrubby. In
summer, the lower elevations appear dull green or
silvery from plants such as saltbush, yucca, and
different forms of cacti. In winter, or if there has
been an unusually long drought, everything dries
up and turns brown. In the autumn the rabbit-
brush, or "chamisa," transforms this semi-arid
world into gold. Fauna is limited to cottontail and
jackrabbits, coyote, bobcat, innumerable lizards,
snakes and birds. There are also occasional antelope and mule deer at higher elevations, and in
the past, there would have been mountain lion.
This is the setting for the site known as Pottery
Mound. This Pueblo Indian village, which derives
its name from the great mass of broken pottery
thickly covering the whole site, has been assigned

to the Pueblo IV period of an established cultural and chronological sequence. The duration of
this particular site falls within the earlier part of
Pueblo IV, or from about A.D. 1300 to 1475.

The southwestern Pueblo area (both prehistoric
and historic) comprises two major divisions—the
eastern and the western. The western Pueblos include the Hopi villages of northeastern Arizona,
and the pueblos of Zuni, Acoma, and Laguna in
western New Mexico. The eastern Pueblos are
located in the Rio Grande valley of north-central
New Mexico, and on nearby tributaries. Geographically, and in other major aspects, Pottery
Mound was a Rio Grande, or eastern Pueblo.
However, other material from the site strongly
bears out western connections with Acoma. The
most important evidence for western connections
may well be the imposing series of mural paintings reflecting similar styles to Hopi.

In 1960, Frank C. Hibben (1960:268–69)
wrote:

> Architecturally, Pottery Mound consists of large
> tiers of adobe-walled rooms surrounding plazas, in
> the plan usual at Pueblo IV sites. Including several
> additions, the structures cover approximately seven
> acres. In several sections the building was three or
> possibly four stories high.
>
> Rio Grande pueblos, in common with other de-
> veloped pueblo structures, usually feature a num-
> ber of subterranean ceremonial rooms or kivas. In
> Pueblo IV times the kivas were usually rectangu-
> lar. There are two major types—the smaller or
> Medicine Society Kivas, which are fifteen to twenty
> feet square, and the larger or moiety kivas ap-
> proximately twice these dimensions. Thus far seven
> Medicine Society kivas have been discovered, and
> one Moiety kiva. All eight of these have paintings
> on the walls.

Subsequently more kivas were opened, and today
we know of seventeen.

Watson Smith (1952:4–5) observed in
his "Kiva Mural Decorations at Awatovi and
Kawaika-a":

At the risk of oversimplification it may be said that among all the Pueblo groups there exist certain societies or fraternities, usually but not always masculine, the primary function of each of which is the periodic celebration of some particular esoteric ceremonial ritual. . . . Some are relatively simple, while others involve a very elaborate paraphernalia, including masks, costumes, altars, wall paintings, and a wide variety of ritual objects. Most, if not all, contain prayers, songs, dances, and various forms of magic, and each is conducted by a hierarchical priesthood, whose membership is correlative with that of a particular society or fraternity. . . .

Although local standards of kiva size and shape are pretty consistent and enduring over fairly long periods of time, kivas vary enormously throughout the Pueblo area. . . . It may contain some or all of a variety of interior features or appurtenances, such as columns or pilasters to support the roof, benches about the walls, fireplaces, ventilator shafts, niches in the walls for the storage of sacred objects, symbolic openings in the floor leading to the underworld, fixtures for the erection of looms, and so on.

Most kivas at Pottery Mound were oriented (altar set up) toward the south or east. Banquettes were usually high, perhaps used for storage. Certain kivas had tunnels leading to other rooms and many had niches. Kivas were roofed with vigas and latillas and brush supported by four upright posts. Some walls were built of solid adobe, while others were constructed of rubble masonry with fresh mud mortar and bracing sticks of wood.

According to Hibben (1975: 16, 141), the following are the numbers of painted layers found in the assumed total of seventeen kivas at Pottery Mound.

Kiva 1	6 painted layers
Kiva 2	18 painted layers
Kiva 3	12 painted layers
Kiva 4	3 painted layers
Kiva 5	(Moiety kiva?) 3 painted layers
Kiva 6	38 painted layers
Kiva 7	38 painted layers
Kiva 8	38 painted layers
Kiva 9	(remodeled version of Kiva 8) 10 painted layers
Kiva 10	(Moiety kiva?) 38 painted layers
Kiva 11	4 painted layers
Kiva 12	38 painted layers
Kiva 13	Uncertain
Kiva 14	Uncertain
Kiva 15	32 painted layers
Kiva 16	32 painted layers
Kiva 17	14 painted layers

It appears that the number of plastered layers from the Hopi sites far exceeded that of Pottery Mound. However, the greater percentage of the plastered layers from the latter site were painted, whereas with the former, a comparatively smaller amount of the total layers contained murals. It would seem that many of the Hopi walls had been left plain white. The layers of Pottery Mound kivas (as at Awatovi and Kawaika-a) were numbered consecutively, in a series, for each wall. The first layer uncovered (which would also be the youngest in time) would be Number 1, and so on until the last layer next to the original adobe wall construction was reached. This layer would be historically the oldest.

For the most part, the pigments used were mineral in origin and undoubtedly were derived from natural deposits in the immediate physical environment such as clay or sandstone stained with minerals. Based on the Awatovi analysis, it is suggested that there was red iron oxide from hematite, azurite, malachite, limonite, uranium oxide, a yellow iron oxide, copper salts, carbon, white clay, and gypsum (a white chalk). The materials available gave the Pueblo artist a basic palette of red, yellow, green, blue, black, and white. The existing paintings show many variations of the primary hues. It seems that pigments were mixed for different combinations, creating secondary and tertiary colors, and diversity within the value and chroma scales such as pink, orange, purple, maroon, brown, and gray. The variations were probably the results of a sense of experimentation as well as some accidents from impurities.

The raw pigments were probably ground with a mano on a metate and were then mixed with a vehicle and a binding medium to cause the paint to adhere to the wall surface. As Smith (1952:30–31) has noted, today the Pueblo method of painting masks, kachina dolls, and other paraphernalia will often combine the vehicle and binder by mixing the pulverized dry pigment into the saliva generated by chewing a variety of seeds, which secrete a vegetable oil. Sometimes, either piñon gum or the juice of boiled yucca plants or squash is used. It seems possible that the same methods were used in preparing mural paint. According to Hibben (1960:269), they could have also used a medium of water and animal grease.

Judging by the existing material, it is probable that a variety of tools was used to apply the paint. The exact nature of their brushes is not known, but it appears that they had both soft and stiff types. In recent times, strips of yucca leaf have been used. These are chewed at one end to remove the pulp and to leave the bare fibers protruding in the form of a brush. Moreover, it is evident that the manner in which brushes were used at Pottery Mound varied a great deal. This can be detected by the dry and wet brush strokes, stippling, splattering, and other techniques. In addition, the surface paint textures found within the paintings make it obvious that the brush constituted only one tool, other possible ones being knives, scrapers, and the fingers or the whole hand.

It seems that the paintings were done on dry plaster, in the manner called "fresco secco," in which the paint forms merely a surface film adherent to the plaster base. In true fresco the paint is applied to damp plaster, with the result that the color becomes permanently bonded to the wall. The "fresco secco" technique at Pottery Mound was used on thin layers of finely prepared adobe plaster, less than ⅛ inch thick. When a new painting was created, the preceding one was coated with a layer of plaster. Thus, the basic adobe wall structure of the ceremonial room would be covered with a series of plastered and painted layers. As at Pottery Mound, the mural decorations at Hopi were applied to these coats of fine plaster using similar fresco secco techniques. Probably they used similar tools, vehicles, binders, and paints from local deposits.

Watson Smith (1952:19) gives four reasons for the probable frequency of renewals of wall plaster at the Hopi sites. These theories may also be useful toward explaining a similar situation at Pottery Mound. They are: the occasional partial disintegration or collapse of parts of the wall, or plastered surface; the desirability of refurbishing the surface in order to obliterate an existing layer that has been blackened by soot; a customary periodic renewal in the nature of "spring cleaning" or, finally, the ceremonial necessity, or practice of obliterating or secreting a sacred object after it has served the religious purpose for which it was made, in this case a mural painting.

Based on ethnographic knowledge, we think that the prehistoric Pueblo Indian also followed a strict ceremonial pattern directly related to his calendar, or yearly seasonal cycle, which could relate to painted plaster renewals. According to Watson Smith:

> The probability of periodic seasonal renewals is supported by analogy to recorded instances among modern Pueblo villages, where it is known to be practiced. In the Hopi villages it seems to be customary for all kivas to be freshly plastered at the time of the Powamu ceremony (or "Bean dance") in February. This is one of the most important of the Hopi ceremonies, and one that in many ways may be regarded as marking the beginning of the ceremonial calendar (Smith 1952:20).

Pueblo World-View

In order to understand the paintings as they might have related to the Pueblo religious calendar, one must look at the Pueblo world-view and consider these four basic assumptions.

1. The paintings are considered to have been religious in character, housed in sacred chambers, and

directly integrated into the total esoteric ritual complex.

2. Prehistoric people of the Southwest viewed nature and the universe in a basic and similar manner. This faith depended on their natural environment—on all the objects and forces of nature they knew from day to day.

3. These people were bound into a world-view which maintained itself in a long, unchanging tradition.

4. The vital relationships between man and nature, a constant flow of mutual giving and receiving, must be considered essential to Pueblo artistic statement.

Man has often personified the forces of nature with a spirit-soul, just as he, himself, had a spirit-soul. When natural phenomena or objects were animated, they became more understood. It was a way of explaining things. Thus cause was explained in relationship to powerful good and evil spirits, which lived in all forms of nature, and which man knew closely enough to fear, love, and respect. As he was motivated by his own inward spirit, nature was motivated. Real personality and animated life were given to the world around him. Therefore, with the power endowed in nature, man must praise and propitiate. Thus were generated the profoundly beautiful rituals and ceremonies—a culminating, dramatic art form, in which the mural paintings probably played an important role.

Elsie Clews Parsons has written:

Not only are the Pueblos basically animists, they are also confirmed anthropomorphists. To a Zuni or a Hopi, little distinction can be made between a spirit and a man. This trait is perhaps most clearly represented in the kachina figures (or their costumed human impersonators) who appear in village ceremonials during various parts of the year. As we shall see, their function is not only to take part in esoteric rituals, but to help the Indian throughout life. (Parsons 1939:198)

According to Frederick Dockstader (1954:9–10), the term "kachina" has three meanings. The word

may be translated as "life father" or "spirit father" (Hopi: *kachi,* life or spirit; *na,* father). This meaning refers basically to the kachinas as spiritual personages or supernatural beings who exercise control over the weather, help in many of the everyday activities of the villages, punish offenders of ceremonial or social laws, and generally act as a link between gods and mortals. The second meaning of the term refers to the masked impersonators who appear in traditional costumes at various ceremonies. When a Hopi wears the costume and mask of a particular kachina, he loses his personal identify and is imbued with the spirit of that being. In reality he is that being. Third, the term "kachina" applies to the small brightly painted wooden dolls, miniature representations of the masked impersonators. The kachinas bring gifts and dolls to children, who receive a careful education in kachina lore, and how to recognize these personages when they appear (the dolls are often used as part of instruction). Some kachinas represent evil or dangerous spirits who come once a year to the villages to frighten children into good behavior.

Each year there is a succession of ceremonies, and their order and occurrence is determined by a calendar based on a combination of solar and lunar observations. It can be outlined briefly as follows from the Hopi calendar:

December	*Winter Solstice (Soyal).* The Sun is coerced back north to begin a New Year.
February	*Powamu ("Bean Dance").* Important start of germination. The bean plants nurtured in kivas. Welcoming the Kachinas back.
July	*Summer Solstice (Niman).* Kachinas go home and carry the people's prayers to the gods.
August	*Snake–Antelope, in alternation with the blue and drab flute societies.* Rain-making ceremonies.

September	*Marau (women's society).*
October	*Oagol (women's society).* The women's societies celebrate a good harvest time.
November	*Wuwuchim.* Ceremonies of the men's initiation societies.

It should be noted that I have listed the Hopi ceremonial cycle only as a frame of reference here. This is not to imply that direct parallels can or should be made between the ceremonial art forms stemming from the particular ritual patterns of these people and those of the ancient dwellers of Pottery Mound. But it should at least present some insights.

Soyal and Mastop kachinas appear at the winter solstice ceremony—aloof and awe-inspiring on the final day of these rites. Another group of kindly Oaqolo Kachinas appear and "open" the kivas so that the kachinas (symbolically) can come out. The Oaqolo also may appear before the Bear dance (or Powamu) and prophesize good crops. Most of the kachinas appear at Powamu including Eototo, the chief, and his assistant, Ahöla. From that time until the final day of the Home Dance in July the kachinas are thought to be in and around the villages and are associated with rainfall, crops, and game (Earle and Kennard 1938:3–5).

As has been indicated previously, kiva walls were probably painted expressly for particular ritual observances. But the broad purpose of such paintings and their integration into the entire complex of ceremonial paraphernalia remains to be considered. Watson Smith has been concerned with the same problem in the Jeddito area and has noted:

> It is well known that the inventory of principal elements involved in most esoteric kiva ceremonials almost always includes most if not all of the following: an upright altar, a sandpainting, an assortment of small items of paraphernalia, and an assemblage of participating persons whose costume and body decoration follow a prescribed pattern, and whose conduct is dictated by an established routine. . . . This altar is erected against the wall of the kiva opposite to the usual raised platform or bench. . . . Upon or against it may be hung or placed an assortment of small objects, such as feathers, corn ears, Pahos (prayer sticks), plants, fetishes, netted gourds, and the like and from the roof above it may be suspended various things as well. This altar normally will occupy only a portion of the center of the entire wall space, leaving unconcealed wide areas on each side and above. In several instances the upright slat altar is replaced by a painted screen which is unrolled and hung against the wall in much the manner and purpose of the backdrop in a modern theater. . . .
>
> Since the slat-altar may be replaced by a painted screen used in the same position, the question at once occurs to us: why could not the upright altar be replaced on occasion by a mural painting in the corresponding position on the wall? . . . That particular mural paintings can be equated detail for detail with particular upright altars is not be be supposed, however, nor are they to be thought of as substitutionary for them. It is more likely that in certain ceremonies the one form of decoration is prescribed rather than the other; and the important point is that morphologically and ritualistically they probably fulfill a like function. (Smith 1952:319–20)

Through the kivas and their painted walls we glimpse the intimate relationship of the spirit and kachina world with the villagers, the need for ritual and ceremony, and the probable development of the mural art form as a manifestation of life experiences and a necessary part of this ritual life. Indeed, the spirit and kachina world may be reflected in the mural art.

Possible Identifications of Esoteric Beings and Their Functions Within Specific Examples of the Mural Paintings

Comparisons with possible counterparts in the prehistoric Hopi murals will aid in a few interpretations of identifications of some figures. In most cases, we do not have enough combined archaeo-logical and ethnological data to tell us exactly who the characters were. Neither Hibben nor his Acoma informants have identified most of the figures, and more evidence must be established before we can interpret the significance of the paintings more comprehensively.

In Kiva 2, layer 1, there is a series of interior kiva scenes which portray a number of chief-like figures with elaborate headdresses and ceremonial spears (Plate 6). Accompanying these figures are other personages such as a "rainbow man" and a woman who appears to be dead and lying on an altar carried on the back of a masked priest (see Hibben 1975:Figs. 14, 49). Other figures hold quivers with arrows, shields, a bow, a club, and a staff decorated with feathers and rattlesnakes. One personage wears the skin of a possible moun-tain lion. There is at least one other woman, who is dressed ceremonially and is wearing many beads. Around the walls are painted cloud and bird forms. Moreover, one can view the storage of headdresses and other paraphernalia, gear such as shields and staffs, and blankets and strings of beads hanging from the walls. On the floor there are storage pots or baskets, and one scene portrays the large figure of a whooping crane (see Hibben 1975:Fig. 17). These painted kiva scenes are from the west and south walls, but they could have run continuously around. Here the viewer is able to glimpse not only the inner world of what would probably have been secret and ceremonial activi-ties within this underground chamber, but also what the chamber would have looked like.

Throughout the Pottery Mound murals occur depictions of various "warrior" figures, or more accurately men in ceremonial costume with huge shields and helmet-like headdresses (although the latter cannot be determined definitely because of their fragmentary conditions) (Plate 7). Such portrayals were discovered for the most part on layer 3 of Kiva 2. Judging from these scattered remains, it would appear that the "warriors" either ran continuously around all four walls of this layer or at least dominated the scene. They carry extremely large round shields from which only their heads and legs show. In most cases these parts of the body are painted a solid color, usually red with black lines around the calves. This could represent body paint, perhaps with yarn tied around the legs, common elements of costuming. The shields are decorated with various designs on their surfaces and black scallop-like fringes around the peripheries. The majority seem to be composed of abstract decorative pattern-ings, although one figure carries a shield with a painted "star head" and feather headdress, while another bears a shield with what looks to be the bottom portions and tail feathers of a bird.

Parsons (1924:5–6, 1939:493) has noted some possibilities for the existence of ritual warriors that relate to the order of yearly Pueblo cere-monies based on an adaptation to the economic round or seasons for farming, weaving, war, hunt-ing, and building. For example, when the Zuni kachinas (the Shalako) depart, there is a hunt ritual; a deer hunt is, and perhaps was, made in advance to secure pelts for ritual use. Rab-bit hunts are held by Hopis to protect fields. Hunts sometimes secure food for the chiefs, their fetishes, or the celebrants. In the past, the "war" organizations with chiefs became "guardians of the outside world" against invasion, witchcraft, and evil spirits.

Perhaps one of the most prominent and vital times for the impersonated warrior to make his appearance is during the nine days of the Soyal or winter solstice ceremony occurring in Decem-ber. This is the time when not only the Hopi but all of the Pueblos know that the sun has trav-eled on his yearly journey as far south as he will go. Watson Smith hypothesizes that several of the Jeddito murals portray an episode in the Hopi Soyal or winter solstice ceremony when the sun must be "forced" to return northward again so that the people will have his light and warmth for the growing season ahead. Within ritual based on this concept, a simulated coercion or battle to produce the results of "victory" over a force of nature would probably be necessary. In addition, Schaafsma (1968:23) has suggested that warrior motifs in nearby Los Lunas rock art may have solstice implications.

According to Smith:

> The identification of this design as representing a symbolic battle seems to have much greater plausibility and may very well be a portrayal of an episode in the Soyal described in some detail by Stephen from his observations in Walpi in 1891. The significant action occurred during the final night of the ceremony, when a series of mock combats were enacted, symbolising the struggle of the people to coerce the Sun northward after his hibernation in the south. The pantomime was carried out by the Chief of one of the seven participating societies, who entered the kiva, received a shield from a spectator, and simulated an "attack" upon a line of other performers, who repelled him. This act was repeated for each of the seven societies, the particular chief in each case representing a different supernatural, and carrying a different shield with varying decorations, but all symbolising the struggle for the return of the Sun.   (Smith 1952:312–13)

This is particularly thought-provoking when we consider the fact that the existing fragments of painted warriors, especially in Kiva 2, definitely suggest that they were arranged in a line, as though standing ready and prepared for ceremonial combat.

At Pottery Mound there is a painting in Kiva 8, west wall, south half, layer 4, which so strongly suggests the portrayal of a War god that an inference is almost inescapable (Plate 8). This personage conveys the feeling of being suspended in air; his body is pointing slightly upward, however, as though he were in the act of flying. Apparently, a profile view was intended because only the one shoulder and arm are shown, and it was determined that the head or face was depicted in profile. On his head is a black, or purplishblack conical cap. The face was too fragmentary to permit a detailed description; however, it appears to have been painted in black, with a white design of some sort upon it. The greater part of the body is hidden by a large circular shieldlike object with the form of an animal skin and tail projecting from the lower end rather than human legs. Whether this figure was portrayed as a half human–half animal, or whether he is merely wearing an animal skin pelt is not clear. The hand is white and is clutching a beautifully rendered bow and arrow, the latter having a perfect point.

My identification of this personage as a War god is based on analogy to a similar figure within the Jeddito murals (Plate 9). Here, there is the portrayal of a figure diving downward in space. The Jeddito figure is also shown with body and head in profile. Smith (1952:302) writes, "The face is black with a white eye and a white footprint, perhaps that of a bear, on its cheek. The head is crowned by a conical white cap and an arrow-point emerges from the mouth." Nothing appears to be issuing from the mouth of the Pottery Mound figure, although the paint could have disintegrated. The Jeddito figure is wearing an animal-skin robe with a tail and an extended leg bound with a tassel. In addition, there is a design painted on it that was identified by a Hopi at Oraibi as a representation of a sun shield with feathers radiating out. As Smith (1952:241–42) has noted, in mythology and ceremony, the sun shield is often carried by one of the Twin War Gods. As previously described, the Pottery Mound figure is portrayed with a shield-like object on his back in an analogous position to that of the painted device on the skin of the Jeddito figure. Whether or not the device of the former was intended as a sun shield is not certain, and unfortunately the entire design upon it could not be reproduced. It is interesting to note, however, that the painted skin robe covers the same portions of the body as does the shield-like object with the projecting skin and tail so that in both examples the same upper parts of the human body are revealed and depicted with neither figure revealing human legs. Finally, the hand of the Jeddito figure is clutching a bow and arrow in the same manner as that at Pottery Mound.

Watson Smith writes,

> One is immediately struck by the similarity of this figure to the Hopi War God images, mainly on the basis of the black faces and conical white caps that seem to be characteristic of the latter, at least at Walpi. The appearances of such images at the Winter Solstice ceremony has been described and the published drawings clearly display the white conical cap. . . .
>
> There would thus seem to be some divergence in the conventional characteristic of the Hopi War Gods, but it should be added that the figure in Test 14 was positively identified by several Hopi as representing one of them. . . .
>
> [A Hopi informant] regarded the cap as characteristic and elaborated his discussion by pointing out that the God carried a chief's staff and bow, had a bear or badger imprint on his face, and a sun shield on his breast . . . The arrow at the mouth he said is the God's breath or spirit. (Smith 1952:302–3)

In addition, records of Pueblo ceremonialism describe the same figure with the conical cap impersonated at various other rituals, such as the Snake ceremony, and the War ceremony at First Mesa Hopi villages. Frederick Dockstader (1954:49) suggests the Jeddito figure may be Ahöla kachina, who wears a conical cap and a painted skin robe. Ahöla, Eototo's partner, follows him during the rites of the ninth day of Powamu ceremony (Earle and Kennard 1938:16). In concluding, however, it would seem a strong possibility that the presence of the conical cap, black face, probable sun shield, bow and arrow, and possibly the bear-paw symbol or other white cheek markings point to the identification of both the Jeddito and Pottery Mound figures as being one of the War gods.

The wall painting in Kiva 8, south wall, layer 5 is composed of a great white circular device with an elaborate display of many variegated feathers around the periphery, possibly a sun shield (Plate 10). Within this is painted a coiled rattlesnake form with a human head, neck, shoulder, arm, and hand. Unfortunately, the face and most of the fingers of the hand are missing: in all probability the hand held an object. Black human hair hanging down on the right side has a long red strip painted down the middle. This could represent adornment, such as a red feather tied in the hair of a ritual performer, and is often seen painted within the black hair of many of the male ceremonial figures at Pottery Mound. The coiled brown snake body has a design of small yellow doughnut-shaped circles superimposed at intervals. The shield-snake form is, in turn, superimposed over the body of a huge elongated animal of a yellow ochre color—possibly a mountain lion with the paws and typical claw-shapes. This body is shown in profile and actually appears to be two "half-bodies" flanking the sun shield in an heraldic design. The sun shield is viewed as war paraphernalia, and its depiction on the kiva wall might point to a ceremony connected with war ritual. The humanized rattlesnake figure is a good example of the Pueblo concept of anthropomorphizing a form of nature. The serpent is given an animated spirit and personality in which the snake and man become as one. The anthropomorphized snake may mirror the Hopi concept of snake-warriors. The human arm and hand, which are missing, might have held war paraphernalia. Parsons (1939:663) has noted that in 1892 during the Snake-Antelope ceremony at Shipaulovi (Second Mesa), the Snake Chief claimed the snakes would go to the house of the sun in the west after the ceremony and would be recognized there by the pollen marks on their backs. As part of the secret rites in the Snake kiva, the snakes were sprinkled with pollen by the chief. This could explain the small yellow painted circles.

Finally, the mountain lion occupies a very prominent place in myth and ritual; this is not surprising when we consider that he is one of the largest and most imposing of the native predators in the Southwest. According to Watson Smith:

> In modern times among the Hopi its [mountain lion] representation in kiva ceremonies seems to be limited to those of the War society at or after the Winter Solstice observances at both Walpi and Hano, to the altar of the Snake society, where it occurs as the central figure of the sand painting (in front of the altar) and to the altar of the Antelope society at Walpi, where stone lion fetishes are sometimes placed near the sand painting. (Smith 1952:202–4)

Moreover, the spear-like form passing through this animal certainly suggests the use of war or hunt paraphernalia in connection with the total portrayal.

There are other examples of the portrayal of snakes in Kiva 8 at Pottery Mound. On the south wall, layer 6, an uncoiled rattlesnake is depicted horizontally behind a kilted human figure holding a quiver in his left hand. The two figures overlap in a typical Pottery Mound artistic style. The heads of both the human and snake are missing, but these appear to be ritual figures painted in a style that suggests an intimate and ceremonial relationship.

The figure from Kiva 8, east wall, layer 1, northeast section is masked and wears a tablita-type headdress with various feathers rising from a rattlesnake skin crown (Plate 11). This personage, who is depicted within the confines of a moon-shaped form, carries a quiver in his left hand. Although the total appearance suggests a kachina representation, the particular identification of this figure and the significance of such a portrayal are unknown.

Various snake motifs occur in Kiva 8, closely associated with stars having human attributes, and depicted in the form of "star-heads" (Plate 12). The most direct examples of this are the paintings at the two opposite ends of the east wall of Kiva 8, layer 7. Each portrays a coiled rattlesnake, the head of which is a round humanlike

form with four large star points on equal sides. This four-pointed shape appears to be characteristic of most of the star forms in the Pottery Mound murals. According to Schaafsma (1992*b*), these four-pointed stars are also an important Rio Grande style rock art motif, commonly occuring with snakes or horned serpents. As in the murals, many have eagle-feather headdresses. The starheads of the two symmetrically flanking snakes at Pottery Mound have eyes and mouths in the form of small crescents pointing downward; the mouth of the figure in the northeast section even has very wicked looking red teeth. The eyes and mouths are white, contrasting sharply against the black faces, giving them a startling appearance. Each figure is wearing a tall headdress of possible eagle feathers. It is unfortunate that the entire middle section of this wall has been destroyed, for these figures apparently flanked a prominent central motif. These round mask-like esoteric looking faces within a star form were termed "soul faces" by Hibben's (1975:134) Acoma informants. It has been thought that they may represent spirits of the dead to whom an appeal for rain and other benefits is made. This possibility could reflect the cult of the dead aspect of the kachina cult. (Adams 1991:35–36)

There are other possible portrayals of kachina figures at Pottery Mound (Hibben 1975). In Kiva 1, north wall, layer 1, for example, insect people or kachinas (possibly grasshoppers or cicadas) are depicted with wings and antenna and jewelry (Plate 13). There are cloud forms above and plant forms in the background. They are painted with meticulous care, as though these elegant personages deserved great attention.

The insect-like personage in Kiva 2, west wall, layer 11, perhaps is a Locust kachina (Hibben 1975:Fig. 18). He is portrayed wearing beads and a pendant and holding a staff decorated with the clawed foot of a bird or animal. He sits in profile within a frame-like shape. At each of the two top corners of this "frame" are perched a macaw or parrot in a flanking or heraldic design.

On the south wall, layer 10 of Kiva 7 is the "Mosquito" kachina (Plate 14) with long proboscis and lacy, gossamer wings. He wears a feather headdress, yarn on the arms and legs, and a kilt and sash, and also sits in profile. Watson Smith identified a similar figure in the Jeddito as a "hummingbird" spirit (see Smith 1952:Fig. 17*f*).

In conclusion, the painted dancing figures of Kiva 8, west wall, layer 1, perhaps the last paintings executed before this kiva was abandoned, should be mentioned (Plate 15). On this wall we may view the portrayal of Pueblo ceremonial dancers and imagine them no longer as painted forms but performers dancing for rain. The southernmost figure is that of a male who wears the typical kilt and sash and a feather headdress. He carries a possible aspergill of feathers and a water pot. According to Hibben (1975:104–5), the aspergill was dipped into the water pot and sprinkled to simulate rain in ceremonies. The central female figure wears the typical Pueblo woman's dress with a sash and also wears a feather headdress. In addition, she carries the aspergill and water pot. The female appears to be wearing a mask. The male face is painted in a solid yellow ochre color with no apparent features. Whether or not this was meant to suggest a mask is uncertain. Between them is an anthropomorphized bird figure, perhaps a Swallow kachina, judging

by the shape of the wings and tail. Unfortunately, the head is missing as in so many of the examples at Pottery Mound. Finally, on the north corner (P. Bryon Vivian, field notes 1960, University of New Mexico) is an upside-down black figure, perhaps some ghostly spirit or ancestor descending from the sky (see Hibben 1975: Fig. 89). Watson Smith found a similar upside-down figure at Awatovi (see Smith 1952: Fig. 53), which was identified as possibly Kokopelli Mana or the Dog kachina, based on the mask appearance.

Conclusion

I have presented in this essay only a small sampling of the rich mural art at Pottery Mound, but I hope to have given the reader a glimpse into a complex and profound world, vastly peopled with kachinas and personages so important in the cosmic and religious drama and daily lives of these ancient people. The anthropomorphized beings in many of the murals appear to be artistic manifestations of the personality and humanized form which the Pueblo Indian gave to the world around him. We know that kachinas, or masked spirits, in ceremonialism today reflect that same humanism. At Pottery Mound, we have uncovered a part of the aesthetic forms and religious functions of that spirit world in the past.

PLATE 1. Twelfth-century stone figurine with kachina-like face from Chambers Great House, NA 8944, Little Colorado River drainage.

PLATE 2. Four Mile Polychrome Bowl with kachina face on snake body, Chevelon Ruin, USNM. *Photo by Peter Pilles.*

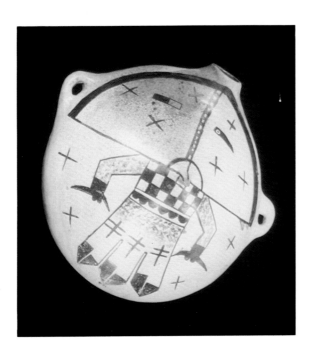

PLATE 3. Late Sikyatki Polychrome canteen with Sun Kachina, FMNH 21174. *Photo by K. Hays.*

PLATE 4. Painted mask on plaster-covered rock. The face has oval eyes and horizontal stripes, Piro rock shelter, Rio Grande Valley, New Mexico, ca. A.D. 1325–1680. *Photo by Polly Schaafsma.*

PLATE 5. Tompiro painted mask and masked ceremonial figures near Abo, New Mexico. Figure at lower left has a star mask. A.D. 1325–1672. *Photo by Polly Schaafsma.*

PLATE 6. Reproduction of Pottery Mound mural believed to depict an interior kiva scene. Kiva 2, west wall, northwest corner, layer 1.

PLATE 7. Reproduction of Pottery Mound mural
depicting two warrior figures with shields. Kiva 2,
west wall, central and right figures of layer 3.

PLATE 8. Reproduction of Pottery Mound mural
depicting a "War God." Kiva 8, west wall, south half,
layer 4.

PLATE 9. Reproduction of Awatovi mural depicting
a "War God." Test 14, room 2, right wall, design 6.
Smith, 1952, Pl. E.

PLATE 10. Reproduction of Pottery Mound mural showing a snake figure, sun shield, and possible mountain lion. Kiva 8, south wall, layer 5.

PLATE 11. Pottery Mound mural of a "Snake-warrior" figure in a round form. Kiva 8, east wall, northeast corner, layer 1.

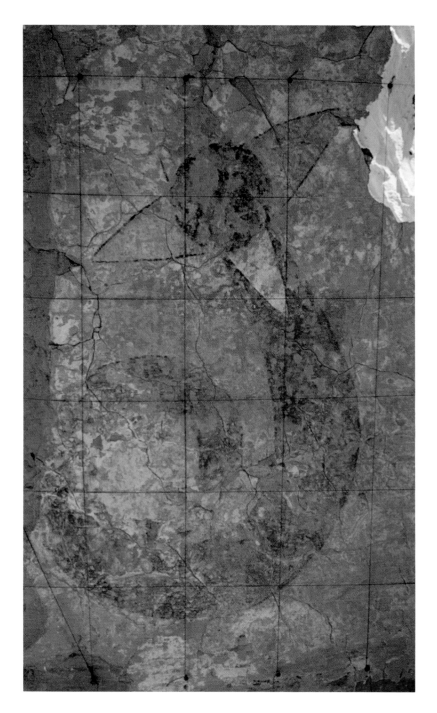

PLATE 12. Pottery Mound mural of coiled snake with star head, Kiva 8, east wall, southeast corner, layer 7.

PLATE 13 *(above)*. Reproduction of Pottery Mound mural of "Insect katchinas." Kiva 1, north wall, layer 1.

PLATE 14 *(right)*. Reproduction of masked anthropomorphized mosquito or insect, Pottery Mound, Kiva 7, south wall, southwest corner, layer 10.

PLATE 15. Pottery Mound mural of a male ceremonial dancing figure. Kiva 8, west wall, southwest section, layer 1.

PLATE 16. Comparison of Ahöla, Wuwuyomo, Wupamo, Ahulani, and Hopinyu masks and similar masks from an Awatovi kiva mural and seventeenth-century pottery: (*a*) Ahöla mask; (*b*) Painted mask from Awatovi, room 788; (*c*) Mask from an Awatovi Polychrome canteen (A.D. 1600–1700); (*d*) Mask from Sikyatki Polychrome canteen (A.D. 1600–1675); (*e*) and (*f*) Ahulani; (*g*) Wuwuyomo; (*h*) Hopinyu; (*i*) and (*j*) Wupamo.

Plate 17. Zuni, Sio, and Hopi Shalakos and associated kachinas.

PLATE 18. Four variations of the Somaikoli kachina.

19

20

21

PLATES 19–23. Examples of different forms of the Zuni Kokkokshi and Hopi Angak'chinas, popularly known as "Long-Haired Kachinas": [only the Hopi are known by this term]
(*19*) Hopi Sio Angak'china;
(*20*) Zuni Upik'aiapona or Atsam Kokkokshi;
(*21*) Red-bodied Zuni Kokkokshi;
(*22*) Zuni Hekshina Shelowa [different from #21];
(*23*) Hopi Katoch Angak'china.

22

23

24   25   26

PLATES 24–27 *(this page)*. Further examples of Long-Haired Kachinas:
(24) Hopi Hokyan Angak;
(25) Hopi Tasaf Angak;
(26) Hopi Sio Powamu Angak. Also called Kokokshe at Acoma, and
Hahawe or Upïk'tamayakwe at Zuni;
(27) Hopi Kotite Angak or Cochiti Angak.

PLATES 28–33 *(opposite)*. Examples of Santa Ana, San Felipe, Zia,
Cochiti, and Hopi-Tewa Long-Haired Kachinas:
(28) Hopi-Tewa Pala Sowichmi Angak'china;
(29) Cochiti Ashuwa or Big Zuni;
(30) Cochiti Ashuwa Li'Kashani or Little Zuni;
(31) Santa Ana Ashuwa;
(32) San Felipe A'shuwa;
(33) Zia Mekatc A'showa.

27

28

29

30

31

32

33

FIG. 570 (41963)   FIG. 572 (41969)

PLATE 34. "Shinumu Statuettes," three Hopi kachina carvings collected by the
Stevenson expedition at Walpi, 1879. *Stevenson 1883: Figs. 570–72, facing
page 396, largest carving, height: 26 in.*

KOKLE

CITOTO

SUMAIKOLI AND YAYA

PLATE 35. Four Hopi kachina figures, watercolor on paper, c. 1900. Originals commissioned by J. Walter Fewkes c. 1900. *Fewkes 1903: Pl. XXXIV; artist unidentified.*

PLATE 36. Zuni Shalako kachinas, gouache on
paper, c. 1930–32. *Artist: Fred Kabotie. School of
American Research, Indian Arts Research Center. Indian
Arts Fund #P94, collected by Alice Corbin Henderson.*

PLATE 37. Tsuku Clown (Sikyatsuku), Hopi, c. 1960. *Artist: unidentified. Maxwell Museum of Anthropology number 64.61.203, height: 13 in., collected by Dorothy Field Maxwell.*

PLATE 38. Snow Maiden (Nuvak'chin Mana) kachina, Hopi, acrylic and oil stain on cottonwood root, 1992. *Artist: Stetson Lomayestewa. Courtesy Maxwell Museum of Anthropology Gift Shop.*

PLATE 39. Heheya's Uncle (Heheya Aumutaka),
Hopi, c. 1950–60. *Artist: Otto Pentewa (attr.),*
Maxwell Museum of Anthropology number 64.61.175,
height: 12.5 in., collected by Dorothy Field Maxwell.

PLATE 40. Shalako Mana kachina, Hopi, c. 1890 or earlier. Acquired c. 1890–95 by private collector Thomas Donaldson from Major J. W. Powell, first head of the Bureau of American Ethnology. *University Museum, University of Pennsylvania, number 38122.*

PLATE 41. "Teu'-Mahs Katchina," Walpi, 1904. Original is
one of a series done at Hopi from life by the California artist-illustrator
Jo Mora. Limited edition color offset reproduction of a watercolor on
paper (580/650). *School of American Research, Indian Arts Research
Center, number 1981.12.22.*

The Evolution and Dissemination of Mimbres Iconography

MARC THOMPSON

SINCE THE discovery of Mimbres ceramics more than eighty years ago, the intended meaning, function, and significance of Mimbres representational pottery have eluded scholars. These black-on-white bowls, often found over the faces of the deceased, exhibit on their interiors painted images of humans, animals, composite beings, and inanimate objects in apparent narrative interaction. Previous interpretations of Mimbres figurative depictions have been derived almost exclusively from narrowly defined, naturalistic, or modern Native American paradigms. The purpose of this essay is to define and demonstrate (1) the meanings of individual and similar images through anthropological analysis of motifs, (2) place these meanings in a temporal and spatial grid as part of an ideological continuum, and (3) reconstruct Mimbres and later Pueblo cosmology. The study presents iconographic interpretations based on comparative analyses of repeated elements and motifs indicating that Mimbres representational figures reflect Pan-American ideologies, mythic traditions, and underworld conceptions shared by ancient, historic, and modern Southwestern Indians.

Anthropomorphic and zoomorphic Mimbres icons (e.g., War Twins, rabbits, deer, and fish) are shown to have been visual metaphors representing culture heroes, celestial bodies, souls of the dead, and other animistic representations, respectively, thought to appear in Mesoamerican iconography at least as early as A.D. 1. Analysis of action and identification of dramatis personae in cognate narrative scenes portrayed on Late Classic Maya (ca. A.D. 600–900) and Classic Mimbres (ca. A.D. 1000–1150) funerary vessels are shown to exhibit structural relationships in mythical and metaphorical content and the importance, as well as the temporal and geographical extent, of the "Hero Twins saga."

Based on intensive and unprecedented examination of images from more than two thousand Mimbres representational bowls, and by comparison to Mesoamerican and Southwestern graphic and mythic motifs, Mimbres iconography can be understood to have existed within a broad ideological context. Further, this study suggests Mimbres figurative bowls were probably made for individuals, depicted scenes from the journey to the underworld, and ultimately accompanied those individuals to the grave. This implies the motifs in bowls may have served as mnemonic devices in rituals (i.e., the enactment of myths) at burials, reflecting a highly structured and multilayered cosmology found throughout Mesoamerica and the Southwest.

Because this essay focuses on Mimbres iconography with respect to its imagery, ideological context, and relative longevity, the significance of kachinas and related imagery are mentioned only briefly. The concentration here is on continuities in Pueblo world-view and ritual rather than on the origin or identification of kachinas. Results of my analyses and interpretations of Mimbres iconography suggest a later date for kachinas and related paraphernalia than among the Mimbres. However, Polly Schaafsma (1992:passim and this volume) presents convincing evidence relating Mimbres figures from ceramics and rock art to later Jornada rock art and subsequent kiva paintings, which suggests that masks, horned or plumed serpents, four-pointed "stars," and twinned rep-

resentations associated with kachina imagery appear and are related within a Mimbres matrix. A few Mimbres bowls might be interpreted as depicting masks. One (see Brody 1977*a*:Figure 18) contains an image of an anthropomorph with horizontal bands from head to foot, a mask, and what appears to be an Awanyu headdress. The body paint or costume is somewhat similar to a Koshare. A second bowl (see Brody 1977*a*:175) combines geometric designs around the interior of a flared rim and surrounds an anthropomorph with stylized, rectilinear limbs and torso, above which a round head and what appears to be a row of oversized teeth, may resemble a Broad-Faced kachina. (See Polly Schaafsma, this volume, for comparative figures in Rio Grande rock art, and Hays, this volume, Figure 6.5 for another Mimbres example).

More than a decade ago Carlson (1982*a*) presented an interesting but ultimately unconvincing paper suggesting the existence of a "kachina cult" among the Mimbres. Although he recognized, cited, and illustrated images of "the Twin War Gods," he failed to document kachina imagery and stated, "The kachina costumes of the present century are rather clearly not depicted on Mimbres pots, a fact indicative of their more recent evolution" (Carlson 1982*a*:153).

Horned serpent elements or motifs, possibly depicted with the Koshare-like image mentioned above, as well as at least four other recorded bowls, have also been illustrated (see Fewkes 1914:Fig. 28, 1923:Figs. 13 and 41; Brody 1977*a*: Plate 11). Again, like putative kachina images, these are rare. Awanyu or horned serpent imagery did exist among the Mimbres; however, its frequency of occurrence is limited. If the horned serpent of the Southwest was ideologically equivalent to the feathered serpent of Mesoamerica, the image was probably emblematic of duality in the Pueblo world (see Eggan, this volume) as personified by the War Twins and Venus (as morning and evening "star"). Mimbres horned serpents may have been precocious precursors to later and related PIV water serpent imagery depicted in petroglyphs, pictographs, and kiva murals. In short, I recognize only a few motifs or elements in rock art related to Mimbres iconography which might be construed as crossreferential images suggesting correspondence in meaning and function to kachinas. At present, it seems more parsimonious to accept a later date, during the fourteenth century (Schaafsma and Schaafsma 1974) for the existence of a "kachina cult" and the widespread appearance of horned serpent iconography within the Southwest.

Mesoamerican Parallels

Analysis and interpretation of Mimbres representational bowls, consideration of the contextual complex (i.e., the esoteric paradigm), and comparative study of related, but ethnically diverse, depictions suggest a florescence of Mimbres representational images between A.D. 1000 and 1150 was neither unique nor isolated in time and space. Researchers since Fewkes (1904) early in the twentieth century have commented on the possibility of Mexican influences in ancient Pueblo ceramic designs. These influences may be viewed more as tangible expressions of widely held concepts reflecting a shared ideology, rather than as continuity in art styles or examples of direct diffusion.

An important problem vexing previous studies of Mimbres painting has been, and continues to be, lack of context. The physical, functional, and ideological contexts are often lacking for Mimbres figurative vessels. Most researchers now agree the vessels were funerary offerings, some agree that they functioned primarily as mortuary goods and fewer, that depicted scenes relate to esoteric rather than mundane or prosaic concerns.

Descriptions of Mimbres representational paintings as "scenes from everyday life" or as expressions of "the sheer ecstasy of living" are no longer tenable. Previous attempts to relate the contextual complex to ethnographically re-corded Pueblo mythology (e.g., Carr 1979) have been only partially successful. While I believe these links exist to some extent, many were destroyed or lost during the contact period with the Spanish, and it seems more productive to explore the evidence for a shared ideology and common cosmology by comparison of contemporaneous Mesoamerican and Southwestern motifs. As Brody (1983:119) has observed, "The Mimbres were as close in time to sixteenth-century Native Mexico as they were in space to the nineteenth-century Pueblos." (The distance from the Mimbres area to Casas Grandes, Chihuahua, Mexico, is but 300 km; from the Late Classic Maya (ca. A.D. 600–900) to Classic Mimbres is a mere century. From the Mimbres to Hopi or Zuni areas is at least 400 km, and the Classic Mimbres period (ca. A.D. 1000–1150) is separated by more than six hundred years from the ethnographically recorded Pueblos.

Lunar Logic: The Rabbit in the Moon

As an example of a pandemic icon and visual metaphor for a celestial body, consider the rabbit in the moon. Rather than a man in the moon, ancient and modern peoples in Mesoamerica and the Southwest described a black rabbit as a shadow on the surface on the moon. It can be seen here (Figure 9.1a) in a telescopic view of a full moon. The rabbit's head faces the viewer's left at about ten o'clock; the ears point to the right at one and two o'clock; the body is between six and nine and the tail is at about four o'clock. A Mimbres representation (Figure 9.1b) shows the same structural relationship with a crescent moon. The same orientation of a rabbit may also be observed in a Late Classic Maya polychrome bowl (Figure 9.1c); note as well this Maya bowl has been ceremonially sacrificed by puncture as were many Classic Maya and Classic Mimbres funerary bowls (see Figure 9.1d). In both Mesoamerica and the Southwest pregnant women were cautioned against exposure to a full moon because of the belief that the child would

FIGURE 9.1*a*. Telescopic view of a full moon.

FIGURE 9.1*b*. Rabbit with crescent moon, Classic Mimbres Black-on-white bowl, Cameron Creek Village. *(Courtesy Southwest Museum, Los Angeles. Photograph from Mimbres Archive, Maxwell Museum of Anthropology, University of New Mexico, Albuquerque.)*

be born with a harelip (Thompson 1939:164–65; Sahagún 1953:8–9; Parsons 1939:181).

The visual metaphor of a rabbit for the moon is most useful in understanding Mimbres iconography because the moon is round and presents a black figure on a white ground as do the interiors of Mimbres representational bowls. Additionally, the moon was also depicted as a vessel (a horse-shoe-shaped container with a rabbit) often represented as filled with water as in the Borgia Codex (1963:10, 55, 71) and the Lápida de Tlaxiaco (Paddock 1966:Fig. 247), both from fifteenth-century Oaxaca. So, in addition to many lunar attributes such as weaving, medicine, and child-birth associated with a female numen, the lunar body or surface was also associated with water, probably a reflection of the watery underworld of the dead in both Mesoamerica (Schele and Miller 1983) and the Southwest (Ellis 1968:70). As a heuristic device we may view the moon (figuratively and literally) as the "ideal type," that

is, a round, black-on-white vessel for numerous Mimbres representational variations. In most Mimbres vessels the rabbit faces left consistent with the lunar surface. In many Mimbres examples (see for instance Brody 1983:Fig. 126; Anyon and LeBlanc 1984:Plates 128*d*, 132*b*, 133*b*) the lunar ideogram is reinforced by rabbits with lunate bodies, or dark bodies which incorporate a white crescent (Brody 1983:Plate 41; Anyon and LeBlanc 1984:Plate 14*d*) which also strengthens the lunar image and visual metaphor. Both motifs (rabbit facing left and dark rabbit with infixed white crescent) are depicted at Kuaua (Coronado State Park, near Bernalillo, New Mexico) on preserved PIV kiva murals in direct association with underworld or spirit beings (see Dutton 1963:Figs. 27, 34 and Plate XX). This traditional motif and its associations may have continued as well in Sikyatki or early Hopi pottery such as a black rabbit within the bowl of a ladle recorded by Fewkes (1973:Plate CXLII*e*).

FIGURE 9.1c. Rabbit in lunar configuration, Classic Maya Polychrome bowl, provenience unknown.

FIGURE 9.1d. Younger twin as lunar rabbit bearing his celestial burden, Classic Mimbres bowl, provenience unknown. (*Courtesy Laboratory of Anthropology, Museum of New Mexico, Santa Fe. Photograph from Mimbres Archive, Maxwell Museum of Anthropology, University of New Mexico, Albuquerque.*)

As an ideal type the moon also represents a supernatural icon and celestial body incorporating multilayered relationships and affiliations associated primarily with night, death and moisture. It is the opposite of the sun which is most basically associated with day, life and desiccation. The former is also primarily female and the latter male; neither is entirely benevolent nor malevolent. Together they form a pair or celestial twain and are a literal reflection of divine duality or sacred plurality represented prehistorically by the "War Twins" and historically personified by Pueblo "War Chiefs."

The Lunar Rabbit and Solar Deer

As night follows day and death follows life, the rabbit (a visual metaphor representing the lunar body) follows the deer (an animal emblematic of the solar disk). The association of the deer with the sun is well established among ancient and

historic Maya (Thompson 1939:150, 1960:230, 231; Schele 1977:52–53, 55; Schele and Miller 1983:46). This association, and that of the rabbit with the moon, are also graphically illustrated in a cosmogram of Late Postclassic Mixteca-Puebla style in the Borgia Codex (Seller 1963:33). Here, above a multilayered cosmos, a rabbit carries the Central Mexican lunar symbol on its back while a deer bears the solar emblem on its body. Seller (1963:33) identified the rabbit and deer as the bearers of the moon and sun, respectively.

Rabbits and deer are common images on Mimbres figurative bowls; the naturalistic paradigm would suggest they are commonly represented because they were observed from nature or were important food sources among the Mimbres. But as Schele and Miller (1983:46) have observed, rabbits and deer share a rather remarkable number of physical characteristics, regardless of their difference in size. These similarities in appearance and behavior include long ears, short tails, split upper lip, timidity, and pellet-like excrement. At Kuaua, when interviewing Native American informants on the significance and identification of certain of the animals pictured in PIV kiva murals, Dutton (1963:158, 162) recorded some confusion among informants about images which appeared to be rabbits but were associated with what appeared to be deer tracks. This association was also articulated by Fred Kaboti (a Hopi artist) when attempting to describe the significance of Mimbres figurative images. With respect to deer, Kaboti revealed, "Insanity can be attributed to this class of animals, which also includes cotton tails and jack-rabbits" and "The deer and the rabbit families are related and have always been regarded as people, especially in legends" (Kabotie 1982:32, 33). Additionally, Kabotie (1982:31) recognized, but did not comment on, the juxtaposition of deer with a sunflower in one Mimbres bowl.

In Figure 9.1d we see a Mimbres version of an anthropomorphized rabbit (note the orientation to the left, lunate body, and rabbit ears and tail) with a stylized burden basket, a probable metaphor for a "bearer." Another Mimbres example (also cognate with the Borgia Codex depiction of the rabbit and deer as bearers of the primary celestial bodies) was illustrated by Bradfield (1929:Plate LXXVI, 306). In this bowl a figure is shown with a deer head above a human body posed in the opposite direction. This traditional motif and association of deer with the sun may have continued in historic Hopi pottery such as two examples of Zuni-influenced Polacca Polychrome bowls illustrated by Wade and McChensey (1981:144, 235). In these (nos. 1746 and 1747), and other bowls from the Thomas V. Keam Collection, are depicted figures of deer alternating with sun symbols dating from between 1740 and the 1800s. This ceramic florescence begins with the appearance of PIV murals between the fourteenth and sixteenth centuries when a profusion of human anatomical parts (hands, limbs, and so on) appear in a style highly reminiscent of

Mimbres depictions such as Sikyatki Polychrome or Jeddito Black-on-yellow bowls (see for example Wade and McChesney 1981:21). This florescence was followed by forced secularization of painted ceramics and discouragement of their use as grave offerings.

The Hero Twins Saga and the Popol Vuh

Another parallel drawn between Mesoamerican and Mimbres depictions of animals is that of bats. It hardly need be emphasized now that paintings of bats, rabbits, deer, or, for that matter, fish probably do not relate to the food quest. Bats shown on both Classic Maya cylindrical vases and Classic Mimbres bowls are usually recovered from funerary contexts and display a similar, sinister quality. Additionally, Mimbres examples usually depict claws and symbols which appear to be related to the underworld (see Brody 1977a: Fig. 157, 1983:Plate 38; Anyon and LeBlanc 1984:Plate 53e, Plate 103f). These symbols or underworld elements are similar to Classic Maya depictions of "death eyes" and crossed bones on bat wings. Finally, Mimbres bats are often shown with the above elements as well as attributes of other animals such as rabbit ears. These composite depictions suggest a rich and multifaceted symbolism found in Mesoamerican iconography that cannot be adequately explained by reference to the natural world. It has been suggested that both Classic Maya and Classic Mimbres depictions of bats refer to "killer bats" (Cama Zotz), which figure prominently in the Hero Twins saga portion of the Popol Vuh (Coe 1973:12, 14; Brody 1977a:206–7). That Classic Maya bats are found on vases and Classic Mimbres bats on bowl interiors does not diminish the obvious similarity of motifs and probable parallel significance.

The Hero Twins saga (Parts II and III) of the Popol Vuh provides a large and intact portion of the ideological context necessary for consistent interpretation of cognate myths and iconographic depictions. Popol Vuh is the most complete and important surviving written account and description of Native American cosmology, mythology, and religion. Originally understood as a sixteenth-century national epic and creation myth of the Quiché Maya of Highland Guatemala, it was transcribed in Mayan with Spanish letters and later translated into Spanish. *Popol Vuh* is now available in three high-quality English translations (Recinos 1950; Edmonson 1971; Tedlock 1985) as well as many other languages. Today, *Popol Vuh* is recognized by informed scholars as a mythic chronicle probably dating to at least as early as the beginning of the Christian era. Many scenes depicted on Classic Maya funerary ceramics are now understood as illustrations of *Popol Vuh* episodes concerning the adventures of the "Hero Twins" (Coe 1975, 1978, 1982, 1989). The basic mythic sequence, narrative events, and characters from *Popol Vuh* appear to have had a widespread currency reflecting a Pan-American ideology.

Briefly, the narrative opens with the creation of the earth, then shifts to the saga of the "Hero Twins." In a series of classic trickster tales, the twins vanquish earthly monsters before they are summoned to the underworld. The "Hero Twins," known as Hunahpú (Hunter) and Xbalanqué (Jaguar Sun) in Mayan, correspond to Pueblo equivalents called "the Little Warrior Twins" in both names and deeds. Among the Zuni they are known as "Ash Boy" and "Echo"; the elder is right-handed and the younger is left-handed. Both are male. Among the Hopi, the elder twin is male and the younger is sometimes female, an interesting parallel as Hunahpú and Xbalanqué of the *Popol Vuh* are finally deified as the sun and the moon, respectively. Xbalanqué also translates as "Little Jaguar Sun" or "She of," that is, a diminutive sun, probably referring to the moon, usually a female deity in both Mesoamerica and the Southwest. Likewise, the Hopi name for the younger, smaller twin translates as "Young Deer," again a diminutive probably referring to a Pueblo version of the association of the deer with the sun, as opposed to the association of the rab-

bit with the moon. In both the *Popol Vuh* (Recinos 1950:119–20; Edmonson 1971:76–77; Tedlock 1985:114–15) and Pueblo mythology (Cushing 1896:381; Parsons 1939:211; Tyler 1986:213), the divine twins are conceived by water. (The adventures and birth of the twins are commemorated in the Navajo names "Monster Slayer" and "Born of Water.") After their birth, the mother of the twins is soon replaced by their grandmother who raises the pair.

In the *Popol Vuh* the first victory of the Hero Twins is over a giant called Seven Macaw (Vucub Caquix, Seven Red Feathers). This monster claimed to be the sun. The twins wound him, but he attacks the elder brother (Hunahpú) and tears his (left) arm off. This motif is seen earliest on carved stelae at the site of Izapa (located on the Pacific slope of Chiapas, Mexico). Izapa lends its name to the distinctive art style thought to have iconographic links with the earlier Olmec Horizon and prefigure in both time and space the Classic Maya developments of the Lowlands. On two stelae (Norman 1976:Figs. 3.6 and 3.3) Seven Macaw, the Hero Twins, a son of Seven Macaw and the severed arm motif can all be identified (for a discussion and identification of these early "Hero Twins saga" motifs see Cortez 1986). The severed arm motif is also depicted in the Late Postclassic Maya Madrid Codex (page 37) as well as the contemporaneous Mixtec Borgia Codex (page 2), which both show a disembodied left human arm in the curved beak of a macaw.

This confrontation is also pictured in several Mimbres bowls including one of unknown provenience in a private collection, one from the Swartz Ruin on the Mimbres River, and another of unknown provenience. The latter was printed in reverse and misinterpreted as a hunting scene by LeBlanc (1983:Colorplate VI, lower right). In these bowls Seven Macaw is depicted as a bruin-like figure (LeBlanc 1983:Colorplate VI) or alternatively as a long-tailed monster attacking the elder twin. In other Mimbres bowls Seven Macaw and the same motif include still other elements such as pointed ears or mismatched feet, one animal and one human. The giant monster (compare pointed ears and head to Fewkes 1914:Fig. 17) is also pictured with a long tail, pointed ears, and mismatched feet, along with his elder son and the twins (see Brody 1977a:Fig. 22), and alone in a bowl with a motif which incorporates the long tail, monstrous head, and one animal and one human foot (Brody 1977a:Fig. 154). Depending on how the missing elements of the motif are reconstructed (see Brody 1977a:Fig. 155) the arm near the mouth of the portrait figure could well be that of the elder twin. In another Mimbres bowl recovered from Boca Ruin (private collection), a bearlike figure is shown in direct association with a disembodied (left) human arm near its mouth. Originally I had simply assumed a bear was the closest approximation to a giant available in the Southwest. However, at Zuni the bear is associated with the War Twins (Tyler 1964:218). Additionally, in the birth of the War Twins recorded from Acoma: "Grandmother feared they would go too far . . . she tried to scare them by telling them the . . . bears . . . would take them off." "There are lots of *cko yo* roaming around the country" (Stirling 1942:94). According to Stirling, the Keresan term *cko yo* refers to both giants and bears.

To retrieve elder brother's lost limb, the twins disguise themselves as healers and pretend to minister to Seven Macaw's wound which they inflicted earlier. But the twins pull the giant's teeth and blind him, rendering him harmless, and Seven Macaw dies. This action is depicted in Figure 9.2*a* in a Classic Maya polychrome bowl where we see Xbalanqué (the younger twin) on the back of the giant Seven Macaw, here shown with a bloody eye and mouth. (Note recognition of the younger twin is confirmed by his right hand on the left eye socket and left arm over the shoulder of Seven Macaw.) In the following Classic Mimbres bowl (Figure 9.2*b*) is a cognate motif. Here we observe a giant avian figure (with pointed ears and long tail) surmounted by the younger twin.

(Note the presence of both unreconstructed arms on the younger twin and the severed arm of the elder twin near the mouth of Seven Macaw.) Similar scenes relating to the defeat of Seven Macaw (depicted as a bear-like figure among the Mimbres) by the twins were also illustrated by Fewkes (1923:Fig. 7 and 16).

Presently, the twins descend to the Plutonian realm where they encounter a river of corruption and other horrors: a journey obviously cognate with that taken by the souls of the dead. By playing tricks, the twins survive in a series of five houses, including one (the "House of Bats") guarded by "killer bats" to which we have already referred and described examples of both Classic Maya and Classic Mimbres depictions on funerary ceramics. Hunahpú is decapitated by a killer bat, but again is made whole by his younger brother. Additionally, the twins must survive in the "House of Knives," the "House of Cold," the "House of Jaguars," and the "House of Fire." Likewise, at Acoma Pueblo (Stirling 1942:96) and elsewhere in Pueblo myth the "Little War Twins" or "Sons of the Sun" were tested in underground chambers (kivas). These were the kivas of wolves, lions, snakes, bumblebees, and hot coals, equal in number and purpose to the denizens or tortures of those described in Maya legend. While in a "House of Gloom" the netherworld lords proffer cigars and pine sticks that must be kept alight throughout the night, but returned intact in the morning. The twins solve this dilemma by affixing fireflies to their cigars and scarlet macaw feathers to the sticks of pine. In the gloom of the underworld the cigars and pine torches appear to be lighted, and the twins are able to return them as requested at dawn. This episode is depicted in the Madrid Codex and a Mimbres bowl illustrated by Fewkes (1914:Fig. 14); in both cases the twins are shown smoking in a reclining position on what appear to be benches.

Eventually the twins willingly suffer death, but this is only temporary. Their bones are ground up and cast into a stygian stream; the bones and

FIGURE 9.2*a* (above, left). The giant Seven Macaw with younger twin on his back, Classic Maya Polychrome bowl, provenience unknown. (*Photograph courtesy Arts 135, Boulogne, France.*)

FIGURE 9.2*b* (above, right). The giant Seven Macaw with younger twin on his back, Classic Mimbres Black-on-white bowl, Mattocks Ruin. (*Courtesy Laboratory of Anthropology, Museum of New Mexico, Santa Fe. Photograph from Mimbres Archive, Maxwell Museum of Anthropology, University of New Mexico, Albuquerque.*)

ashes reform and the twins reappear transitionally as fish (an important visual metaphor for life after death and passage through the watery underworld). Fish in an otherworld stream may also symbolize the entrance to or the surface of the underworld at Izapa (Norman 1976:Fig. 3.43) where paired fish are depicted in the current of a linear body of water in direct association with a death's head at the bottom of a stela tableau. A similar motif at the bottom of a PIV mural at Kawaika-a (Smith 1952:Plate D) was recognized by Carlson (1982*a*:154) as depicting fish and other aquatic animals in a Pueblo version of the "watery underworld." In Mimbres iconography, fish are the second most common animal depicted accounting for about 15 percent of representational figures. Fish are depicted singly, or as nearly identical or similar pairs, in narrative scenes and most often with leglike appendages rather than ventral

fins. These paired limbs are distinct from either anal or dorsal fins in most depictions. Paintings of paired fish emphasize duality (Figure 9.2*c*) or depict slight decorative or color differences seen in body markings (Figure 9.2*d*). In other cases, paired fish are nearly identical, but close examination reveals that one is larger than the other, indicating the individual identity of the larger, older twin. In some cases the differences are dramatic, but the pair is connected by an umbilical-like line from mouth to mouth (Anyon and LeBlanc 1984: Plate 37*d*). Fish are rarely paired in simple bilaterally symmetrical or mirror images. Other examples are also depicted with obviously anthropomorphized limbs, illustrating the transition from fish to human form. These may be paired or single portrait representations with obvious human arms or legs.

In the *Popol Vuh* the twins reappear, after their

FIGURE 9.2*c* (right). Paired fish, Classic Mimbres Black-on-white bowl, Cameron Creek Village. *(Courtesy Laboratory of Anthropology, Museum of New Mexico, Santa Fe. Photograph from Mimbres Archive, Maxwell Museum of Anthropology, University of New Mexico, Albuquerque.)*

FIGURE 9.2*d*. Twinned fish, Classic Mimbres Black-on-white bowl, Pruitt Site. *(Courtesy Mimbres Archive, Maxwell Museum of Anthropology, University of New Mexico, Albuquerque.)*

death, as mermen: "On the fifth day they appeared again and were seen in the water . . . both had the appearance of fishmen" (Recinos 1950:155). Numerous Mimbres bowls illustrate the transition from dead souls (represented by fish) to fishmen (see Brody 1977*a*:Fig. 153), 1983:Colorplate 40; LeBlanc 1983:Colorplate VI, lower center, printed in reverse; Anyon and LeBlanc 1984:Plate 98*d*) and finally, the reappearance of the twins apparently swimming in the water without fish bodies, but note paired fishtails, left and right (Brody 1983:Fig. 94). The final part of this episode appears in a Mimbres bowl (Brody 1983:Colorplate 28), picturing the elder and younger (diminutive) twins emerged, but still tenuously attached to a clearly depicted, anthropomorphized catfish. Quoting again from the *Popol Vuh:* "The two of them looked like channel catfish when their faces were seen" (Tedlock 1985:149). The Mimbres artist obviously took great care to illustrate numerous catfish barbels (as well as human limbs) on this example. However, a study of Mimbres fish designs (mired in an ethnocentric and naturalistic paradigm) attempted species identification and suggested this fish" is (incorrectly) identified with catfishlike barbels" (Jett and Moyle 1986:704). A PIV mural fragment from Kuaua presents a further link between Mimbres mythic depictions and more recent Pueblo motifs (Dutton 1963:Plate XXV). Here the twins are presented on either side of a niche: on the right side is the elder, light-colored, right-handed twin, associated with the sun; on the left is the younger, dark-colored, left-handed twin associated with the moon. (Polly Schaafsma, personal communication 1992, notes that paired horned serpents in kiva murals often appear on either side of niches.) Additionally, coupled catfish appear in another kiva mural fragment at Kuaua (Dutton 1963:Plate XVI; see also Creamer and Haas 1991:96). In this example two catfish are shown ventrum to ventrum (note the paired eyes, barbels, and dorsal fins) in a motif similar to that in Figure 9.2*c* (the logo for the Maxwell Museum of Anthropology).

In the final episode of the Hero Twins saga, the brothers once again are victorious over the lords of the underworld (i.e., they defeat death) when Xbalanqué dismembers and beheads Hunahpú, then brings him back to life. (It is of some interest that Hunahpú, the older and more masculine twin, loses his arm once and his head twice.) The above motif is first recognized at Izapa on Stela 21 (Norman 1976:Fig. 3.20) where we see the younger, left-handed twin (a knife in his left hand, his brother's head in his right hand) standing over the decapitated body of Hunahpú while a lord of the underworld watches from a palanquin born by two underlings. A cognate motif is also presented in two Mimbres bowls (Fewkes 1923:Fig. 13 and Brody 1977*a*:Plate 11). In both, the younger twin holds a knifelike object in his left hand while he grasps the head of his brother in his right hand. Additionally, the younger twin wears what appears to be an Awanyu headdress and the older twin's head remains tenuously attached by a "thread of life" to his body. The lords of death are so enthralled by this final performance that they demand to be sacrificed in a similar manner as well. The twins oblige them but do not bring them back to life, assuring the possibility of life after death for all who must journey through the underworld. At last, Hunahpú and Xbalanqué are apotheosized as the sun and the moon, respectively. Thus, the twins show the way through the underworld, which all the defunct might survive, and like the twins, successful souls will eventually rise and be seen as the stars of the night.

Other Macaws, Parrots and Red Tail Feathers

Another dramatic constellation of parallel elements found in Mimbres pottery and PIV kiva mural paintings are associated with macaws and other parrots. The scarlet macaw (*Ara macao*) is of particular importance as it is indigenous only to tropical Mexico, yet ancient macaw (as well as other less exotic parrot) remains and feathers have been recovered throughout the Southwest at Mimbres, Anasazi, Hohokam, and Sinagua pueblos (Bradfield 1925:176, 1928:159; Jenks 1929:352; Smith 1952:180; Judd 1954:263, 264; Ellis and Hammack 1968:28; Hargrave 1970). Additionally, studies of macaw skeletal materials and architectural features demonstrated that macaws were bred for trade at Casas Grandes in northern Mexico. Trade in scarlet macaws from Mexico to the Southwest may have begun as early as A.D. 1 at Snaketown (Mckusick 1974:283) and continued intermittently through the sixteenth century among Rio Grande Pueblos (Smith 1952:180; Hargrave 1970:50; Ellis 1976:100).

Early on, Fewkes (1914:Fig. 27; 1973:Plate CXLIII) recorded examples of parrots on both Mimbres and later Sikyatki ceramics. Mimbres parrots (recognized by their recurved beaks) are pictured singly, in association with burden baskets (Anyon and LeBlanc 1984:Plates 58*c* and 67*b*), as well as in direct association with anthropomorphs (Brody 1977*a*:Fig. 141, 1983:Color-plate 22). Additionally, parrots in the presence of anthropomorphs are often depicted on hand-held rings. Many of these elements and related parrot motifs are also depicted in PIV murals at Awatovi (Smith 1952:183), Kuaua (Dutton 1963), and Pottery Mound (Hibben 1975) as well as in Rio Grande rock art near Albuquerque where they are also shown in what appear to be cages. Most striking are the combined elements of hand-held rings (Dutton 1963:Fig. 23; Hibben 1975:Fig. 46), burden baskets and women, kachinas, or spirit beings holding parrots (Hibben 1975:Figs. 16, 18, 38, 39, 45, and 98). It might be tempting here to interpret these obviously cognate motifs through the naturalistic paradigm (e.g., the human figures pictured with parrots, rings, and other elements such as cages and sticks are parrot trainers, and the scenes represent nothing more esoteric than people with pet birds). Examination of the motifs and the Mesoamerican and Southwestern contextual complexes reveals more complex and significant associations. In numerous depictions of parrots with anthropomorphs (see Brody 1977*a:*Fig. 141, 1983:Colorplate 22) the females (identified by breasts) are also depicted with parrotlike faces or masks (see also Polly Schaafsma, this volume). Additionally, male and female anthropomorphs (Brody 1983:Colorplate 22) may represent the War Twins, as suggested by the light (female) and dark (male) coloring of their bodies. This coloration pattern with what appears to be a light-colored female and a dark-colored male is repeated in another Mimbres bowl (Brody 1977*a:*Fig. 148) which I interpret as a portrait of the War Twins. A similar and perhaps related motif of light and dark/left and right is combined in at least two figures (Dutton 1963:Plates XXII and XXX) representing duality at Kuaua.

The association of the twins with apparently docile parrots suggests to me the *Popol Vuh* episode in the "House of Gloom" when the twins used scarlet macaw tail feathers to represent burning pine torches. Also, the giant Vucub Caquix (Seven Red Feathers), who claimed to be the sun, suggests a long-lived and widespread association of scarlet macaw feathers with the sun. Today at Izamal, Yucatán, the winter solstice is still celebrated when Kinich Kak Moo (Sun-eyed Macaw) sets above an Early Classic pyramid. Likewise, studies of macaw skeletal elements in the Southwest (Mckusick 1974:276; Di Peso et al. 1974:273, 599) indicate many macaws were sacrificed at about eleven and a half months, approximating the arrival of the vernal equinox. While it is well worth considering Brody's (1991:130) cautionary note that "barring assurance of clear, direct, and, above all, unmodified discussion of information from past to present, oral transmission of information from any Pueblo IV art or art style by modern Pueblo people, no matter how well informed or well intentioned . . . is based on modern practices" (i.e., ethnographic analogy,

or the Native American paradigm). It also seems apparent that a consistent significance, through time and space, applies to ceremonial use of scarlet macaw feathers (see Cushing 1896:386; Ellis 1986:65).

Conclusions

On the basis of the foregoing highlights from an intensive examination of more than two thousand images from Mimbres figurative bowls, the following conclusions are presented:

(1) Representational Mimbres depictions are of supernatural figures, underworld characters, mythical creatures, and celestial bodies.

(2) Analysis of action and identification of individuals permits chronological ordering of motifs from episodes recorded in Mesoamerican and Southwestern myth and folklore. This allows for visual reconstruction of oral traditions into a pictorial "Book of the Dead" comparable to that from ancient Egypt.

(3) These bowls were made for the dead and depict scenes from the journey to and through the underworld. The bowls may also have served as mnemonic devices in rituals (enactments of myths) at burials and probably reflect a highly structured and multifaceted cosmology found throughout Mesoamerica and the ancient Southwest. Additionally, painted Mimbres figurative motifs may have played a role analogous to that of scenes from the *Iliad* and *Odyssey* found on Archaic Greek vessels.

While most of our ancestors may have been fleeing Norman knights in England or witnessing the collapse of the Holy Roman Empire on mainland Europe, and while the balance of power in Mesoamerica shifted from the Late Classic Maya to the Early Post-Classic Toltec regime, ancestors of modern Pueblo Indians buried their dead with black-on-white pottery below the floors of Mimbres villages and continued to live in them. Analysis of Mimbres figurative motifs indicates the florescence of Mimbres motifs between A.D.

1000 and 1150 was neither unique nor isolated in time or space. Comparison to late Pueblo motifs suggests some motifs and meanings did not die with the end of the Classic Mimbres Period any more than they began with the second millennium A.D. As Brody (1991:122) has succinctly stated, "Kachina societies, Rio Grande style rock art and kiva murals form so interconnected a triad as to appear to be all parts of a single phenomenon."

In summary, interpretation and consideration of the contextual complex (physical, functional, and ideological) suggest Classic Mimbres bowls carried a series of related, metaphoric messages from a nonliterate society reaffirming the immortality of the human spirit.

ACKNOWLEDGMENTS

I am grateful to Polly Schaafsma for inviting me to present and publish this paper. I also wish to thank J. J. Brody for encouraging me to attend and participate in the Kachina conference. *Dedico este artículo a mi amigo perdido, José Antonio Villarreal.*

10

The Interconnection
Between Western
Puebloan and
Mesoamerican
Ideology / Cosmology

M. JANE YOUNG

Various scholars have suggested that western Puebloan ideological systems—such as those manifested in the kachina cults of the Hopis and the Zunis—are derived largely from concepts that originated in Mesoamerica (Anderson 1955; Ellis and Hammack 1968; Ellis 1989; Kelley 1966; Parsons 1933; Schaafsma and Schaafsma 1974; Schaafsma 1975). Whether one posits that the kachina cult came to the Southwest only relatively recently, for instance, around A.D. 1325, or much earlier, there is no doubt that the extensive although intermittent contact between the peoples of Mesoamerica and the American Southwest has resulted in a number of striking parallels in world-view and religious practice, as well as in the more practical domains of agriculture and textile and pottery production. It is now known that extensive trade networks existed between the two groups and that cultural items and ideas were exchanged as well as trade goods over a long period of time: the precursors to the modern-day Puebloans adopted maize, beans, and squash—later to become central foods in their diet—along with the techniques for cultivating them, from Mesoamerican peoples at an early date. Maize domesticated in central Mexico was being grown, at least sporadically, by the ancestral Puebloans at around 1000 B.C. (Ford 1981). It seems unlikely, then, that the food-stuffs were adopted entirely apart from the socio-religious complex to which they were central (Kelley 1966). As anthropologist Florence Ellis suggests, it is difficult to imagine that the seed and the techniques for growing corn were trans-mitted without added instructions as to the gods and rituals believed to be essential for an eventual successful harvest (1989:3).

Nevertheless, at the present there are scant archaeological data to support a northward trans-mission of ideology from Mesoamerica to the American Southwest during the middle to late Archaic period (ca. 1500 B.C. to A.D. 100); per-haps this is due to the fact that ritual parapher-nelia and other items of material culture from this early date have not survived the ravages of time (Kelley 1966; McGuire 1980). There is some evi-dence that prayer sticks were deposited in caves by the Archaic cultivators of maize in the South-west (Martin et al. 1952), but there is little else that relates to the Mesoamerican religious com-plex that may have come with the maize. One may not, however, conclude from this that there was no ideological impact between these cultural groups; rather, we must look towards the less easily quantifiable and less tangible areas of cos-mology and world-view to begin to formulate an idea of the extent of Mesoamerican ideological in-fluence on ancestral western Puebloan cosmology and, hence, astronomical practice. Although this influence was certainly pan-Puebloan, I focus on the western Pueblo groups of Hopi and Zuni be-cause they have been subject to less Spanish and Anglo influence than the Eastern puebloans.

One means by which to explore this Southwest-Mesoamerican connection is to look for parallels in iconography; I do not mean to suggest, how-ever, that I advocate comparisons based strictly on stylistic criteria such as one would find in a study of correspondences between masks of west-ern Puebloan kachinas and the codex depictions of various Mesoamerican deities. I am more con-cerned with similarities between religious con-cepts—such as those illustrated by the paral-lel functions and attributes of the supernatural beings—than with pictorial/stylistic correspon-dences between representations of deities (these parallels are outlined in Table 10.1). Further-more, it must be stressed that it is highly unlikely that the ancestral Puebloans adopted Mesoameri-can concepts without subjecting them to change and variation. Certainly differences in climate and ecology would have necessitated adjustments, but it is also significant that the character of these Southwestern peoples tended to be dynamic: they borrowed much from surrounding groups, but tended to mold what they adopted to their own particular cultural style (Ellis 1989).

To keep this essay to a manageable length, I will limit my discussion of Mesoamerican ideol-ogy to the Valley of Mexico, focusing particu-larly on the Aztec pantheon of the late Post-Classic Period (largely from the early fifteenth to the early sixteenth centuries A.D.). The Aztecs did not, however, exist in isolation from the rest of Mesoamerica and their culture was sub-ject to many influences both from peoples in nearby geographical areas and from the perva-sive ideologies of earlier cultures. Indeed, it is quite significant that scholars have delineated im-portant cultural similarities between Mesoameri-can and Southwestern peoples that precede the Aztecs (P. Schaafsma and M. Thompson, this vol-ume). This influence through time and over space is integral to the hypothesis that, in addition to their tribal god, Huitzilopochtli, the Aztec religion was dominated by three gods who ap-pear to have persisted since Olmec times, their forms only slightly changed (Covarrubias 1946; Ellis 1989; Joralemon 1976; Nicholson 1976; von Winning 1976). These deities are Huehuetéotl, the Old Fire God, descended from the Olmec serpent-jaguar with flame eyebrows; Tlaloc, the

TABLE 10.1. Parallels in the distinguishing characteristics of Aztec, Hopi, and Zuni deities.

Aztec	Hopi	Zuni

Ometecuhtli/Omecíhuatl ——— dual creative principle ————————— **'Awonaawil'ona**
   (primary generative pair)

Tonatiuh ————————— sacrifice, ferocity, eagle ——— **Tawa**
   (sun)   (sun)

Chalchiuhtlicue ——— jade/turquoise ————— **Huru-ing Wuhti**
   (Goddess of Water)   (Goddess of Hard Substances)

Coatlicue ————— fertility ————— **Hahai-i Wuhti** ——— **Ahea (Hemokatsiki)**
   (Mother of Gods/   (Mother of Gods)
    Goddess of Earth)

                         "seven ears of corn,"
Chicomecóatl ——— fertility, sustenance ————————————— Seven Corn Maidens
   (Goddess of Sustenance and Corn)

Huixtocíhuatl ————— salt, rain, feathered staff ——— Salt Old Woman ——— Salt Old Woman
   (Salt Goddess)

Xólotl ———⌐ conical caps, ————————⌐
   (Venus, Twins)   ⌊ morning & evening star ————⌊— Twin War Gods ——— Twin War Gods

Quetzalcóatl ——— dignity, bringer of corn ——— **Eototo** ————— **Pautiwa**
   (Wind,   ⌐— leader of rain spirits   (Father of Gods)
    Venus,
    Twins,   ⌐ conch shell, rain, ⌐
    Plumed Serpent) ⌊ fertility, serpent, ⌊
            — rain, serpent, goggle eyes ——— **Palölökong** ——— **Kolowisi**
                                   (Horned Water Serpent)
          — serpents ———
Tlaloc ———— goggle eyes, serpents ——— **Hilili**
   (Rain)
         — star, dignity, conical cap, rain ⌐
        — rain, fertility ——— **Sotuknangu**
        — scalping ———

       — turned up beak ———
       — stars on mask ——— **Ahul**
       — growth, fertility ———

       — growth, fertility ———
Centéotl ⌐— growth, fertility ——— **Alosaka/Muyingwa**
   (Male Corn God)

       ⌐— nadir/underworld, rebirth ⌐
Xipe Tótec ———— death, rebirth ——— **Masau**
   (Earth & Rebirth/
    Underworld & Death)   ⌐ death, bloody face, ⌐
Mictlantecuhtli ————⌊ skeleton, trickster ⌊
   (Death)
       — old fire god ———   ⌐— spots on mask ——⌐
Huehuetéotl ⌐— young fire god ——— **Somaikoli** ——— **Shulawitsi**
   (Old Fire God) ⌊— old fire god ——— **Kawikoli**

Xochipilli ——— games, dances, flowers, love, sun's deputy, butterflies ——— **Paiyatamu**
   (Spring)

representative of water and growth who was derived from the Olmec dwarf or infant symbolic of maize; and Xipe Tótec, the patron of spring and the annual rebirth of plant life, whose progenitor was the Olmec masked god.

Of these three, perhaps the most important was Tlaloc, the rain god. He was frequently pictured with his eyes encircled by raised rings, originally in the forms of two snakes that represented rain clouds—this has been described as a goggle-eyed effect (Furst 1974:69–71); further water symbolism is seen in Tlaloc's down-turned and cavernlike mouth, pointing to his association with caves and underground springs (Ellis 1989; Grove 1970:11, 32; Joralemon 1976:37–40). In certain depictions he is clutching lightning bolts, rendered in other portrayals as serpents (Ellis 1989; Nicholson 1976:168), and in some representations he wears a fringed kilt signifying rain (Anton 1969:Plate 101; Peterson 1961:Fig. 31).

Paralleling its importance in Mesoamerica, a rain/water cult, seemingly derived from the Tlaloc cult, took hold rapidly and at an early date in the Southwestern United States. Polly Schaafsma has pointed to Mesoamerican prototypes for many of the iconographic features of the Jornada rock art style which first appeared in the Southwest sometime around A.D. 1050. Of particular note in this respect are the goggle-eyed Tlaloc-type figures (see P. Schaafsma, this volume, Figure 7.1) and possible representations of Quetzalcóatl found in this rock art style complex. Schaafsma concludes that there is a logical historical and cultural connection between cults such as that of Tlaloc and Quetzalcóatl in Mesoamerica and the later Pueblo kachina cult (Schaafsma 1975). Of course, it is not surprising that the cults of Tlaloc and Quetzalcóatl—deities of the rain and wind that often brings rain—spread so rapidly, for both the Mesoamericans and the ancestral Puebloans faced the contingencies of sustaining an existence dependent on agriculture in a frequently dry and somewhat capricious climate.

I will turn now to a comparison of some aspects of the western Puebloan pantheon and cosmological concepts with those of the Mesoamericans (see Table 10.1 for a diagram of the parallels drawn throughout this discussion). I regard this sort of comparison as a necessary first step in delineating the range and extent of the interactions between the two groups that had a major effect on their perceptions of astronomical phenomena as well.

To start with cosmology, the Aztecs and their predecessors posited a dual creative principle: Ometecuhtli and Omecíhuatl—a male god and female goddess who are never represented pictorially. According to one legend, this pair had four sons "to whom they entrusted the creation of the other gods, the world, and man" (Caso 1958:10). These four sons, associated with the cardinal directions and their corresponding colors were the Red Tezcatlipoca, the Black Tezcatlipoca, the White Tezcatlipoca or Quetzalcóatl, and Huitzilopochtli, the Blue Tezcatlipoca. Although there are diverse opinions about this, there appears to be some similarity between the Mesoamerican generative pair and the Zuni primary principle of light and life: 'Awonaawil'ona. This term is used as an epithet both for the Sun Father and the Moon Mother, translating in the plural as "The Ones Who Hold the Roads" (Tedlock 1979:499). A major difference, however, is that in addition to this male/female pair, the Zuni term refers to an entire class of supernaturals—"the sun, the earth, the corn, prey animals and the gods of war" (Bunzel 1932a:486). The Hopi also ascribe subsequent generations to a male-female creator pair (Parsons 1939:212–13).

Both the western Puebloans and the Mesoamericans believe that the sun travels from its eastern to its western house during the course of the day—the Aztecs considered these houses to be paradises to which certain people went upon death (Caso 1958:58–60; Parsons 1939:212). Just as the Aztecs and Mayas perceived the universe to be layered, so do the Zuni, although not in a nine underworlds/thirteen heavens pattern (Caso 1958:60–65; Henderson 1981:83). Instead, for the Zuni there are four underworlds, each associated with a tree and a direction; four upperworlds, each associated with a particular kind of bird; and in the middle, the familiar world, adding up to nine levels in all (Tedlock 1979:499).

The six points of orientation emphasized by the Hopis and Zunis correspond in many respects to those of the Aztecs and Maya, although the colors they assign to those directions are somewhat different, and the western Puebloans, at least in some cases, refer to semi-cardinal, or solstitial, directions rather than the cardinal directions of the Aztecs and Maya (Caso 1958:10–11; Henderson 1981:83; Stephen 1936:51, 961, Fig. 483; Young 1985:18; Young in press). For all four groups, the ritual direction is generally counterclockwise (Henderson 1981:83; Parsons 1933:618–19; Young in press). Both Mesoamericans and Puebloans include two points which refer to an up-down dimension, or zenith and nadir, in their directional scheme. Thus, while four is an important ritual number for these peoples, so is five, signifying four plus the center which also includes the vertical dimension: up, down, and center (frequently, the zenith and nadir are included as discrete points: the ritual number then becomes seven). The Hopi and Zuni associate separate colors with the zenith and nadir, but the Maya used green to symbolize the entire up-down dimension, including the center (Henderson 1981:83). The concept of the center has great significance for the western Puebloans as it did for the Mesoamericans. Just as the Aztecs were induced by Huitzilopochtli, their tribal god, to leave their mythical homeland and undertake long wanderings in search of their ideal abode, so, after they left the four underworlds, the Zunis traveled for a period described by some as four days and others as four years until they reached their ideal home, "the center" (Caso 1958:34–35; Young 1985:14). The western Puebloans and the Mesoamericans do not limit their directional associations to colors, but extend them to include almost everything

in the world—birds, mountains, trees, animals, and so on—in a vast network of symbolic associations (Caso 1958:11; Young 1985:16–18). In the Aztec pantheon, certain of the gods, including the rain gods, were related to the directions, as were human beings whose directional associations were determined by the day on which they were born (Caso 1958:11). Similarly, the Zuni assign the rain priests, or *'uwanammi,* and the Hopi, the Cloudyouths, to the six directions. These Puebloan Chiefs of the Directions are also intimately associated with mountain tops, as were the Aztec rain gods, or Tlalocos: thus both groups perceive a fundamental relationship between mountain ranges and rains (Caso, 1958:42; Parsons 1933:612).

Western Puebloan and Aztec beliefs about reincarnation also reveal certain similarities. The Aztecs held that there had been four previous creations which were destroyed in cataclysms and that the fifth and final existence would also succumb to destruction (Caso 1958:14–17). The Zunis, too, foresee the end of the current world: whereas the Aztecs predicted destruction by a great earthquake, the Zunis say that "at the end . . . our tools and utensils and everything we have will rise against us; the stars will fall and we will all be boiled by a hot rain" (Tedlock 1975:270).

Similarly, for both the Zunis and the Aztecs there are different afterlives, depending on the position one held in life. The Zunis believe that deceased Rain priests join the deified Rain priests of the six directions, just as the Bow priests and members of the beast god societies join their deified counterparts. Members of kachina societies become kachinas upon death and may return among the living as clouds. When a person goes through four reincarnations, that person can choose to return among the living as an animal, depending on the knowledge acquired in life. Young girls and uninitiated boys become turtles or watersnakes (Tedlock 1979:507). In contrast, the Aztecs believed that where a person's soul went after death was determined not by that person's conduct in life, but rather by the manner of death and occupation in life. The souls of those who fell in combat or died on the sacrificial stone went to the eastern paradise of the sun; thence they would return to earth after four years, transformed into hummingbirds and other exotic birds (Caso 1958:58–64). To the western paradise went women who died in childbirth; they were believed to have possessed great magical power. Those who died by drowning, by the strike of a lightning bolt, and from other illnesses that were thought to be related to the water gods went to the paradise of the rain god Tlaloc in the south—a place of fertility where all kinds of trees and foodstuffs existed in abundance (Caso 1958:60). Those not selected either by the sun or Tlaloc went to Mictlan in the north and underwent a series of magical trials, passing through nine hells until after a period of four years they reached their final rest. In a somewhat related vein, the Zunis believe that after one has died four times—descending death by death through each of the four underworlds—one returns to the place where the people originated (Tedlock 1979:508). Finally, the Aztecs believed that children who died before they reached the age of reason joined the dual creator gods in the thirteenth and highest heaven—perhaps to become the new human race when the present one is destroyed in the great earthquake (Caso 1958:64).

Lack of space precludes a detailed comparison of western Puebloan and Mesoamerican ritual practice, but I will briefly summarize some of the most important similarities. The ritual life of both groups included or includes a period of fasting and continence for four days before the enactment of some ceremonies; the performance of certain rituals that could be described as "killing the god"; rites of running and kindling new fire with a wooden drill; various sorts of divination, including perceiving omens in the appearance of certain birds or certain types of phenomena such as water and fire; burning offerings of food

to the deities; using ritual shields and crooked staffs; and observing a period of idle days at the end of the ceremonial-calendrical year (Parsons 1933). Of special note is the Zuni practice of dividing the months into three groups of ten, as well as that of dividing the forty-nine-day Shalako count into four periods of ten days each with nine remaining: Parsons describes this as an Aztec, not a Puebloan count (Parsons 1917:187; Parsons 1933:626; Stevenson 1904:108).

Having given a brief introduction to the Mesoamerican and western Puebloan world-views in general, I will turn to an examination of the similarity in function and attributes of the various deities of both groups, beginning with the sun (see Table 10.1 for a graphic depiction of these similarities).

Sun

Although different deities took on the role of the sun during the four previous creations, the Aztecs seem to have perceived the sun as an entity distinct from these other deities. This sun, Tonatiuh, was invoked by various names, including "shining one," "beautiful child," and "eagle that soars," and was generally represented by a disk—such as the one that makes up the core of the Aztec calendar stone (Caso 1958:32). In the center of the disk Tonatiuh is depicted with his tongue hanging out; his hands, at the side of the disk, are tipped with eagle claws clutching human hearts (Caso 1958:33). It is of note that one aspect of this Aztec sun is eagle, for the Zuni beast god of the zenith is sometimes eagle, and sometimes, Knifewing—the mythical creature with wings and tail of knives—although this being is not synonymous with the Sun Father (Young 1985:18). Furthermore, the Aztec equation of the sun with sacrifice and a measure of ferocity, as illustrated by his eagle claws clutching human hearts, is reiterated in a Hopi myth in which "Sun had to be helped to move on across the sky by killing a child," and his daily movement depended on some form of dying at various times and "on ritual racing by the town youths" (Parsons 1939:212). The sacrifices that accompanied Aztec sun worship were thought to provide sustenance to the sun who could only be kept alive by life itself; this underscores the reciprocal relationship that existed between the Aztecs and their deities—a characteristic of Puebloan relationships with the supernaturals as well (Caso 1958:12). Despite Hopi and Zuni legends hinting at human sacrifice to the solar deity, however, the most prominent feature of the sun is kindness and helpfulness. The Hopi describe their sun god, Tawa, as "young, handsome, gentle, kind, and helpful" (Colton 1959:80). When impersonated, Tawa wears eagle and parrot feathers inserted in a plaited corn husk in a circle around his face like the rays of the sun (Fewkes 1903:138–41).

Goddesses of Water

According to some Hopi myths, the wife of the sun is Huru-ing Wuhti, the goddess of hard substances, that is, turquoise in particular or wealth in general (Voth 1905:1–9). This personage appears in kachina form as a chief kachina (Wright 1977:37). It seems likely that this deity parallels the Mesoamerican Chalchiuhtlicue, "the lady of the jade skirts," who was the goddess of water and, according to different legends, the wife or sister of Tlaloc, the rain god (Caso 1958:42–44). Chalchiuhtlicue was the special patroness of the sea and much revered by fishermen. However, for those who traded in salt, there was another patroness, Huixtocíhuatl—either the sister or daughter of Tlaloc and Chalchiuhtlicue (Caso 1958:44–45). This goddess may have been a precursor to Salt Old Woman at Hopi and Zuni—an extremely important personage who brings rain as well as salt (Bunzel 1932d:1035). The Zuni kachina of Salt Old Woman carries a feathered staff with which she pulls down the rain clouds—a feature quite similar to the befeathered stick of the Aztec salt goddess (Bunzel

1932d:1032 and Pl. 42). Furthermore, the Aztec story of the banishment or departure of the salt goddess seems to be a variant of the Western Puebloan tale in which Salt Old Woman is offended by the way she is treated and goes away to the south (Bunzel 1932d:1031–35; Sahagún cited in Parsons 1933:628).

Wind and Rain

The Aztecs assigned Quetzalcóatl to the cardinal direction west and the color white, and regarded him as a creator god along with the Black Tezcatlipoca. Their colors are opposite, reflecting the fact that so are their personalities: the struggle between these two gods seems to symbolize the struggle between good and evil in the universe. Whereas Quetzalcóatl was a beneficent god and a hero—the discoverer of corn and the founder of agriculture and industry—the Black Tezcatlipoca was a god of darkness, the patron of sorcerers and evil ones; yet he was also the patron of warriors and the discoverer of fire. Tezcatlipoca means "mirror that smokes" and he is generally depicted wearing such a mirror at his temple and another in place of his right foot which was torn off by an earth monster (Caso 1958:10, 14, 25, 27–30).

The image of Quetzalcóatl in the Codex Borbonicus reveals certain important distinguishing attributes (Caso 1958:19, 21–33). For instance, he carries in one hand an incense pot with its handle in the form of a serpent. Covering his mouth is a red mask in the form of a bird's beak; in some representations this beak is also set with the fangs of a serpent. This particular mask identifies Quetzalcóatl as the god of wind, in which form he was worshipped under the name of Ehécatl, "wind" (Caso 1958:22). On his head is a conical cap made of ocelot skin. His breastplate, described as the breastplate of the wind, is made from the transverse cut of a large seashell; perhaps it is this sort of association which links a spiral form with wind as well as with water, an association which seems to hold in the Southwest as well as in Mesoamerica (Ellis 1989; Fewkes 1892a:20; Young 1985:16).

Like many other Mesoamerican deities—and, as will be shown, Puebloan deities as well—Quetzalcóatl comprised a number of different and seemingly unrelated aspects synthesized in a single god. Furthermore, he was an extremely ancient god, known among the Maya as Kukulkán and Gucumatz (Caso 1958:25). He was Quetzalcóatl, the god of wind, life and morning, sun during one of the ages of creation, but he was also the planet Venus—the god of twins and monsters (Caso 1958:23). His name literally means "the plumed serpent" but also translates somewhat esoterically as "the precious twin" (Caso 1958:24). The second meaning refers to Quetzalcóatl as representing Venus, or the morning star; while his twin brother, Xólotl, represented Venus as the evening star (Caso 1958:24). It has been suggested that the apparent motion of Venus—its appearance as evening star, its disappearance, and its reappearance as morning star—is symbolized in an Aztec myth about Quetzalcóatl and his twin brother Xólotl (Caso 1958:24). According to this myth, the two descended to the world of the dead where they underwent various trials, finally asking Mictlantecuhtli, the god of the underworld, for the bones of the dead so that they could bring about a new creation. After escaping from this god they reappeared and re-created man. Quetzalcóatl then discovered corn, showed the people how to weave and do mosaic work, and taught them science; in fact, it is he who endowed humans with "the means to measure time and study the movements of the stars" (Caso 1958:25). Quetzalcóatl not only invented the calendar, but he also designated specific days for the performance of ritual activities. In his benevolent aspect Quetzalcóatl is the essence of saintliness (Caso 1958:26): his life of fasting and penitence and his priestly character resemble the qualities of the Zuni Pautiwa, chief of the kachinas, who "displays the most honored of Zuni virtues, dignity, kindliness, and generosity, and

also beauty" (Bunzel 1932c:909). Pautiwa brings the Corn Maidens to Zuni after Shalako, inaugurates the winter solstice ceremony, and comes at the new year with the crooks of appointment for the principal kachina personators of the coming year (Bunzel 1932c:909). Furthermore, like Quetzalcóatl, Pautiwa makes up the yearly ceremonial calendar.

In his manifestation as Venus, as well as in his aspect as sun, Quetzalcóatl is strikingly parallel to the Zuni and Hopi Twin War Gods (Caso 1958:15, 23–27): at Zuni, these twins are sons of the sun who represent the morning and evening stars and are sent to the fourth underworld to bring the people to the surface of this earth (Parsons 1939:236n, 239–42; Young and Williamson 1981:184; Young 1985:12). This connection between the western Puebloan War Gods and Quetzalcóatl, especially in his guise as horned and plumed serpent, is further strengthened by the frequent co-occurrence of stars and horned serpents in Pueblo IV rock art as well as in the Pottery Mound kiva murals (Hibben 1975:Fig. 34; Schaafsma 1980:265). Additionally, in a Hopi kiva mural at Awatovi painted during the late fifteenth or early sixteenth century, a figure, closely corresponding to the Hopi and Zuni War God images, is depicted wearing a conical cap very much like those worn by Quetzalcóatl in various codex depictions (Ellis 1989; Hibben 1975:Fig. 28; Smith 1952:302–3, 316–18, Figs. 28i, 65a, Color Plate E; Stevenson 1904: Plates 137, 138). As mentioned earlier, Polly Schaafsma (1975) has documented similar Quetzalcóatl-like figures with conical caps in Jornada style rock art at Hueco Tanks State Park, Texas, and in Pueblo rock art in the Tompiro and Southern Tewa provinces (P. Schaafsma, personal communication). These figures are associated with cloud and water symbolism as are the Hopi and Zuni Twin War Gods and the Hopi deity Sotuknangu. According to Schaafsma and Schaafsma (1974), the Jornada complex was Mexican-derived and appeared in the Southwest at about A.D. 1050. A further link with Mesoamerica is demonstrated by the fact that the western Puebloans make miniature weapons, such as bows and arrows, as well as rain-associated shields and lightning sticks for the Twin War Gods (Parsons 1939:305–7)—an offering paralleling that which the Mesoamericans made to their own war gods (Parsons 1933:617).

Quetzalcóatl may also be linked to the Hopi deity Sotuknangu, "god of the sky, the clouds, and the rain . . . good, dignified, and powerful" (Ellis and Hammack 1968:41). He is personated only occasionally and then may be masked or unmasked (Colton 1959:78). His white mask is topped with one vertical horn colored blue and slightly curved at the tip. In some depictions his face is marked with cloud designs. In his left hand he carries a netted gourd of water and in his right hand a lightning stick (Fewkes 1903:178, Plate 58: Stephen 1936: Plates V, VI). When not masked, the personator of Sotuknangu wears a star-shaped hat from which feathers hang over his face (Colton 1959:78). This deity is described as "both Star and Lightning, the god who kills and renders fertile and who initiated the practice of scalping" (Parsons 1939:178). Thus we see in this Hopi god one version of Quetzalcóatl, with traces of Tlaloc (rain, fertility), and also Xipe Tótec, who was ritually honored by the taking of scalps (Parsons 1933:617).

While strongly resembling the Hopi and Zuni Twin War Gods, Quetzalcóatl is also akin to the Zuni and Hopi horned or plumed water serpent, although Tlaloc also figures in this association. The Hopi horned water serpent is called Palölökong and plays a central role in a dramatic ceremony in late February or early March when puppet effigies of this serpent knock down miniature corn fields and fight noisily with the Mudheads (patterned after Zuni clowns) amid loud roars made by actors blowing through empty gourds (Fewkes 1900:605–29; Stephen 1936: 287–349; Young 1986:5–6). The Zuni horned water serpent, Kolowisi, figures prominently in the initiation of boys into the kachina society and the performer who creates the serpent's roar blows through a conch shell (Bunzel 1932*d:*975–80; Stevenson 1904:94–102). As mentioned earlier, Quetzalcóatl's breastplate is also made from a conch shell, perhaps symbolizing a wind / water / spiral relationship that is also integral to this Zuni drama. Anthropologist Florence Ellis notes that at both Hopi and Zuni, the Mudheads are fertility figures and have the thick-ringed goggle eyes and thick-ringed mouth reminiscent of Tlaloc (1989). Of course, a number of Hopi and Zuni kachinas also exhibit such goggle eyes. Similarly, the Hopi and Zuni horned water serpent puppets have goggle eyes, which are filled with corn kernels and the seeds of important plants: this points to a water / fertility association which is characteristic of both Quetzalcóatl and Tlaloc (Caso 1958:15, 24–27, 41; Young 1986:17). There is an apparent sun-serpent antagonism in the Hopi performance: the puppets of Palölökong push aside the sun symbols in the curtain as they dart at the imitation hills of corn; the Hopis believe that if the horned water serpent is not properly propitiated, it might hinder the journey of the sun along the horizon (Fewkes 1897:270–71). Yet, the horned water serpent is also connected with agricultural fertility, as indicated by the seed-filled eyes of the puppets. Similarly, the puppet figure at Zuni spurts forth water from a scared spring as well as grasses which symbolize the long life of the initiate into the kachina society (Young 1986: 15). Finally, both the Hopis and Zunis believe that the horned water serpent has the power to send floods and controls the underwater springs—in this respect he is much like the Mesoamerican Tlaloc (Caso 1958: 42). In one Zuni tale, the sacrifice of a boy and girl to the horned water serpent causes the flood waters to abate—a practice similar to the Mesoamerican tradition of child sacrifice to the mountain rain gods (Caso 1958:42; Parsons 1933:616; Young 1986:29–30).

Mothers of the Gods / Goddesses of Fertility

The Hopi and Zuni puppet performances described above reveal an important link between the mother of the gods, also associated with fertility, and the horned water serpent: this female deity, called Hahai-i Wuhti at Hopi (see P. Schaafsma, this volume, Plate 4, left) and Ahea or Hemokatsiki at Zuni, suckles the horned water serpent puppets and offers them sacred corn meal—an act of propitiation that serves to quell the antagonism of the serpents toward the young corn plants (Young 1986). The Puebloan mother of the gods is similar to the Mesoamerican Chalchihuitlicue, goddess of water, described earlier (Caso 1958: 15, 41). She also resembles the Aztec mother of the gods and old goddess of the earth, Coatlicue, who is sometimes depicted carrying a child in her arms (Caso 1958:12, Ellis 1989). The Hopi Hahai-i Wuhti is the first image presented to new born babies (Wright 1977:56). Her mouth is turned up in a perpetual smile and her cheeks are red disks. In her right hand she carries a gourd of water and frequently in her left an ear of corn or a tray of corn meal—thus she may also be connected with the Mesoamerican goddess of sustenance, Chicomecóatl, who is called "seven ears of corn" (Caso 1958:45; Fewkes 1903:76; Stephen 1936:297–98).

Gods of Death and Rebirth

Xipe Tótec was mentioned earlier as a deity who had his origins in Olmec ideology: the god of spring and the annual rebirth of plant life. Yet the Aztec added a terrifying aspect to this god who became the Red Tezcatlipoca. As "our lord the flayed one," his cult consisted of flaying a slave and covering a priest with the victim's skin, symbolizing the arrival of spring, when the earth covers herself with a new coat of vegetation (Caso 1958:47). Xipe thus reveals characteristics similar to those of the Hopi Masau, deity of earth and rebirth as seen in spring growth and renewal, but

also god of the underworld and death (Ellis 1989; Parsons 1939:183, 789–90): it is perhaps because of this dual and contrasting role that the Hopi describe him as one "who does things by opposites" (Titiev 1944:72n). The patron of travelers as well as the Hopi Old Fire god, Masau is personated with or without a mask, his face painted red or blotched with blood (Colton 1959:78; Fewkes 1903:90; Parsons 1939:184). According to the Hopi origin myth, the people first met Masau in his unmasked form as they emerged from the underworld. Although they were terrified of him, he spoke kindly to them and in his earth deity guise gave them land to plant (Voth 1905:12–13). In his gruesome aspect as god of the underworld—especially his appellation of "skeleton"—Masau resembles the Aztec god of the underworld, Mictlanteceuhtli, who is frequently depicted with his body covered with bones and wearing a human skull for a face mask (Caso 1958: 56; Voth 1905:12–13). Although he is most often characterized as kindly though fearsome, Masau is infrequently described as a thief, liar, and practical joker; these qualities further link him with Mictlanteceuhtli, who, according to some accounts, was "double-dealing and mistrustful" (Caso 1958:24; Stephen 1929:55–57).

Father of the Gods

Masau is related to and in some respects almost antithetical to one of the most important Hopi personages—Eototo. Called the "father" or chief of the kachinas, as is the Zuni Pautiwa, Eototo controls the seasons and is sometimes referred to as the husband of Hahai-i Wuhti, mentioned earlier as the mother of the kachinas who suckles the Horned Water Serpent during the Palölökonti ceremony (Parsons 1939:175, 205; Wright 1977:34). According to both anthropologist Florence Ellis and kachina-doll collector and scholar Harold Colton, "Eototo knows all the ceremonies . . . and leads in the spring Bean dance at which kachinas of all types appear, though emphasis is on those wearing the flowers and butter-flies of spring"—for the Hopi this comprises a "re-turn of the gods ceremony" (Colton 1959:22; Ellis 1989). Just as Masau's mask is of the helmet-type with circles for mouth and eyes, so is Eototo's, although Eototo lacks Masau's many-colored spots; while Masau carries yucca whips in his hands, Eototo carries a pouch of sacred meal in one hand and a gourd of sacred water in the other (Fewkes 1903:Plate 14, 90–93). Anthropologist and archaeologist Jesse Fewkes suggests that the similarity in symbolic designs on the masks and costumes of these two kachinas shows that these two gods are "virtually dual appellations of the same mythological conception" (Fewkes 1903: 93). Interestingly, the Aztec gods who corre-spond somewhat to these Hopi gods are also symbolically linked to one another. As just men-tioned, Masau is related to Xipe Tótec, who as god of seed time and planting is in turn linked to Tlaloc, and Tlaloc resembles Eototo to a great degree. As chief of the kachinas or rain-fertility spirits, Eototo holds a position similar to Tlaloc who is leader of the Aztec Tlalocos or rain spirits. Furthermore, Eototo's prominence in the Hopi "return of the gods ceremony," which is part of the pre-planting ritual of Powamu or the Bean dance, corresponds to Tlaloc's role in the Aztec preplanting celebration (Ellis 1989; Parsons 1933:625). Like the Powamu, the Aztec festival was also known as "when they eat bean food" (Spence 1912:48; 56–58).

Gods of Germination

Another Hopi deity who, like the Mesoameri-can Tlaloc, could be described as "he who makes things gorw," is Alosaka or Muyingwa, the Hopi patron of reproduction for man, animals, and plants (Caso 1958:41; Colton 1959:79). Predomi-nant features of his mask are two mountain-sheep horns curving backwards, while the lower section of his mask is black (Fewkes 1903: Plate 59, 182; Stephen 1936:Plate VII). Interestingly, although

a god of earth and growth, Muyingwa is also called "chief of the nadir" and "father of the underworld," a description which calls to mind Xipe Tótec's dual function as a god of death and rebirth (Parsons 1939:178). This Hopi god of growth in a slightly different form appears as the Hopi chief kachina Ahul, who is also the lieu-tenant or companion of Eototo; both Ahul and Muyingwa are described as germ-god kachinas (Colton 1959:20; Wright 1977:35). On the back of Ahul's many-colored cloak is painted a likeness of Alosaka, who is responsible for the germina-tion of seeds (Colton 1959:32); Alosaka is also depicted in the center of the shield carried by the personator of the sun during the Walpi win-ter solstice ceremony (Fewkes 1918:502, Pl. 2). Of course, in this aspect of enabling the germina-tion of seeds, both Alosaka / Muyingwa and Ahul resemble the Aztec Centéotl, the male corn god (Caso 1958:46). Ahul is further characterized by a turned-up beak and a mask painted over with stars; in some depictions he carries a gourd full of sacred water, and in others a bundle of bean sprouts (Colton 1959:20; Fewkes 1903:Plate VII, 74). One can see in certain of these characteristics of Ahul a similarity to Tlaloc, who may also have stars scattered over his mask (Caso 1958:40). But Ahul fulfills a function parallel to Quetzalcóatl, too, in his guise as the White Tezcatlipoca, water and fertility deity (Caso 1958:9, 23–26). Accord-ing to Ellis, the turned-up beak of Ahul is related to some Mesoamerican depictions of Quetzalcóatl as Ehécatl, the wind god (Ellis 1989).

Fire Gods

Both the Hopis and the Zunis have a dual counterpart to the Mesoamerican Old Fire God, Huehuetéotl—in western Puebloan ritual drama these roles are played by a youth and an older man. At Hopi the older fire god is Kawikoli and the younger is Sumaikoli, a possessor of powerful magic who kindles new fire during a spring fes-tival and carries it to the shrines of the fire god at the four solstitial points (Fewkes 1903:131). Kawikoli and Sumaikoli live on the edge of a mesa and are regarded by the Hopis as kind and helpful (Colton 1959:85; Fewkes 1903:131). Of course, Masau is also a version of the Hopi Old Fire God, and the shrines at the four solstitial points are dedicated to him—evidence perhaps of a symbolic association between sun and fire. The new fire ceremony itself may be a ritual enactment of the rekindling of the sun's warmth in the spring which causes the growth of young plants; it is also a dramatization of that part of the emergence myth in which Masau teaches the Hopi the use of fire (Titiev 1944:135). Furthermore, Stephen suggests that the Hopis regard the speed with which this new fire is kindled as an omen of the good or ill that the coming year will bring (Stephen 1936:964n). At Zuni the kindling of the new fire is a crucial part of the winter solstice ceremony—throughout the ten days of the solstice observances, the fire is tended and watched over by an older man of the Badger clan appointed by the Zuni priests (Bunzel 1932c:637, 659). This man, in turn, selects the personator of Shulawitsi, the young fire god, from among the young boys of his own family (Bunzel 1932d:959). The young fire god lights signal fires prior to Shalako, "the coming of the gods ceremony," and leads the Zuni "council of the gods" into the village (Bunzel 1932d:958–61). The colored spots on Shulawitsi's black-painted body and mask suggest gleaming sparks and resemble the multicolored disks on the mask of the Hopi Masau (Tyler 1964:125). The western Puebloans create new fire by the friction produced from a wooden drill, and they carry it out from the kiva; the Hopis perform a ritual in that kiva for Masau. Similarly, the Aztec produced new fire with a wooden drill and carried it out from the temple of the Aztec fire god (Sahagún cited in Parsons 1933:621). In both Mesoamerica and the Southwest, the fire gods and their societies are extremely old and important aspects of ceremonial life.

Gods of Music, Flowers, and Love

The attributes of the Mesoamerican and western Puebloan gods of love, music, and flowers point to another sun / fertility parallel. The Aztec god of summer, Xochipilli, is called the "prince of flowers" and symbolizes dances, games, and love. His symbol is formed by four points signifying the heat of the sun. He is adorned with flowers and butterflies and carries a staff on which a human heart is impaled. As a god of summer and fertility he is also connected with Centéotl, the Aztec corn god (Caso 1958:47). Xochipilli seems to be a prototype for the Zuni Paiyatamu, the gay and youthful fluteplayer associated with music, poetry, flowers, and butterflies, who is also described as the Sun's deputy (Bunzel 1932a:530). According to Zuni mythology, Paiyatamu became enamored of the chaste Corn Maidens who brought corn to the Zunis (Stevenson 1904:48): at first his passion frightened them and they fled, but he was also instrumental in causing their return (Stevenson 1904:56). It is of note that the Aztec goddess of sustenance, Chicomecóatl, was also called "Seven Ears of Corn" (Caso 1958:45)—a striking parallel to the seven Corn Maidens associated with Paiyatamu at Zuni. These seven maidens represent corn in the colors of the six directions plus the center which is symbolized by sweet corn (Cushing 1896:433). There is also some indication that the Zuni Corn Maidens symbolize the seven stars of the Big Dipper. The Zuni word for this constellation means "seven ones," and Cushing explains that the Zunis first planted corn in the spring "by the light of the seven great stars which were at that time rising bright above them" (Cushing 1896:392; Young and Williamson 1981:183–84, 191).

Conclusion

Although there are many other parallels to be explored in establishing the connection between

Mesoamericans and western Puebloans, what I have outlined points to a number of significant similarities in the cosmological outlook of both groups. Not only do many of the Puebloan deities and kachinas seem to be based on Mesoamerican prototypes, but the entire Puebloan religious perspective is also shaped by a belief in the reciprocity between human beings and supernaturals—the interdependence of the people and their gods—which harkens back to the Aztec premise that sacrifices provided necessary nourishment for the gods. The Zuni Sun Father, for instance, sent his sons, the Twin War Gods, to bring the ancestral Zunis out from the fourth underworld, not only because he took pity on their miserable semi-human existence in the darkness, but also because he wanted their offerings and prayers; and both the Hopi and the Zuni perform ritual activities that are aimed at helping the sun to complete his daily and annual travels. Furthermore, as we have seen, many of the western Puebloan kachinas and other deities—such as Masau, the Hopi earth and death god, and the horned water serpent—have the same sort of dual or multiple personalities, sometimes demonstrating conflicting aspects as well, that characterized the Aztec gods. Interestingly, the Hopis say that the horned water serpent came "from the Red Land of the South," and that he is a patron of the Water-Corn clan, which "also came from that Red Land" (Parsons 1939:184–85).

A pervasive theme in both the cosmology of the western Puebloans and that of the Mesoamericans is the necessary interrelationship of sun and water as the basis for human and agricultural increase or fertility. This significant association is exemplified in the Zuni myth that ascribes the birth of the Twin War Gods to the union of the sun's rays with the foam of a waterfall (Cushing 1896:381; Stevenson 1904:24). Sometimes this sun / water

relationship is antagonistic, however, as when the horned water serpent who controls the underground springs causes a flood, which destroys the benefits wrought by the sun in the Hopi and Zuni fields; or when the Aztec gods who took on the role of sun destroyed four consecutive creations by invoking water, wind, rain, and jaguars (Caso 1958:15).

Finally, this sun / water cult is the basis of the all-pervasive directional scheme, with its accompanying color symbolism and emphasis on ritual numbers such as four and five, employed by both the Mesoamericans and the western Puebloans. The vast network of symbolic associations generated by these two principles is derived not only from the apparent motion of the sun, but also from the belief in its interconnection with rain and water more generally. Although the western Puebloan semi-cardinal directions refer to the solstice positions, they also refer to four oceans and to the areas in which the rain priests dwell; similarly, the deities the Aztecs associated with directionality were related to both the sun and water.

This discussion has been necessarily general, but I hope that it will provide an impetus for more detailed contextual analyses of the range and extent of the interactions between the Mesoamericans and western Puebloans—interactions that had a major effect on their perceptions of astonomical phenomena as well. Certainly we see a common focus on observing the ordered motions of the sun, the moon, Venus, and various constellations which are central to the interlocking spheres of religion, ceremonial practice, and world-view. Nevertheless, the Southwest-Mesoamerican connection is a complex and complicated scheme to unravel, and many questions concerning its nature and impact are yet to be answered.

ACKNOWLEDGMENTS

I am grateful to Polly Schaafsma for reading and commenting on this chapter, which is based on a paper delivered as part of the Recursos of Santa Fe seminar she organized entitled, "World View and Ritual: Kachinas in the Pueblo World," October 4–6, 1991. I also thank Robert H. Leibman for his help in devising Table 10.1, as well as his patience in helping me solve yet another series of mysterious computer glitches. This chapter is a revised version of a chapter (published under the title, "The Southwest Connection: Similarities Between Western Puebloan and Mesoamerican Cosmology") included in a volume edited by Anthony F. Aveni, *World Archaeoastronomy* (Cambridge: Cambridge University Press, 1989). This was a volume of selected papers from the Second Oxford International Conference on Archaeoastronomy held at Mérida, Yucatán, Mexico, January 13–17, 1986. I am grateful to Cambridge University Press for giving me permission to publish this chapter in another volume. Although I dislike publishing a similar article in two different volumes, I was persuaded to do so on the basis that the readership of a book focusing on the Pueblo kachina cult would likely be quite different from that interested primarily in world archaeoastronomy.

11

Pueblo Ceremonialism From the Perspective of Spanish Documents

CURTIS F. SCHAAFSMA

Before the appearance of a wealth of archaeological evidence concerning kachinas (Adams 1991; Brody 1991; Griffith 1983; P. Schaafsma 1980, 1992*b*), scholars relied mainly upon ethnographic evidence to propose theories about the origin and early distribution of the kachina cult (Anderson 1951, 1955, 1960; Parsons 1930). The minor attention paid to historical evidence (Anderson 1956; Dockstader 1985) seems often to have been lost in general discussions. This heavy reliance on ethnographic evidence led to a false emphasis on Zuni Pueblo as the source of the cult (Anderson 1960; Parsons 1930). Anderson's summary article on the topic only mildly corrected the situation, since he mainly argued that Acoma also contributed to the formation of the kachina cult (1960:376). A consideration of the original Spanish documents and the dislocations caused by Spanish colonial practices reveals a very different picture from the one available from viewing the topic primarily from the ethnographic situation. One cannot deal with this topic without a thorough consideration of the historical evidence.

Two key points emerge from a review of the documents. One is the evidence that from ca. 1610 to 1639 there was a real break with the past

Catholic ✓

pop ▵

ceremonial practices, and the Pueblos were effectively converted to Catholicism essentially in the manner described by Benavides (Forrestal 1954; Hodge, Hammond and Rey 1945), Fray Juan de Prada (Hackett 1937:106–15) and others. The second is the evidence for major population dislocations and mixing of Pueblo peoples during the first century of Spanish colonization, especially from ca. 1670 to ca. 1706. The result of these changes means that the Pueblo cultures after ca. 1706 would have been very different from those existing before 1598. These changes have to be taken into account when assessing the validity of the prevailing bias that the Pueblos encountered by Anglo ethnographers after ca. 1880 were an essentially unbroken cultural continuum with the prehistoric past, as stated by Basso:

> Unlike many regions of North America, where Indian populations had been decimated by disease, destroyed by arms, or forcibly removed from their original homelands, the Southwest in the late 1800s contained a number of native societies that persisted in situ and were essentially intact. (1979:14–15)

This lack of cultural continuity between the prehistoric Pueblos and those studied by ethnographers after ca. 1880 due to the disruptions of the Spanish colonial period was well addressed by Wilcox (1981). What is the case in a general sense is even more exaggerated in religious matters which are delicate and easily disrupted, especially since they were the direct target of seventeenth-century Spanish missionaries. All of this has immense implications for the question of the origin and prehistoric distribution of the kachina cult. Any conclusions about this topic based primarily upon ethnographic evidence are almost certain to be faulty and of little value.

The historical evidence indicates that kachinas were a dominant feature of eastern Pueblo religion, especially the Southern and Eastern Tiwa, Piro, Tompiro and Southern Tewa or Tano Pueblos (Figure 11.1) at the time of initial Spanish contact (ca. 1540–1610). The kachina cult among

the eastern Pueblos was quickly suppressed by Spanish missionary activities after ca. 1610 but somehow remained strong enough to experience a widespread resurgence during the confused time of church and state strife that reached a culmination in the 1660s. The resurgence in the 1660s was quickly extinguished. There was a widespread revival of kachina dancing following the 1680 Pueblo Revolt while the Spaniards were away, but this too was quickly suppressed after 1694 when the missionaries arriving with Vargas were stationed in the Rio Grande Pueblos (Espinosa 1988:xvii). After the June 4, 1696, revolt (Espinosa 1988) the documents are essentially silent about kachina ceremonies anywhere in the eastern Pueblos, giving the impression that kachina ceremonies originated primarily among the western Pueblos of Acoma, Zuni and Hopi (Anderson 1951, 1960).

Our impression in 1974 was that the ethnographic distribution of kachina religious practices was largely the result of dislocations caused by Spanish settlement and the effects of missionary efforts:

> One of the most obvious reasons for the greater complexity of the cult today among the western Pueblos is that these villages escaped the intense oppression inflicted on all of the eastern villages and particularly on the kachina cult by the Spanish friars in the 1600s, who attempted to eradicate native religious practices in order to replace them with Catholicism. (Schaafsma and Schaafsma 1974:543)

The situation was undoubtedly very complex, and in addition to the reduced impact of the Spaniards on the western Pueblos of Acoma, Zuni, and Hopi because of their distance from the area of actual Spanish settlement (primarily in the Rio Grande valley) there is good reason to believe that many Pueblo people left the Rio Grande region and moved to Acoma, Zuni, and Hopi to escape from Spanish domination and continued to practice their indigenous religion in these hinterlands.

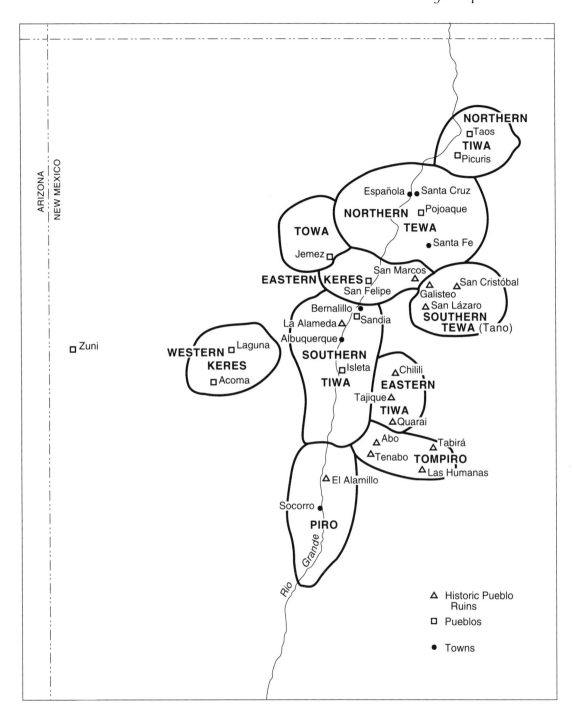

FIGURE 11.1. Map of the Rio Grande valley showing some of the historic pueblos and major linguistic divisions.

Many of these dislocations took place at the time of the 1680 rebellion and the subsequent return of the Spaniards in 1692. The documents newly translated by Espinosa (1988) disclose that no pueblos were occupied in the Rio Grande valley below San Felipe Pueblo between 1692 and 1696 (Figure 11.1). The entire southern Rio Grande Tiwa and Piro districts (Marshall and Walt 1984; C. Schaafsma 1987) below San Felipe were abandoned. Additionally, the Tompiro, Eastern Tiwa (Ivey 1988; Mera 1940), and Tano districts were also abandoned.

Some of the few displaced people who can be identified in the period 1692–96 are the Tanos or Southern Tewas from San Lazáro and San Cristóbal who were living in the Santa Cruz valley east of modern Española (Espinosa 1988). It is possible to keep track of these Southern Tewas and follow them after the June 4, 1696, rebellion to Hopi where some of them settled Hano (Stanislawski 1979). However, many other displaced Pueblo people probably also moved into the western Pueblos without much notice to the Spaniards and without maintaining their identities as did the Tewas at Hopi. Ellis discussed the post-1680 dislocations of the Southern Tiwas (1979:353–54) and was of the opinion that modern Isleta Pueblo was formed after 1742 by Tiwa refugees returning from Hopi (1979:354). On the one hand, these displaced people undoubtedly added their particular practices to those already at Hopi, leading to the increased complexity of the kachina repertoire in the west; on the other hand, it is likely that the more conservative followers of the kachina religion stayed at Hopi and only those willing to return to the Catholic church came back to the Rio Grande valley. Anderson took the inflow of refugees to Hopi into account and recognized the fact of "Tusayan having been for a long time an asylum for refugees from the Spanish-controlled east, who of course brought their own kachinas and kachina observances with them (1960:381)." All of these

pre-1750 population dislocations undermine the validity of the post-1880 ethnographic evidence laboriously sifted and weighed by Parsons (1930) and Anderson (1951, 1955, 1960).

Griffith (1983) felt impelled to finally lay to rest Parsons's proposal that kachinas developed after the Spaniards arrived in a complex emulation of Catholicism, an effort that pervades Dockstader's (1985) and Anderson's (1951, 1955) treatments of this topic as well. Griffith concluded his summary of this subject by stating that "It is indisputable that some form of masking existed in the Greater Southwest in pre-hispanic times" (1983:764), and that "not only was there masking, but it was recognizably kachina masking" (1983:766). Griffith would thus have been in basic agreement with Fred Eggan, who maintained that "the kachina societies, thought to have been introduced from the south in the fourteenth century, are found in every group, except the northern Tiwa pueblos of Taos and Picuris" (1983:739).

In order to gain perspective on Parsons's viewpoint it is appropriate to recall what she originally proposed:

> At Zuñi early in the nineteenth century the mission was withdrawn to be reëstablished only a few years ago. My guess is that a great deal in the nature of ceremonial adaptation followed the withdrawal of the Franciscan mission at Zuñi. The native hierarchy took over functions of the Franciscans; and the *kachina* cult throve and blossomed. . . . The *kachina* cult spread from Zuñi, whence in fact it is still spreading, to the Hopi, through the associations with the immigrant group probably Keresan, that had settled at Sichumovi after living some time at Zuñi; to Acoma, where there was no resident missionary; to Laguna; likewise to the Eastern Keres, to Jemez, and circling out, to the Tewa, and even to Isleta and Taos. No doubt even in the eighteenth century this process had begun, but it was in the first half of the nineteenth century, I surmise, that a great impetus was given to the distribution. (1930:597)

One can refer to Anderson (1951, 1955, 1960) for the involved replies to this proposal, as well as to Dockstader (1985). It is important to note that both Ralph Beals (1932) and Leslie White (1934) quickly made contrary responses to Parsons's proposal. In part, Parsons's perspective can be treated as bygone scholarly history, but one wonders to what degree it echoes in the background for those who still view the origin of the kachina cult among the western Pueblos. It is well to remember that Parsons's account is almost totally based upon ethnographic information, and she apparently only partly modified her views in later years (Anderson 1960; Griffith 1983). Parsons regarded the kachina cult as largely based on Catholic prototypes and believed that it came into being in the late 1700s or early 1800s, when the Zuni religious leaders took over the former functions of the Franciscan missionaries.

It is hard for me to understand how this view can mean much today given the wealth of archaeological information bearing on the topic that clearly demonstrates that kachinas were widespread throughout the puebloan world after A.D. 1300 (Adams 1991; P. Schaafsma 1980) and have roots in the Mimbres rock art and ceramics extending to ca. A.D. 1000 (P. Schaafsma 1992*b*; 1980). Griffith in discussing kachina masks in the Southwest took the specific position that the kachina cult was derived from Mesoamerica by way of Casas Grandes (1983:764–65). In the post 1300 pueblos of the southwestern United States, kachinas would seem to be a late manifestation of a practice that pervaded the summer–rain–dependent, corn–growing cultures of Mesoamerica for centuries before 1300. As J. O. Brew suggested long ago (1943), the kachina cult appears to be derived from the ancient, deeply rooted Tlaloc complex of Mexico.

Anderson summarized the early Spanish documents pertaining to the Pueblo kachina cult (1951; 1956) and especially the extraordinarily detailed accounts of the 1660s dealing with the resurgence of kachina ceremonies at the direction of Governor Don Bernardo López de Mendizábal. In our earlier treatment of kachina origins in the Southwest (Schaafsma and Schaafsma 1974:543) we referred to the extensive work of Anderson (1955:410; 1956; 1960) and agreed with his evidence that Spanish accounts of the mid-1600s demonstrated the kachina cult was flourishing everywhere among the eastern Pueblos at that time, with the minor exception of the Northern Tiwa. Our impression was that the resurgence of kachina dances in the 1660s represented the revitalization of religious practices common in the 1580s, when the Chamuscado-Rodriguez and Espejo expeditions visited the Pueblos of the Rio Grande valley (Anderson 1956:31; Beals 1932; Hammond and Rey 1929, 1966; White 1934), and that they had existed long before the Spaniards arrived. Diego Pérez de Luxán stated of the Southern Tiwa that "throughout this nation they have many masks which they use in their dances and ceremonies" (Hammond and Rey 1929:79). Anderson (1956:31) accepted Bandelier's summation that "the dance was early prohibited, but was never completely suppressed. . . . One of the first things the Pueblos did after the expulsion of Otermín from New Mexico was to re-establish the Cachinas" (Bandelier 1890:150–51).

Many of the documents referring directly to kachinas appear in records of the Inquisition or "Holy Office" between 1660 and 1664 relating to the trials of Governor Don Bernardo López de Mendizábal and Nicolás de Aguilar (Anderson 1956; Hackett 1937). Governor Mendizábal was in New Mexico from July 1659 until November, 1661 (Hackett 1937:168) and Aguilar was *alcalde mayor* of Las Salinas (Hackett 1937:152). Mendizábal had been accused of giving the Indians permission to perform kachina dances against the wishes of the Catholic priests, and Aguilar was accused of passing on the governor's orders to the Pueblo Indians in his jurisdiction. The dances are described in considerable detail, and in all instances the Catholic priests regarded the dances as a return to ceremonies that had been conducted before the Spaniards arrived in New Mexico. For example, Fray Nicolás de Chávez stated in 1660, "This dance had been done away with among the Christians until Don Bernardo López de Mendizábal came as governor" (Hackett 1937:152). Fray Chávez's description of the kachina dances is typical of the many descriptions that were presented in the hearings:

> He heard it said publicly in New Mexico that Don Bernardo López de Mendizábal had given his permission for the Christian Indians to perform their ancient and modern dances, among them that of the *catzinas,* which is a dance of the heathen in which the Indians dress themselves in peculiar garments, concealing only their private parts, smearing their entire bodies with earth, and covering their faces with masks like hoods, leaving only a small hole through which they can see a little. Only the men perform this dance, and when they dance it some of them beat the others with palm leaves over their entire bodies until they draw blood. (Hackett 1937:152)

Fray Nicolás de Freitas described the kachina dance on a high hill in sight of Isleta Pueblo and made it clear that this was a return to dances that had been conducted before the Spaniards arrived:

> The Indians of the pueblo of La Isleta had danced the *catzinas* on a high hill which is in sight of the pueblo, with express idolatry of the devil, giving thanks because, due to the action of Don Bernardo López de Mendizábal, they had again returned to the old times of their idolatry and heathenism. (Hackett 1937:157)

In other words, in the early 1660s the Pueblo Indians of the southern Rio Grande valley below Albuquerque were once again doing kachina dances, as they had been doing before the Catholic missionaries arrived.

It is well to bear in mind that Parsons had the notion that the early Spanish chroniclers did not mention masked dances (1930:594). It would

seem that she mainly was referring to Benavides (1930:593) who was in New Mexico between 1626 and 1629 (Forrestal 1954; Hodge, Hammond and Rey 1945). By Benavides's time it appears that kachina dances in the eastern Pueblos had been replaced by Christianity. It was during Benavides's administration that the New Mexican missions entered their "golden age" (Forrestal 1954:xx). In other words, if one is reading Benavides as the main source of historical information about Pueblo ceremonies, nothing about kachina dances is likely to appear because the eastern Pueblos had probably stopped doing them, at least in any manner that was observable to the missionaries. They may have still been done at Hopi and Zuni, but Benavides did not go the western Pueblos. As Griffith noted (1983), many of the pertinent documents, such as Hackett (1937), were not published until after Parsons had presented her views. Once again, the picture derived from ethnography ca. 1930 is in need of major revision in the light of the Spanish documents, many of which have become widely available in English only since 1928.

One of the odd notes to this earlier literature is the manner in which Anderson subscribes heavily to a Zuni and Acoma origin of the cult, accepts the Parsonian ethnographic view that "The Tiwa, except perhaps Sandia, have borrowed less of the kachina cult than any of the other tribes" (1960:380) and yet was fully aware of the wealth of documentary evidence for kachinas throughout the Southern Tiwa and Piro Pueblos in the 1660s (1960:382, 1956). He noted this anomaly, but did not really correct the ethnographic interpretation on the basis of the historical evidence. It appears to me that Anderson never escaped from the grip of Parsons's ethnographic vision, and that accounts for the ambivalence in his work.

Historical Summary

To gain perspective on the many accounts describing the kachina dances of the Rio Grande area in the 1660s (Hackett 1937), it is well to review the documentary evidence from the time of initial contact in 1540 until the events of the 1660s and even later until the 1770s.

CORONADO, 1540–42 √

Most of the documents relating to the Coronado expedition were translated and published by Winship (1896). Even though the Coronado party spent a considerable time in what became known as New Mexico, there is essentially nothing that can be sensibly related to the masked dances described in the 1660s. In a letter Coronado wrote to Viceroy Mendoza on August 3, 1540, he noted, "So far as I can find out, the water is what these Indians worship, because they say that it makes the corn grow and sustains their life" (Winship 1896:561). A similar account appears in the anonymous "Relación del Suceso" that is similar to that of Coronado, but refers to the use of prayer sticks which are planted at springs:

> Their rites and sacrifices are somewhat idolatrous, but water is what they worship most, to which they offer small painted sticks and feathers and yellow powder made of flowers, and usually this offering is made to springs.   (1896:573)

There are minor descriptions of ceremonies, but I can find no mention of masked dances. In part, this lack of references to masked dances in the Coronado documents may have allowed the ethnographers through ca. 1930 to believe that the documents overall did not refer to kachinas. Beals astutely noted, "The reason there are so few references to masked dances in the Southwest was [that] . . . the Spaniards . . . rarely mentioned anything which was the same or similar to Mexican customs" (1932:168). This was probably the case for the Coronado party.

CHAMUSCADO-RODRIGUEZ, 1581–82 √

Hernán Gallegos wrote an account of this expedition which is generally quite reliable (Hammond and Rey 1966). As was stated in a testimony Gallegos made in Mexico City on May 16, 1582, "he wrote it from time to time as the events took place and as he observed them" (Hammond and Rey 1966:138). A valuable secondary account of the expedition was written in 1584 by Obregón (Hammond and Rey 1928). Gallegos's account is particularly valuable because this was the first party to enter New Mexico since the Coronado expedition of forty years before, and there had been very little alteration of the indigenous culture due to Spanish settlement and no missionary activity aside from whatever minor impact resulted from the Coronado expedition. His account of a ceremony is repeated here because it can be related to the later ceremonies recorded in the 1660s:

> The *mitotes,* or ceremonial dances, which they perform to bring rain when there is a lack of rainwater for their cornfields, are of the following nature. During the month of December the natives begin their dances, which continue more than four months, at intervals of a certain number of days —every fortnight, I believe. Attendance at the mitotes is general, so the people gather in large numbers, though only the men take part, the women never. The ceremonies, which begin in the morning and last until evening, are held around an altar maintained for this purpose and continue throughout the night. An Indian chosen for the occasion sits elevated in their midst, and the participants dance before him. Close to this Indian are six others holding fifteen or twenty sticks. They walk about and dance. During each movement of the dance, one of them steps out and puts into his mouth seven sticks, three spans in length and two fingers in width. When he finishes putting them in his mouth and taking them out, he pauses, seemingly fatigued. Then he dances with two or three of the said sticks in his mouth. Next, the man who is seated as "lord" receives seven lashes from whips made of light flexible willow for that purpose. These lashes are administered by the Indians standing close to him, for he has six Indians on each side who lash him thirty-six times in the course of each movement, in such a manner as to draw blood, making him look like a flagellant. After inflicting the original seven lashes, they continue to dance

and to give him an equal number of lashes until they make the blood flow as if he were being bled. Although they do this until it seems that he will collapse, he shows no sign of pain. On the contrary, he talks to a large snake as thick as an arm, which coils up when it is about to talk. The whipped "lord" calls to it, and the reptile answers in such a manner that it can be understood. We thought this snake might be the devil, who has them enslaved. For this reason God our Lord willed that the settlement and its idolatrous people should be discovered, in order that they might come to the true faith. . . .

When this is over two Indian coyotes appear and go around among the dancers, howling in a startling and pitiful manner. As soon as the mitote has concluded, the flayed lord makes an offering of a certain number of sticks, adorned with many plumes, so that the people may place them in the cornfields and waterholes; for they worship and offer sacrifices at these holes. The natives do this, they say, because then they will never lack water. The flayed are so badly lacerated that their wounds do not heal in two months. The participants are so neat and well adorned in these mitotes and dances that the spectacle is well worth seeing.   (Hammond and Rey 1966:99–101)

Gallegos does not specify where he observed this ceremony, but since his party spent the greater portion of their time in and around the Rio Grande valley, it would seem likely that he observed it among the Rio Grande Pueblos. The party did, however, go to Acoma and Zuni. Because they did not go to Hopi, the ceremony could not have been observed in Hopi. The connection with rainmaking and the use of prayersticks would relate it to the ceremonies described in the Coronado period as well as later kachina ceremonies. The role of the flagellant caught the attention of the Spaniards and is a feature of the ceremonies that is mentioned in many of the later accounts, including Benavides's (Forrestal 1954:35) and those of the 1660s (Hackett 1937:158).

ESPEJO, 1582–83

Shortly after the Chamuscado-Rodriguez party returned to Santa Bárbara in what today is southern Chihuahua, the party led by Antonio de Espejo went to New Mexico (Hammond and Rey 1966). Diego Pérez de Luxán prepared a report on the expedition which is comparable to that of Gallegos in its detail and in the fact that it is essentially a diary maintained during the trip (Hammond and Rey 1929, 1966). Antonio de Espejo himself wrote a useful account of the trip after his return to Mexico (Hammond and Rey 1966). Obregón in 1584 also wrote a secondary account obtained by him from Bernaldino de Luna, a member of the party, which agrees very closely with the accounts of Luxán and Espejo (Hammond and Rey 1928:315–41).

When in the Southern Tiwa province along the Rio Grande, Luxán recorded, "Throughout this nation the people have many masks which they use in their dances and ceremonies" (1966:177). This would provide quite reliable evidence that the Rio Grande Tiwa people made use of masks, in ceremonies that in the 1660s would be called *catzinas*. This is the same quote to which Beals (1932) referred in his response to Parsons.

In his account Espejo described extensively the Piro Pueblos and made an interesting comparison with the Indians of Mexico: "In the painting of their houses and in other matters—relating to their dances and music and so forth—these Indians are very much like the Mexicans" (1966:220). Also in the Piro area, Espejo stated that "The natives have some small stone idols which they worship" and wayside shrines "where they place painted sticks and feathers" (1966:220). Espejo described the dance at Acoma and noted that they used live snakes (1966:225).

The basic ceremonies in the Rio Grande valley Pueblos described by the two expeditions of the 1580s (Hammond and Rey 1966) are essentially the "idolatrous practices" that the Spaniards set out to eradicate after the beginning of the settlement led by Oñate starting in 1598 (Hammond and Rey 1953). The basic attitude of the Spaniards toward the native religion was concisely summarized by Gallegos when he said:

> We thought this snake might be the devil, who has them enslaved. For this reason God our Lord willed that the settlement and its idolatrous people should be discovered, in order that they might come to the true faith. (1966:100)

OÑATE, 1598–1610 √

There are extensive records of the Oñate period (Hammond and Rey 1953) but very few useful descriptions of the ceremonies that the Spaniards were seeking to abolish. Many of the accounts are like that of Oñate himself in his March 22, 1601, letter when speaking of the activities of the friars:

> They all began at once to baptize the people and to learn the vernacular language of each Indian nation in order to minister to them in their own tongue. Some forty or fifty thousand persons are now peaceful, undisturbed, and obedient. They respect and obey the priests. (1953:619)

It is often overlooked that missionary activities during the Oñate period were erratic and unsettled, with many of the original friars returning to Mexico City by 1601 (Scholes and Bloom 1944, 1945). As Scholes and Bloom state, "Information is also very inadequate for the period from 1601–10. Such information as is available indicates that missionary activity was concentrated in the Tewa and Rio Grande Keres districts" (Scholes and Bloom 1944:329). Scholes and Bloom present good documentary evidence that in late 1609, near the end of Oñate's tenure, there were only two or three friars in New Mexico and "it may be assumed that missionary activity was at a minimum when Oñate's government came to a close" (Scholes and Bloom 1944:330). In other words, while there was a great deal of impact on the Pueblos during the Oñate period, the influence of the missionaries remains uncertain, and it is hard

to imagine that the native religion was replaced to any major degree by such a small number of friars, especially in the Pueblos outside of the Tewa and Rio Grande Keres. Significant changes really seemed to wait until the 1610 arrival of additional friars with Governor Peralta (Scholes and Bloom 1944:330). It is after 1610 that missionary activities really began. Espinosa said that "the early decades of the seventeenth century witnessed a period of phenomenal success by the Franciscan missionaries sent there" (Espinosa 1988:xv). It really appears that the Pueblo Indians, especially those in the Rio Grande Valley region, actually accepted Christianity and stopped doing their ancient ceremonies during this early period of missionary activity ca. 1610–26. By the time Benavides arrived in 1626, native religion was evidently largely supplanted by Christianity.

BENAVIDES AND PEREA, 1626–1639 √

The well-known accounts of New Mexico by Fray Alonso de Benavides published in 1630 (Ayer 1916; Forrestal 1954) and 1634 (Hodge, Hammond, and Rey 1945) present a picture of the Pueblos' genuinely having accepted Christianity and terminated their ancient ceremonies. This interpretation is at variance with the notion that the old ceremonies persisted in secret throughout the early Spanish missionary period. For example, Dockstader in his review of the early Spanish period regarded the resurgence of kachinas in the Rio Grande Pueblos such as Sandia as the revival of "something which I suspect had never really died—and the success of the Revolt only strengthened their tenacious hold on masked ceremonies" (1985:68).

Benavides was the custodian and commissary of the Franciscan missionaries in New Mexico from 1626 when he arrived with twelve new missionaries to join the fourteen already there (Forrestal 1954:4) until he left New Mexico in the autumn of 1629 (Forrestal 1954:5). It is important to note that he overlapped the stay of Fray Estévan de Perea, his replacement, for several months from the spring of 1629 until the autumn of 1629 (Forrestal 1954:5). This accounts for some of the summaries of the same events in the "True Report of the Great Conversion" published by Perea in 1632 (Bloom 1933; Hodge, Hammond and Rey 1945:210–21) and the memorials published by Benavides.

Benavides presented a glowing account of the success of the conversion, as in the 1634 chapter entitled "The Indians, after baptism, observe our holy Catholic faith well":

Once the Indians have received holy baptism, they become so domestic that they live with great propriety. Hardly do they hear the bell calling to mass before they hasten to the church with all the cleanliness and neatness they can. Before mass, they pray together as a group, with all devotion, the entire Christian doctrine in their own tongue. They attend mass and hear the sermon with great reverence. They are very scrupulous not to miss, on Saturdays, the mass of our Lady, whom they venerate highly. When they come to confession they bring their sins, well studied, on a knotted string, indicating the sins by the knots; and in all humility, they submit to the penances imposed on them. . . . During Holy Week they flagellate themselves in most solemn processions. They take particular care in bringing their children to be baptized. . . . When they fall sick, they at once hasten to confess, and they have great faith and confidence in the priest merely laying his hands upon their heads. They are very subservient to him. . . . They all assist in a body in the building of the churches with all good will, as can be seen by the many we have built, all spacious and neat. The first of their fruits they offer to the church in all reverence and good will. Lastly, they are all very happy and recognize the blindness of idolatry from which they have emerged and the blessings they enjoy in being the children of the church. This they often admit. (Hodge, Hammond, and Rey 1945:99–100)

A similar summary of the success of the conversion appears in Benavides's 1630 *Memorial,* in which he refers to the short time in which the conversion had taken place:

Therefore today they are so well instructed in everything, especially in what pertains to the Faith and Christianity, that it is wonderful to consider that ever since they began to be baptized less than twenty years ago, and particularly during these last eight years when the harvest of souls has been most abundant, they have given the impression of having been Christians for a hundred years. Whenever we pass along the roads and they see us from their pueblos or fields, they all come out to greet us very joyfully, saying: "Praised be our Lord Jesus Christ! Praised be the Most Blessed Sacrament!" When we arrive at their pueblos, they receive us with bouquets of flowers and present us with fish or whatever they have; and the captain of the pueblo welcomes and greets us, saying, among other like things, that as priests of God we honor their pueblos, where they had previously lived as savages. . . . Ever since God created them, this land and its inhabitants were subjects of the demon and, until recently, his slaves, the entire country being covered with estufas of idolatry. . . . But today, after so few years, all that region is covered with churches and with crosses set on pedestals, and its inhabitants greet one another aloud in words of praise for the Most Blessed Sacrament of the Altar and for the Most Holy Name of Jesus Christ. . . . It is a land in which the atmosphere seems to have been corrupted by the presence of the demon and made uninhabitable, but it has now become completely changed and pleasant because the Blessed Sacrament . . . has been carried through it in the processions. (Forrestal 1954:36–37)

That Benavides's account of the success of the conversion was widely accepted by the church authorities can be seen in the *Petition* of Fray Juan de Prada, Commissary-General of the Province and Custodias of the Order of Saint Francis for all of New Spain, written in 1638:

In the most important of these pueblos thirty convents have been built, in addition to many other churches in the smaller villages which are called *visitas.* From these convents fifty religious of my Order [go forth and] administer, without giving way under the labor or yielding to fatigue . . . their labors and operations . . . have been marvelously fruitful, for not only have they taken from the devil the control over as many souls as have been baptized and reduced to the bosom of the Church, but idolatry has been banished and only the true Lord of earth and heaven is worshipped. Furthermore, where there were nothing other than the ceremonial chambers of barbarous idolatries to-day temples may be seen that are frequented by Christians, who acquaint themselves with the Christian faith and good customs. (Hackett 1937:108–9)

In all of these accounts, as in that of Fray Juan de Prada, speaking of the fifty Spaniards residing in Santa Fé, there is revealed a dark side that the Spaniards stood ready to enforce the "conversion" if any of the converted Pueblos should wander:

These Spaniards occupy themselves in bearing arms in defense of the reduced Indians against the barbarous and ferocious heathen who are in the habit of making attacks upon them. They serve also in putting fear in the subjected ones in order that they may not rebel and forget their obedience to the king, our lord, as well as to their ministers of instruction. (Hackett 1937:108)

At the hearing of Nicolás de Aguilar in Mexico City on May 11, 1663, there is an account of the kinds of punishments that the friars utilized in suppressing the native ceremonies, in particular at Hopi and Zuni:

He also declares that about eight years ago when . . . Fray Salvador de Guerra was *guardián* of the pueblo of Jongopabí, they took from the Indians a great amount of cloth and [other] tribute. The Indians went to the custodian to complain, or else to the governor. When the Indians returned to the said places, Fray Salvador had them brought to him, and he went into their homes to search them. He found some feathers, or idols, and consequently seized [the people] and ordered turpentine brought so as to set fire to them. [The witness] does not know how badly he mistreated them all, but he does know a few of them who are marked by the burns. One of them he sent to his pueblo. The Indian was about to die of his burns and could not walk. Fray Salvador provided him with a horse, the Indian dying soon

after in spite of this. . . . He has also heard it said that these religious of Saint Francis caused some Indians in Moqui to dress as very penitent hermits; they walked about praying in penitence, carrying a cross and some large beads, and wearing haircloth shirts. They cooked [only] some pots of herbs for them to eat, so that the Indians were about to die, and complained. (Hackett 1937:141)

One of the few continuities in pueblo ceremonies that can be discerned in Benavides's writings is the role of the flagellant. Since this practice was well described in the 1580s, and also was part of the revived ceremonies in the 1660s, Benavides's account should be repeated:

When they were about to choose one of their number as captain, they assembled in a plaza and tied him naked to a pillar. Then they all flogged him with some cruel thistles and afterwards entertained him with farces and other jests. If during all this he remained completely unperturbed, neither crying nor making grimaces at the one nor laughing at the other, they recommended him as a very valiant captain. And in this way the demon kept them deceived by a thousand superstitions. (Forrestal 1954:35)

From all indications, Benavides himself did not witness ceremonies of this nature, but he was passing on stories about the former rites of the pueblos, "When they were pagan" (Forrestal 1954:34). By 1629 they did that no more.

Fray Estévan de Perea remained in New Mexico until he died there. "By the time of his death in 1639, the New Mexico missions had reached the peak of their development" (Forrestal 1954:xxi). The conversion of the Pueblos during the period ca. 1610–39 apparently was as complete as the conversion of the Yaquis by the Jesuits at the same time in Sinaloa and Sonora (Hu-DeHart 1981). "The period of decline which began soon after was brought on principally by strife between the military and religious authorities" (Forrestal 1954: xxi). Perea was no stranger to this strife, having been Governor Peralta's jailer at Sandia Pueblo in 1612 (Bloom 1933:215). "Between 1645 and 1675 there were several unsuccessful attempts at armed rebellion" (Forrestal 1954:xxi). In other words, there seems to have been a "golden age" from about 1626 to 1639 (Forrestal 1954:xx), followed after about 1639 by a gradual deterioration of the entire relationship between the Spaniards and the Pueblos. As Espinosa summarized things, "Towards the middle of the century, however, oppressive treatment of the Indians by unscrupulous Spanish governors, compounded by economic hardships, weakened respect for all Spanish authority and led to constant hostile acts and plotting by rebellious Pueblo Indian leaders" (Espinosa 1988:xv). The fate of the late seventeenth-century Franciscan missions of New Mexico was very much like that of the early eighteenth-century Jesuit missions of Sinaloa and Sonora and was related to the same process of secularization of the tight communities originally established by the missionaries (Hu-DeHart 1981).

The Spaniards were either extemely naive or there was a real break of kachina ceremonialism among the Rio Grande Pueblos in the early seventeenth century. If the latter view prevails, it should have many ramifications about the continuity of pueblo religion. At a minimum, Pueblo religion after the conversion period would have to be a revival with indeterminable alterations from the prehistoric period, and one cannot discount the accommodation of an equally indeterminable amount of Christian influence. This latter circumstance could account for the kinds of things Parsons was pointing toward (1930).

THE REVIVAL OF KACHINA DANCES IN THE 1660s

There is little question that the revival of kachina dances in the 1660s was linked very directly to the well-known strife between the Spanish governors and the Franciscan missionaries. Most of the documents dealing with this subject in Hackett (1937) are drawn directly from the Inquisition records of the trial of Governor Mendizábal and *alcalde mayor* Nicolás de Aguilar. The whole episode seems to have begun when Governor Mendizábal attended a kachina dance at Hopi and decided that it was not bad and that the Indians should be allowed to do it. One of the primary complaints against Mendizábal was that he had blatantly permitted the Indians to do kachina dances when he was fully aware that the Catholic priests had forbidden them. Not only did he direct them to do that, but he arranged for the dances to be conducted in the Plaza of Santa Fe (Hackett 1937:209). Aguilar described the visit of Mendizábal to Hopi, where he observed a kachina dance and decided there was nothing wrong with the dances, and thereafter ordered the dances to be conducted throughout his jurisdiction and that the friars were not to interfere:

[The witness says] that in that kingdom the Indians were accustomed to perform a dance, which consisted of their coming to the plaza in very ugly masks, each one bringing in his hand some of the fruits which they eat, tied with a maguey cord, and depositing them one after another in a circle in the plaza. The Indians then put on masks representing aged persons and walk among the fruit, making ridiculous figures. Other Indians, either belonging to the place or strangers, come as freely as they wish. He who dares enter the circle to take the fruit, does so; he seizes what he wants, and flees. The Indians in the masks try to stop him and strike him with little paddles which they carry, whereupon those who are caught pay those who catch them, and so on until [the fruit is gone]. But the religious of that kingdom have undertaken to say that this dance is wicked and diabolical, and they stopped it. When Don Bernardo went to govern that kingdom he, seeing that the dance was not evil, permitted it, and it was performed, though the friars continued to say it was evil. But the accused has paid particular attention to these dances, and has found nothing bad in them. . . . [Aguilar says] that the incident of dancing the *catzinas* was not due to him, but to Don Bernardo López de Mendizábal, who ordered it danced in the entire kingdom. Once, upon the day of San Miguel, the Indians told him that they desired to perform this dance, and he told them to dance it, provided they should do no sinful thing, that being the thing which the fathers *doctrineros* reprehended.   (Hackett 1937:141–42)

In regard to Mendizábal having been aware of what he was doing, the following account from 1664 indicates the opinion of the priests:

> Nor can it serve as an excuse to the accused to pretend ignorance of the evils comprised in these dances; for it was enough to know, as he did know, that they had been forbidden to the Indians by the parish ministers ever since the beginning of the conversion until that time, wherefore he should have assumed that they had legitimate reason. . . . He had brought about a meeting of the [Indian] judges of the pueblos in the vicinity of Santa Fé, and had made them perform dances, even the *catzinas*, whereby the remainder of the kingdom was scandalized, for the people had never seen these dances and considered them idolatrous and diabolical. [To this charge] the accused responded that they did not know what they were talking about; that the *zarambeque* and other dances which the Spaniards danced were not prohibited, that he had detected no superstition in the *catzinas* . . . and that they might dance them as long as he was governor.   (Hackett 1937:208)

In the continuing round of allegations and charges made against Mendizábal, there are very detailed descriptions of the kachina dances and dancers, many pertaining to the Eastern Tiwa Pueblos of Tajique and Chilili as well as the Southern Tiwas near Isleta and Piro Pueblos like Alamillo (Hackett 1937). In the course of these long descriptions, the friars describe the flagellation that seems to have been a regular feature of the dances from the 1580s, through Benavides's time and at least until the 1660s. A comparison between these descriptions and modern Hopi kachina dances and dancers will reveal many similarities. Anderson prepared a summary list of such traits (1956:42). These accounts do not leave much credibility to Parsons's 1928 notion that the kachina cult was an emulation of Christianity. Certainly, the Span-

iards summarizing the dances for this trial did not see the kachinas as an emulation of Christianity.

Of particular interest are the several accounts of the kachina dances that were held during this period in Santa Fe at the invitation of the governor:

> The accused also ordered the Indians of his district to go to Santa Fé and dance the *catzinas*, and they donned their costumes and their devilish masks in the very *casas reales*, from which place they went out upon the plaza to dance. The accused gave them watermelons and other things customarily used and offered during these dances. . . . He also told the Indians to go ahead and perform the *catzinas*; that the fathers were a lot of drunkards, and that their sowings were just like the *catzinas*. . . . The accused said publicly in a loud voice in the corridor of the *casas reales* . . . that if it were not for the necessity of upholding his dignity as governor he would himself go out and perform those dances, and for a little he would do it anyway.   (Hackett 1937:209)

A similar account of the kachina dances in Santa Fe appears in a letter of Fray Garcia de San Francisco dated October 13, 1660, and received in the Holy Office on January 22, 1661:

> When the Indians came to the governor to complain that the religious would not allow them to perform certain superstitious dances of idolatrous character, he said: "They are a thing which the religious abominate, so let them come and dance them." And the Indians of the neighboring pueblos gathered in the villa, and they dressed themselves in their abominable masks in a hall of the palace, and performed the dances, offering to the devil watermelons and other things. These dances were often repeated in the palace and on the plaza. They are called the *catzinas*, and are prohibited by all the devout ministers who have been here.   (Hackett 1937:156)

Fray Nicolás de Freitas testified on January 24, 1661, that the kachina dances in Santa Fe had taken place "about the end of September or the beginning of October of the past year, 1660," at the command of governor Mendizábal (Hackett

1937:158). While detailed, and indicative of the politics of the period, the dances at Santa Fe are an oddity and do not reflect the wide resurgence of kachina dances in nearly all of the pueblos.

More instructive in the larger setting is the account by Esteban Clemente, the native Indian governor of the Pueblos of Las Salinas (the Eastern Tiwas and Tompiros) (Ivey 1988) and the Tanos. Clemente, a very capable interpreter of six Indian languages of New Mexico, composed a letter in the presence of Fray Diego de Santander at San Buenaventura de Humanas mission on November 30, 1660, in which he described the kachina dances in general and specifically those among the pueblos of his jurisdiction:

> As to what are the *catzinas* which the Indians of this land dance, and why they do it, I say that I certify and make oath that some of them have very ugly painted masks; certain of the Indians put them on and go to dance in them, and make the people think that they come from the other life to speak to them. There are other dances in which they fast; they fast as many days as they can, and afterward the one who has fasted distributes some feathers to those whom he knows, who are the fortunate ones. On the day on which the *catzinas* are to be danced they sweep the plaza of the pueblo, and the faster, as an acolyte, places on the ground some feathers and flour, and he who fasted stands upon it; they do the same thing when they reach the north, west, and south sides of the pueblo. They lead him to an underground room to give him certain drinks; all this they do in order to have good fortune and to be brave. There are other dances called *catzinas*, in which many people come out with masks on, to dance in the costume of men and women, all of them being men. The purpose for which they do this is not known. They perform other dances, in which they worship an idol, and each one offers him whatever he likes, and they set up an altar. These are the *catzinas* which I know to be evil, although I have heard that there are others; but as I have not verified these superstitions I do not certify to more than this. I also certify and make oath that in the pueblos of Cuarac and Taxique, in my jurisdiction, Captain Nicolás de Aguilar, *alcalde mayor* of these

> pueblos, commanded the Indians to dance the *catzinas*, and they danced them. . . . All this is the truth and I have seen it and heard it, and because there is no notary nor is one made use of in this land, I certify and make oath on my own behalf to all that is herein contained. Dated in the pueblo of Xumanas, November 30, 1660.   (Hackett 1937:165)

The above account by Esteban Clemente is of extraordinary importance because he was a Pueblo Indian, was in a position of political importance in the Jurisdiction of Las Salinas, and knew the languages of the area, presumably those of this jurisdiction, which would include Eastern Tiwa (spoken at Chilili, Tajique, and Quarai) (Ivey 1988:24), Tompiro (and thus, Piro as well), and Tano or Southern Tewa. As an overview summary, it should be regarded as applying to the Tompiro Pueblos (Abo, Humanas and Tabirá), the Eastern Tiwa (Quarai, Tajique and Chilili), and the Tano (San Cristóbal, San Lázaro, Galisteo and perhaps Keres-speaking San Marcos; Figure 11.1). One can readily infer that in 1660 kachina dances were being conducted in all of these Pueblos.

The whole episode with Governor Mendizábal and Nicolás Aguilar terminated with the arrest of Mendizábal by Juan Manso representing the Holy Office on November 22, 1660, at Los Mansos and his transportation to Mexico City (Hackett 1937:168), where he was placed in the "secret prison." Subsequently, Aguilar was arrested by the Holy Office in Isleta Pueblo on April 11, 1662, and taken to Mexico City to the "secret prison" (Hackett 1937:169). The hearing of Mendizábal's case ended in March 1664, at which time he was very ill. Mendizábal died in the secret prison on September 16, 1664 (Hackett 1937:227). Aguilar was convicted, fined, and banished from New Spain.

The full range of testimonies submitted in the trial of Mendizábal make it clear that kachina dances in the Rio Grande Pueblos were widespread during his tenure. For example, Captain Juan Griego testified in November 1661 that "the *catzinas* were danced with Mendizábal's permission in Sandia, San Marcos, and Galisteo" (Hackett 1937:183). In November 1661 Captain Juan Varela de Losada also testified "[that they danced the *catzinas* in the pueblo of La Alameda in December of 1660.] He saw the flat roofs of the pueblo full of people . . ." (Hackett 1937:183). In September 1661 Captain Andrés Hurtado testified that the Indians of Alamillo, one of the Northern Piro Pueblos (Figure 11.1), said to him that Mendizábal ordered them to dance the *catzinas*, "threatening them with punishment if they did not dance them" (Hackett 1937:186). Captain Hurtado also stated that Father Francisco de Acevedo collected the masks in the Pueblo of Alamillo (Hackett 1937:186). On September 18, 1660, Fray Nicolás de Chávez testified that "they found that the Indians of Pujuaque were dancing the *catzinas* in the darkness of night right in the plaza of the pueblo, which is very small. They were singing their songs in their own language . . ." (Hackett 1937:152). Overall, these accounts make it clear that in 1660 there were kachina dances in the pueblos of the Piro, Tompiro, Eastern Tiwa, Southern Tiwa, Hopis, Keres, Northern Tewa, and Tano or Southern Tewa (Figure 11.1).

TERMINATING THE REVIVAL

The revival of kachina dancing was abruptly terminated by the arrival on April 28, 1661 (Hackett 1937:166), of Fray Alónzo de Posadas, the commissary of the Holy Office in New Mexico and the chief representative of the Inquisition. He proceeded to terminate the dancing of the kachinas throughout New Mexico, as he documented in this letter to the Holy Office dated May 23, 1661:

> I arrived in the *custodia* and kingdom of New Mexico on April 28th of this year, 1661. . . . As is publicly and notorously known to all the inhabitants of this kingdom, and as I found in this *custodia*, the Indians are openly idolatrous, dancing superstitious dances with permission of Don Bernardo López de Mendizábal, governor of these provinces.

> Knowing the great danger to their souls which falls not alone upon the natives but also upon those who see these dances, especially those of low degree, such as the *mestizos* and mulattoes . . . and it being my duty to provide the remedy, both because I am custodian and ecclesiastical judge, and because I am the commissary of your very illustrious lordship, I commanded Father Fray Diego de Santander to read . . . the letter in which the various illicit dances are prohibited by your lordship. It was read in this convent of La Isleta on that day at high mass; and I was afterward told by a Spaniard that there had been [maintained] openly in this pueblo a council chamber or room below the ground, which was full of idols, offerings, masks, and other things of the kind which the Indians were accustomed to use in their heathenism, and that the same condition prevailed in the rest of the pueblos, or at least in most of them. I ordered the father secretary to take with him the father *guardián* and minister of this convent and two other Spaniards, and go to this council chamber or temple, for such they say it appears to be, and take away all the paraphernalia and . . . bring them, which they did. I then sent orders to all the other ministers of this *custodia* to do the same thing, and to report everything to me, and if anyone tried to prevent their doing it they were to advise me at once, giving all details . . . and I have heard that a great quantity of objects of this kind has been collected as a result. (Hackett 1937:166–67)

The orders of Posadas were carried out and the kachina dances terminated, with many masks collected and destroyed. Anderson cited a December 8, 1661, letter to the Inquisition in Mexico City in which Posadas reported a "total of more than 1600 masks found (1956:38)." As Anderson observed, this quantity of masks "certainly indicates a very flourishing mask cult" (1956:38).

KACHINA RELIGION CONTINUITY DURING THE CONVERSION

One of the nagging considerations is how the knowledge of Pueblo ceremonialism survived through the years of the conversion so that the revival in 1660 was possible. Some suggestion of this is provided in the May 21, 1661, account of events at Quarai by Thomé Dominguez, retired *sargento mayor* of Isleta:

> He also deposed . . . that a very old Indian in that pueblo had sent word to them to come out to receive him, and that they had done so. . . . They asked the old man who he was, for they did not know him. He said to them: "Don't you know me? I am not surprised, for you have kept me in exile for so many years, but now I am coming back because now you are living as I desire; now I am going to be happy among you, wherefore I bring you this fir branch in my hand. (Hackett 1937:178–79)

Were there people who remained in "exile," living outside of the converted pueblos in the hills who were able to revive the ceremonies that had been put aside for nearly fifty years? It is hard to really know much about this period, but accounts like this suggest that pueblo ceremonies were kept alive by people who were not converted, and lived outside the pueblos maintaining the knowledge of the old ceremonies sufficiently to be able to teach the others when the occasion arose as it did during the 1660s.

Since Mendizábal started the whole affair by witnessing kachina dances at Hopi, where they were "accustomed" to performing the dances (Hackett 1937:141), the Hopis obviously kept at least some of the ceremonies going there. Some of the knowledge about conducting the ceremonies in the mid 1600s could therefore have reached the eastern Pueblos from Hopi. There is the account from an eastern pueblo that even those thirty years old "still recall the shadows of their heathenism" (Hackett 1937:151), suggesting that even those obviously born after the missions began knew some of the songs and ceremonies. Some of the secluded rock art locations away from the pueblos, like those near Abo, Tenabó, and Tajique may have been places where the old ceremonies and songs were preserved in secret (P. Schaafsma 1980; 1992*b*). Clearly future research is needed on this topic.

KACHINA CEREMONIES AFTER 1661

After Posada's suppression, there is very little indication that kachina dances were conducted in the eastern Pueblos for the next twenty years. However, following the 1680 revolt, many of the eastern Pueblos revived the ceremonies as was well documented by Otermin's finding and burning of masks and ceremonial paraphernalia when he came back in 1681 (Anderson 1956:42–43). This revival seems fully appreciated by most scholars concerned with the history of the kachina cult in the Southwest (Adams 1991). However, the documents of the 1660s show that the 1680 revival was a secondary revival of ceremonies that were deeply rooted in the eastern Pueblos and were fully developed in the eastern Pueblos at the time reliable chronicles appeared in the 1580s.

Following the return of Vargas in 1692 there is very little mention of kachinas or other Pueblo ceremonials in the documents leading up to the June 4, 1696, revolt (Espinosa 1988). The many letters and reports from the missionaries in the pueblos during the 1694–96 period are extremely detailed about events and practices in the eastern Pueblos, and there is little to suggest that kachina dances were in any manner apparent to the missionaries. If there were any kachina ceremonies taking place among the eastern Pueblos, they had become deeply hidden and kept from the view of the Spaniards. By the time of the 1776 inventory of the Pueblos conducted by Fray Francisco Atanasio Domínguez (Adams and Chavez 1956) there is nothing to suggest that kachina dances were being conducted in any of the Rio Grande pueblos. If they were active, they were so well hidden that they escaped his inquisitive eye and were apparently unknown to the resident Franciscan missionaries—many of whom had lived in the pueblos for years. Whatever the fate of kachina ceremonies in the eastern Pueblos after 1692, there is little question that the earlier documents make it clear that kachina ceremonies were a dominant feature of the eastern Pueblos at the time of contact and somehow were retained in enough viability to be strongly revived during the 1660s and during the period 1680–92 while the Spaniards were gone.

Conclusion

No discussion of kachinas in the Southwest can ignore the wealth of information latent in the documents of the 1660s. The picture of widespread and deeply rooted kachina ceremonialism among the eastern Pueblos at the time of Spanish contact is fully in agreement with the wealth of archaeological information that is now available (P. Schaafsma 1980, 1992*b*). We should also now firmly lay to rest Parsons's 1928 proposal that kachinas developed at Zuni after ca. 1800 when the Franciscan missionaries left and the Zuni hierarchy took over the former functions of the missionaries. The kachina religion was fully developed in all the southwestern Pueblos long before the first Europeans set foot in the New World.

12

The Changing Kachina

BARTON WRIGHT

O NE OF THE concepts that seems far too prevalent in the Southwest is that petroglyphs, pictographs, ceramic representations, kiva murals, and the like can be easily identified with contemporary kachinas. Such a contention is fraught with problems, some of which have been addressed through current research and some which have not. Foremost among these problems is an accurate identification of a group producing a given ideogram and the ability to separate it from neighboring areas. It is insufficient to identify a depiction as belonging to a prehistoric region, as these area divisions are far too broad in scope to allow meaningful comparisons with contemporary pueblos. It also seems unlikely to me, in the light of our current knowledge of kachinas, that comparisons that cross great stretches of time or space are very meaningful. Usually these efforts are long on archaeology and short on kachina identifications. It would seem much better to work from the known to the unknown and far more likely to succeed if a contemporary village was contrasted with a temporally remote relative in the same region. An ideogram from Awatovi might be compared to one from Kawaika-a, for instance, or one from Walpi against one from Sikyatki. This would have some assurance of a coherency of imagery that could be extended in time.

A facet of this same problem arises in the identification of the personae that are being portrayed. The criteria that are used must be distinctive and not of a nature so general that it incorporates a broad spectrum of representations. Based on superficial resemblances it is easy to say that a combination of bulging eyes and a great mouth full of teeth represents a Whipper kachina rather than a class of beings or that the presence of a humpback and a flute indicates the kachina Kokopelli. In the first instance at least one of the many interpretations possible could just as easily be a Chief of Direction, the deity Masau, the ogre Soyoko, or the gentle kachina Ho-ote, to name but a few. In the second the ideogram could be Kokopelli, or Ololowishkya, or a dancer, a hunter, a trader, or a representation of the locust who is not a kachina but a fragment of folklore. Among the Hopi alone there are various classes of beings, some of whom are deities, others that may be divinities, some who are chief kachinas, other dancing kachinas, as well as priests, folk heroes, and animals. To indiscriminately call them all kachinas without understanding their differences and to base comparisons with different areas on their superficial resemblances is to obscure any meaningful understanding of the phenomena.

Assuming that one has isolated a given area and identified a particular ideogram as a kachina, then one is faced with the problem of change. Do kachinas change, and if so, how rapidly? An example of the difficulties involved is present in one of the most often-quoted identifications of a kachina: that of a painting from Room 788 at Awatovi (Plate 16). Watson Smith, in his report on the kiva murals (1952:304–5), states unequivocally that "no probable, possible shadow of doubt, no possible doubt whatever" exists but that the figure represented is of Ahöla as he appears at Powamu. He then qualifies this by saying, however, that there is also a strong resemblance to the Wuwuyomo and Wupamo masks and to Ahulani and Hopinyu. The criteria that Smith lists by which he identifies the kachina

Ahöla are the following: a circular mask with a divided face of two colors and the presence of a black triangle on the lower part of the face. The two halves of the face are decorated with stars as are the large quartered ears. The head is decorated with what appear to be two red macaw feathers at either side of an eagle feather placed slightly above each ear. It is possible that a third set was placed on the crown of the head.

An examination of the kachinas he lists discloses some interesting data revealing that neither characterization of Ahulani (Figures 12.1e, 12.1f) (Fewkes 1903:pl.LX; Colton 1959:164) resembles Ahöla in the slightest, nor does Hopinyu (Fig. 12.1b), whose helmet is hemispherical, not circular, and who possesses a snout, and whose face is divided horizontally below the eyes as well as vertically. The only similarity is the presence of stars on a partially divided face. Wupamo (Figures 12.1j and 12.1k), who varies by mesa, is generally pictured as he appears on First Mesa with a circular mask surrounded by alternating eagle plumes and small branches with soft feathers attached. However, the face has no features that resemble the Awatovi painting with the exception of the face being divided in different ways. The Wuwuyomo (Figure 12.1g) has a similar circular mask with three eagle feathers alternating with small branches holding soft feathers around its periphery. The face is divided, with one side being yellow and the other brown and both sides being decorated with black stars or crosses. The bottom of the face has a black triangle with no black bar below and it has a large curled snout. Ahöla (Plate 16a), whom the Awatovi figure is identified with, has a circular mask with a corona of eagle feathers and red horse hair around it. The face is divided both horizontally and vertically, and on either side of this division the face is yellow and brown with black crosses or small dots as decoration. A black triangle is inserted into the dark bar that lies across the bottom third of the face, and from it protrudes a curled yellow snout. The Awatovi mural figure (Plate 16b) lacks a snout and has elaborately decorated ears with a quartered design sprinkled with stars and turkey-feather pendant earrings. The black triangle on its face and the corona of feathers is set more in the fashion of Wuwuyomo than Ahöla. There is, however, more similarity between Ahöla and Wuwuyomo than there is between the mural painting and either of these two kachinas.

Interestingly enough, a canteen of Awatovi Polychrome (A.D. 1600–1700) was recovered from the site of the same name by Helen Naha that shows Ahöla almost exactly as he appears at First Mesa today (Plate 16c). This would seem to indicate that the Awatovi painting is not that of Ahöla but of a related kachina that has been lost. Additional support for this hypothesis comes from a second canteen found at Sikyatki Village. This canteen of Sikyatki Polychrome (A.D. 1600–1675) is decorated with an image (Plate 16d) that is much closer in detail to the being shown on the wall of Room 788 at Awatovi. All this exercise does is to point out that the criteria used in identifications should incorporate every available detail before naming it a particular kachina and submitting it to print.

On the subject of change, one of the most common statements regarding Hopi kachinas is that their chief kachinas never change (Earle & Kennard 1971:7). This appears to be an assumption based, at least for the present, on studies that may be of inadequate historical depth and on the statements of those who possess the chief kachinas but do not have a method of recording historical data other than through oral tradition. The resulting conclusion is that the chief kachinas or *wuye* are unchanging and certainly in the case of Ahöla this would appear to be true. It is not necessarily true over a period of time, however. The presence of Ahöla on the Awatovi Polychrome (A.D. 1600–1700) canteen indicates that this particular kachina at least has remained relatively unchanged for over three hundred years. In addition, there are other ceramic reproductions of Ahöla-like beings from both Pottery Mound and

Matsakya that could possibly extend this representation another two hundred years (Smith et al.: 1966, Fig. 77b, also Fig. 77c).

Despite the apparent longevity of some chief kachinas there are processes whereby change can and does occur often within a relatively short interval. Variations can appear that will eventually shift not only the structure within which these beings act but their appearance as well. These changes or modifications can have a definite effect on the interpretation of some archaeological phenomena and historical movements, as well as adding to our understanding of cultural processes.

To enumerate some of the ways in which even the most important kachinas may change it is easiest to begin with the obvious and proceed to the more obscure processes. A few of these processes are as follows:

1. Outside interference
2. Intercultural drift
3. Variations on a theme

Of these the impact of outside interference on the kachinas is the most easily traced, for it is the result of European beliefs and mores which have been clearly expressed. While it is possible that the Spanish were not the first to affect the kachina cult and its representations, they were certainly the first to record their efforts to eradicate or change these native beliefs.

The Spanish priests, regardless of when or where they came into the Southwest, were intent upon a single objective; namely the immediate conversion to Christianity of any Native American encountered. This goal was most easily achieved by either subverting or eradicating whatever native religion was found. For the Pueblo people it consisted of an intensive effort to exterminate any ceremonies or manifestations of the kachina cult (see C. Schaafsma, this volume). These Spanish programs have been thoroughly documented by historians, but mainly they consisted of the destruction of kivas, altars, masks, dolls, and if need be the individuals associated with them. The results were not only the loss of ceremonial gear but also the decimation of native priests, chiefs, and elders—in other words, those whose ceremonial knowledge was the greatest. Thus, in addition to the destruction of the materials of religion the Spanish destroyed centuries of accumulated ceremonial knowledge, contributing to a steady diminution of individuals who knew the exact content of their religion of which the form and function of the kachinas is an integral part. These losses required some form of adaptation to continue a ceremony or to prevent a particular kachina from being lost when the primary steward of such information had been killed. The impact of the hiatuses in ceremonialism created by the Spanish cannot be overemphasized. If Spanish actions were sufficient to reduce the number of inhabited pueblos from sixty-six to twenty in their first two hundred years (Spicer:1962:266), consider what the internal disruption within each village must have been. Regeneration of any element undoubtedly required the combined knowledge of every individual even remotely concerned with the affected portions of their religion.

Although not directly attributable to the Spanish Christianization policy, the Hopi Shalako serves as a case in point to illustrate how the loss, reaction, and adaptation of a religious element can be handled and its effect upon the iconography.

In 1853–54 and again in 1866–67 smallpox epidemics devastated the Hopi villages. In between came a disastrous drought accompanied by raids from the Apache, Navajo, and in one instance by a troop of the United States Army who mistakenly presumed First Mesa to be inhabited by Navajo. The entire village of Sichomovi stood virtually abandoned (Bartlett:1936:36), and the inhabitants of almost every other village suffered enormous losses of life primarily from smallpox, but also from starvation and the raids. To survive, many of the Hopi fled to either the Zuni or the Havasupai for refuge. Because most of the major ceremonialists are usually elderly they are always in a high-risk category, and it seems safe to assume that among the uncounted dead there must have been many whose religious knowledge was of prime importance. The effect of this period on the Hopi would have been similar to the Spanish impact on the Rio Grande villages.

Some of the results of these circumstances can be seen in the records of early ethnographers. Foremost is the presence of a new kachina, the Sio Shalako, whose first appearance came in 1870 and second in 1893 (Stephen:1936:412–54; Parsons:1939:509n, 864, 972–73, 1097, 1104). Through ethnographic reports of this event it is possible to trace some of the changes in the form of the kachinas and the format in which they appeared.

Ethnologists have mistakenly assumed that the appearance of the Sio Shalako was an effort by the Hopi to borrow the totality of the Zuni Shalako (Wright 1984) whereas it seems far more likely that it was an attempt to replace the Hopi Shalako lost during the devastating period of the 1860s. Support for this contention comes from the fact that First Mesa had originally possessed a Hopi Shalako ceremony, but in 1893 the Hopi stated that it had not been given for over thirty years. Furthermore, masks of these early Hopi Shalako from First Mesa have surfaced in collections and been photographed within the last quarter-century. And last, when the Hopi borrowed the Shalako from Zuni it was originally presented in the ceremonial format of the Hopi Shalako but then became progressively more distinctive until by 1916 it was a unique ceremony. This Sio Shalako (Plate 17), a new kachina, combined elements of both the Hopi and the Zuni Shalako and became one of the sacred beings of the Badger clan.

The primary differences between the Sio Shalako and the Zuni Shalako is in the dress. The Sio Shalako comes garbed in a full skirt of eagle feathers as did the Hopi Shalako. The face, however, is the same as that of the Zuni, but it is marked by a black band behind the bulging eyes.

It is in the personnel of the Shalako procession where the changes are most apparent. In the 1893 performance, the first recorded, there were four Sio Shalako (Zuni has six), two males and two females. They were preceded by four Wuwuyomo rather than the Council of the Gods as at Zuni. Leading was Eototo and following was Hahai-i Wuhti with the warrior Akush guarding. Two of these kachinas, Eototo and Hahai-i Wuhti, are present in the format of the Hopi Shalako. The presence of the Wuwuyomo and their guard Akush appear to be a Hopi version of the Zuni Council of the Gods. The only beings that can be called Zuni in this group were a chorus of Koyemsi and two Salimopaiya. However by 1916 the constitution of the group had shifted until there were four Sio Shalako, all male, led by Shulawitsi and four Saiatasha and accompanied by four Yamuhakto and a chorus of Koyemsi. This is a distinct shift from the earlier Hopi version to one more definitely related to the Zuni Shalako.

The lost Hopi Shalako, formerly found on all three mesas, returned to the Second Mesa village of Shungopavi by a strange set of coincidences. When Fred Kabotie was working in the basement of the New Mexico Museum of Fine Arts as a young man he came upon two very large tablitas which he recognized as Hopi Shalakos from the descriptions of his grandfather. He painted a picture of the two kachinas accompanied by Eototo and Hahai-i Wuhti and sold it. (This picture eventually ended up in the Department of the Interior in Washington, D.C.) On a trip home before selling it Fred showed the picture to his grandfather, who in tears told him that they had not been able to give the Hopi Shalako since he was a boy. In conference with other old men from Shungopavi and, although the painting had been sold, from drawings made by Fred and an examination of two petroglyphs near the village, they arrived at the appearance and an approximation of the personnel and format of the ceremony. The accompanying Tukwinong kachinas and their Manas were retrieved from their hiding places as

well as the Sotuknangu and Danik'china, and in 1937 the Hopi Shalako was given once more after a lapse of over seventy years. However, through a somewhat ironic twist, the tablitas Fred had seen were not from Second Mesa as he believed but from First Mesa. Even so, they must have been very similar to those with which Fred's grandfather and uncle were familiar.

In the intervening years the Hopi Shalako has been given at Shungopavi in 1952, 1957, 1968, 1972, and 1981, and in that interval the kachinas associated with the Shalako pair have changed (Eototo did not appear in 1972 or 1981). The faces of the Tukwinong Mana and Tukwinong Taka have changed their symbols. In 1957 the face of the Mana was very plain, being divided vertically by a single black line with the right side painted yellow and the left blue and set with triangular eyes. The terraced tablita bore no designs at all, but by 1981 the tablita had a cloud design, the face divided by a broad black-and-white line. The right side of the face was painted white and the left side yellow, while the lower margin had a row of red clouds, and the eyes were painted realistically. The face had become almost an exact copy of the First Mesa Tukwinong Mana as represented by the masks sold from that location. The Tukwinong Taka, whose headdress consisted of three white tablets or slabs rimmed in black, acquired a tripartite cloud symbol on the outer ones. Added to the spruce that covered the face were long cattails that hung to the knees where before these festoons were much shorter and more mosslike. No information exists on possible variations in the appearances of the Sotuknangu and Danik'china.

To summarize what occurred in the span of less than one hundred years: there was the appearance of a new kachina, Sio Shalako, who was added to the roster of the Badger clan; the adoption by the Hopi of the Zuni kachinas of Saiatasha, Hututu, Yamuhakto, the Salimopaiya, and possibly a Zuni version of Kokosori; and the reintroduction of the Hopi Shalako at Shungopavi alone. Here within four decades there has been the disappearance of one kachina and changes in the appearance of at least two others to conform to kachinas of a different time and village.

In the second instance, that of cultural drift, the Somaikoli is an excellent example. This supernatural, the so-called Blind Kachina, is a curing kachina among the Northern Tewa as well as in all of his appearances among the eastern Pueblos. Presumably Somaikoli was brought with the Tewa in the 1700s when they migrated down the Rio Grande and across through Laguna/Acoma to Zuni and finally to the Hopi mesas. Somaikoli is present in all of the pueblos along this route as well as in the Tewa village of Hano and in the Hopi villages of Walpi and Mishongnovi, although only the last four villages are considered here (Plate 18). Folklore has it that Somaikoli arrived quite late at Mishongnovi, but the date is not verifiable other than it was after he appeared at Walpi, which followed his arrival at Hano.

As a kachina Somaikoli belongs to the Yayatu, a society of magicians, who can control fire and space as well as cure various ailments. The kachina is believed to be lame as well as blind, and thus at Laguna he is the patron of the Saiyap society, which cures for lameness, while at Zuni the masks belong to the Shumaakwe Society, which cures for blindness. Among the Tewa he also cures for blindness, but regardless of the village in which he appears he is always led by the Yayatu.

Although the form of the performance and the cast of participants remains unchanged, as this kachina passes from one village to the next his appearance changes. Apparently when the ceremony moves to a new village its function may take on a new dimension as well. Consequently when Somaikoli arrived at Walpi the Yayatu, who controlled fire, as well as the kachina became linked to Masau, who also controls fire. Masau's power with fire seems to be one that involves warmth and germination in darkness and inevitably this is associated with fertility. Hence by the time Somaikoli reached Mishongnovi his function was as much for fertility as for curing.

In each of these four villages where Somaikoli comes, the kachina has seven different aspects so that a proper representation of his appearance among the Hopi, Zuni, and Tewa would entail twenty-eight variations in his mask and parts of his costume.

The third example is popularization or variations on a theme. When popularization occurs the result is the appearance of multiple variations of a kachina which may appear only within a particular pueblo or among many neighboring villages as well. The Zuni Kokkokshi (Plate 21) essentially identical to the Hopi Sio Angak'china (Plate 19) are almost the epitome of such a thematic variation. The Kokkokshi are considered to be the first kachinas of the Zuni. They represent the children lost in the water while crossing the river near Kolhuwabaw'a where their spirits drifted down to that sacred lake to become the first Kokkokshi (Cushing:1896:412–54; see Tedlock, this volume). They are considered to be the beautiful kachinas, kind, gentle, the ultimate rain-bringers who are to be equated with the Shiwanni. Their songs are distinctively different, being far more melodic than rhythmic. Because of their sacrosanct nature every aspect of their appearance at Zuni is so rigidly controlled by tradition that no variation is possible. But there are a number of other kachinas that are variations of this kachina at Zuni which are not considered to be as sacred as the Kokkokshi and consequently can be changed. Despite any and all changes these secondary kachinas are recognized as being derivative from the Kokkokshi. The process whereby this occurs has not been studied, but hypothetically it could occur where tradition controls so tightly that the creative urge is stifled. But if a kachina is produced with just enough variation to prevent confusion with the original then the songs may be changed and the dance may occur at a different time. Other kachinas may accompany them, or the dance form may alter slightly.

Whatever the mechanism is that allows this process to occur at Zuni it has produced, in addition to the Kokkokshi, Upikaiapona or Atsam

Kokkokshi (Plate 20), the Hekshina Shelowa or red-bodied version (Plate 22), the Upikaiapona Tamayakwe, Whopone Shelowa, and possibly others such as Hahawe. To the east at Acoma the kachina appears under its own name of Kokokshe but at Laguna it is Koapeauts, a version more like the Shiwanni. The kachina surfaces in Cochiti in three different forms, as a Shiwanni and in the Big and Little Zuni Dances or Ashuwa (Plate 25) and Ashuwa Li'kashane (Plate 30). It is present in Santa Ana and San Felipe in two different dance groups of Ashuwa (Plates 31, 32) a name undoubtedly derived from Ashiwi-Zuni. At Zia these two dance groups are the Mekatc (Plate 33) and Croyati Ashuwa, and in Jemez the impersonation is known just as S'urni (Zuni).

To the west the Hopi seized upon this kachina and with their usual creativity produced a large variety of Angak'chinas, the Loose or Long-Haired Kachinas that are the homologues or equivalents of the Zuni Kokkokshi and its derivatives (Plates 19, 23; 28–30; 24). Thus one finds the Sio Angak'china (Plate 19) which is the homologue of the Kokkokshi, but then there is also a Hopi version of the same kachina that differs only in the presence of the colored teeth above the beard. They also produced a homologue of the Zuni Uikaiapona Tamayakwe or Santa Ana Angak'china which is danced both with and without a mask. An older form of the Long-Haired Kachina is the Hokyan Angak'china (Plate 24) described by Stephen (1936:280–369) in the 1890s.

The Bare-Footed or Katoch Angak'china (Plate 23) is a Hopi version of the Zuni Hekshina Shelowa (Plate 22) except that it comes without moccasins. Another form of the kachina is attributed to the Tewa and is called the Pala Sowichmi Angak' or the Tewa Red-Bearded Long-Haired Kachina (Plate 28), which is very similar to the Zuni Whopone Shelowa, the Santo Domingo and Santa Ana Ashuwa and the Jemez S'urni. With little change in costume, body, color, and face decoration the Long-Hair can become the Tasaf Angak'china (Plate 25) or the Cochiti Long-Hair, Kotite Angak'china (Plate 27). There are other derivatives among the Hopi such as the Talawi-pik' Angak'china who wears lightning upon his head or the Pushung' Angak' who drums.

Thus this single impersonation of the Zuni Kokkokshi has, like a starburst, produced well over two dozen related kachinas in at least a dozen different pueblos but over what length of time this occurred remains unknown. It is possible to determine additional relationships within this kachina cluster, but for the moment their diversification is sufficient to emphasize the fact that all kachinas change because they are not only a religious statement but also a creative outlet and consequently are subject to improvisation. The reasons they change, the rate at which they do, the differences by kachina type, and the form these changes will take are all variables which if understood more fully could be projected back in time.

13

Kachina Images in American Art: The Way of the Doll

J. J. BRODY

IMAGES OF kachinas were, and are, made to serve a variety of purposes related to the sacred realm within the societies that use them.[1] My essay discusses the transformation of these images into secular art objects. As such, they now serve novel purposes for the societies where they are made, as well as for the Euro-American ones that conducted the transformation. How, why, when, and for what reasons were kachina images initially acquired by Euro-Americans, and when and why and in what senses did they become classified or reclassified as art objects in their new settings?

The Euro-American classification of kachina images as art was a gradual process rather than a single act. It often occurred far removed in time and space from the point of acquisition, and it involved several different subcategories of Euro-American art. Further, classifications of appropriated kachina images as one thing rather than another changed over time and across social space, so that we observe a dynamic process that can inform about general relationships between art-classification systems and quite other distinctions in the communities that create and utilize those systems. Other observations may also be made, especially of crosscultural behaviors, for the idea-

When he claims to be solitary, the artist lulls himself in a perhaps fruitless illusion, but the privilege he grants himself is not real. When he thinks he is expressing himself spontaneously, creating an original work, he is answering other past or present, actual or potential creators. Whether one knows it or not, one never walks alone along the path of creativity. (Claude Lévi-Strauss 1982:148)

All in all, the creative act is not performed by the artist alone; the spectator brings the work in contact with the external world by deciphering and interpreting its inner qualifications and thus adds his contribution to the creative act. (Marcel Duchamp, in Lebel 1959:78)

tional transformation within the Euro-American world of kachina images into art also had effects on the makers of those images and their communities.

My paper thus differs from the others in this volume in some critical respects. Whereas the others discuss the complex totality of kachinas in terms of native perspectives and contexts, my concern is only with the images, their acquisition by alien societies, and their consequent transformation into art by acts of imagination which we call "classification." I concentrate my attention upon the position of kachina images as aesthetic objects within two historically related but distinct non-native art-classification systems: that of Euro-American, industrial world societies from about the mid-nineteenth century to the early years of the twentieth, and that of the "international" (really global) art community of the twentieth century. I further limit my discussion to the expression of those two systems in the United States.

The objects of my focus are the pictures and carvings of kachinas that were acquired by Euro-American collectors since about 1850. The fact that most were made by Hopi artists is of limited interest to this discussion, and, because my primary attention is upon the world of the collectors rather than of the makers and original users of kachina images, the histories of kachina societies and of earlier kachina imagery, and any meanings that kachinas have for any Pueblo people that are unrelated to the transformation of their images into one or another class of Euro-American art are not considered. There is a kind of crosscultural symmetry here, for I also pass over many issues of world-view, history, and philosophy that drove, and still drives, Euro-American, global, industrial, and postindustrial art communities to take kachina images as well as many other objects of alien, nonindustrial societies and transform them into appropriated arts.

The positions I take here may be objectionable from at least two perspectives. First, they can appear to validate the cultural imperialism that is often expressed when one society appropriates objects from another for uses which transform their meanings utterly. Second, they can appear to trivialize the expressive content of objects and the intended social usages and meanings which inspired, and, in this instance, still inspire their creation (Berlo and Phillips 1992; Price 1989; Torgovnick 1990).[2] Both interpretations are explicitly rejected. The acquisitions, transformations, and appropriations on which I focus occurred and continue to occur as series of associated events triggered by the intrusion of industrial world societies upon the Pueblo universe. History happened, and kachina images became several different kinds of "art" within the larger American society.

I argue that their transformation to one or another kind of art was primarily a response to their formal, aesthetic qualities rather than to any local conditions which caused them to be created in the first place. Therefore, examination of the visual attributes of kachina images on the one hand and of the art-classification criteria of the intruders on the other is essential to gain understanding of the visual and social dynamics of these observed phenomena. The fit between the physical qualities of the objects and any of the imposed alien art classification systems, always expressed by aesthetic judgments, was never stable. Those judgments thus become a measure of the changing social values that were placed on the objects after their removal from original contexts.

Because aesthetic considerations play so important a role in the transformation process, examination of form is the route by which we learn how objects are classified as one thing rather than another. And, since all art classifications are also expressions of value applied to special forms of social communication, locating the social positions of the different art classification systems will expose social meanings that may otherwise be masked. Kachina images can then be recognized as the physical manifestations of complex, open-ended social interactions which make them potentially pertinent to all people.

Collecting Kachina Images

Before about 1920 very few kachina images were acquired as objects of art by their original Euro-American collectors. Most were thought of primarily as ethnographic specimens, as curiosities, or as tangible souvenirs of travel to an exotic place or to the experience of an exotic culture. After about 1920, except for paintings on paper, which are a special case, kachina images were primarily acquired as either generic souvenirs of travel to the Southwest ("curios") or as ethnic "craft-art" objects. Transformation of any kachina image into some other, higher-status category of art generally occurred only after further transfer of possession, and usually in places far distant from their source.

Although images of kachinas seem not to have been collected by Euro-Americans until after the middle of the nineteenth century (Dockstader 1985:101–4), they were known of in various media long before then, having been loosely described by Spanish chroniclers in the sixteenth century and then systematically destroyed by Spanish missionaries for reasons of ideology in the seventeenth (Smith 1952:73–75; see Vivian, this volume, Figure 8.4).

Initial collecting was at Hopi of carvings called *tihu,* now commonly referred to as "kachina dolls." That form of kachina image may not have been as common in 1852, when it was first described by Anglo-Europeans, as it became by the early 1880s, when railroads made the Hopi Mesas somewhat more accessible to curious outsiders (Dockstader 1985:77). By then, most Pueblos other than Hopi and Zuni had effectively cut off access by outsiders to their kachina imagery. Thomas Keam, however, was already well established at his Keams Canyon Trading Post just east of Hopi First Mesa, supplying tourist and curio markets and scientific collectors with kachina

carvings (Wade and McChesney 1980; Figure 13.1). Kachina carving proliferated during the 1890s, and by 1900 some were being made specifically for sale to outsiders (Erickson 1977:24–27).

Systematic institutional collecting began in 1879 with James Stevenson's Bureau of Ethnology expedition to the Southwest (Stevenson 1883:307–422; Plate 34). By 1900, well over a thousand kachina carvings had been acquired at Hopi as ethnographic specimens by such museum professionals as John Wesley Powell, Jesse Walter Fewkes, George A. Dorsey, and Stewart Culin, sometimes for resale to other institutions or individuals. Many hundreds more were sold as curios, and during the 1890s a few large private collections were assembled. Those gathered by southern Californian photographer Adam C. Vroman and his neighbor, writer George Wharton James, later became the core of the large kachina doll collection of the Southwest Museum in Pasadena (Kenagy 1989). Both Vroman and James were avid collectors of Indian objects who had close associations with the Arts and Crafts movement. They seem to have been among the first to consider the carvings as aesthetic objects (Kornstein 1985; Kenagy 1989:13).

While some carvings were certainly acquired directly from Hopi people by short-term visitors, transactions could be difficult without the help of middlemen. Thomas Keam, his friend the ethnologist Alexander Stephens, and H. R. Voth, the Mennonite missionary and amateur ethnologist, all lived at or near the Hopi mesas during the 1880s and 1890s, and all acted as purchasing agents for American and European museums and private collectors. Between 1899 and 1901 Frederick Volz's trading post at Canyon Diablo near Hopi First Mesa became a distribution center for kachina dolls that may have been made for the tourist trade. Some four hundred of these were wholesaled to the Fred Harvey Company in 1901, and in 1904 almost two hundred found their way to the Carnegie Museum of Natural

FIGURE 13.1 Curio Room of Captain Keams,
Keams Canyon, Arizona, 1897. (*Photo by Adam
Clark Vroman. Courtesy Seaver Center for Western History
Research, Natural History Museum of Los Angeles,
negative* V-505.)

History in Pittsburgh by way of George Dorsey,
who bought them from the Harvey Company. He
may have perceived them as "authentic" ethnographic specimens rather than curios (Bol 1991;
Harvey 1963:38–39, 46; Figure 13.2).

Manufacture and sale of Hopi kachina carvings as curios for tourists became proportion-
ately more important as the twentieth century
advanced. Even before World War I, automobile
travel had made Hopi somewhat more accessible,
and paved roads after World War II simplified
access considerably (Goldwater 1969:4). Long before then, however, innovations in wholesaling
made Hopi kachina carvings broadly available,

and they became a generic kind of southwestern souvenir. The Harvey Company through its Albuquerque Indian Department, established in 1902, became a major outlet on both retail and wholesale levels, serving all markets. Other of their retail outlets included as many as seventy-five Harvey Houses associated with the Santa Fe Railroad, and the company supplied many other, sometimes far distant retailers (Harvey 1963:33–34). Meanwhile, its Indian Department, managed by Herman Schweizer, remained a major provider of ethnographically documented kachina images to museums and private collectors until mid-century.

Large collections of kachina carvings continued to be acquired directly or with the help of middlemen by American and European ethnographic museums during the first two decades of the twentieth century, after which older examples became scarce (Kaemlein 1967). Marketing by specialized, elitist, "primitive art" and "Indian art" galleries became important only after World War II. Since then, art galleries and art auction houses in large metropolitan centers have served as important redistribution agents for carvings collected decades earlier and inherited by a new generation of owners—or museum curators—who may have had little interest in them. Those located farthest from the Southwest seem most likely to specialize in older carvings.

After about 1925 museums and juried arts and crafts fairs in the Southwest became major sales outlets for new kachina images, now including paintings on paper. These served also as critical interfaces between the makers and alien purchasers. Until about 1970 nearly all jurors were Anglo-American curio dealers, collectors, or museum curators, who by the simple act of awarding or not awarding blue ribbons exerted great influence on both market prices and aesthetic decisions made by collectors, dealers, and makers of kachina images.

By 1931 the Museum of Northern Arizona in Flagstaff was an active promoter of kachina carv-

FIGURE 13.2. "Volz-type" Hopi kachina doll, "Honawuu/Bear Katcina Tihu", c. 1900. Acquired by George Dorsey of Chicago's Field Museum of Natural History from the Fred Harvey Company, ca. 1903. Purchased by the Carnegie Museum of Natural History, January 1904. (*Courtesy Carnegie Museum of Natural history, number 3165-193.*)

ings as an ethnic craft-art, soliciting them from carvers at Hopi for its annual "Hopi Craft Exhibition." It codified aesthetic qualities that it thought desirable, established stylistic authenticity for those images that met its aesthetic standards, and certified authenticity of subject matter (H. Colton 1940, 1959; M. R. Colton 1938). In addition to its many exhibitions and authoritative publications, from about 1933 it hired Hopi kachina carvers to demonstrate their craft and interact with museum visitors (Anonymous 1966). During the 1960s its gift shop became a major retail outlet for kachina images and other Indian arts and the model for similar shops at most other museums in the region.

Paintings of kachinas on paper became an important art at Hopi during the twentieth century. The first were probably those commissioned by Fewkes in 1900 and published by the Bureau of American Ethnology as "The Codex Hopiensis" (Fewkes 1903; Plate 35). Fewkes was inspired by recently published Mexican codices to have Hopi artists make kachina pictures on paper in order to study native religious symbolism (Fewkes 1903:15). He interpreted the mixed-media paintings in terms of contemporary theories of cultural evolution and folklore and compared the pictures favorably to Mexican and Mayan codices, though without committing to any aesthetic judgment of the Mesoamerican pictures. His primary concerns were with "aboriginal character" and the utility that kachina pictures had to him in provoking discussion among Hopi people about their religious beliefs (Fewkes 1903:16). Native reaction to the exercise soon became negative, and almost two decades passed before Hopi artists again made kachina pictures on paper. The art they created was first made in far-distant Santa Fe, New Mexico.

Fred Kabotie (ca. 1900–1986), while a teen-aged student at the Santa Fe Indian School in 1918, is credited as the first modern Hopi easel painter. His earliest watercolors were made as an extracurricular activity in the living room of Elizabeth DeHuff, wife of the school superintendent. By choice he painted kachinas and other ceremonial subjects that reminded him of home, for "loneliness moves you to express something of your home, your background" (Kabotie 1977:28). Soon another young Hopi, Otis Polelonema (ca. 1900–1981), joined what became an art group, and the two together created a new Hopi kachina art that was outside the framework of traditional Hopi usages and forms of kachina imagery. Their paintings were exhibited along with those by others of the group in 1919 at the Fine Arts Museum of the Museum of New Mexico in Santa Fe (Anonymous 1919). They painted other subjects also, and the entire exhibition was purchased by the writer Mabel Sterne, later Mabel Dodge Lujan, a major force in the burgeoning modernist wing of the Taos art colony.

Polelonema continued to paint, often on commission, after his return home in 1922, but he appears to have had few Hopi followers (Seymour 1988:247). Kabotie stayed in Santa Fe until 1930, enjoying the patronage of its intellectual community, which was in fact international. In the 1930s a few other Hopi painters of kachina images who worked in urban settings were greatly influenced by both Kabotie and Polelonema (Plate 36). Kabotie's influence at Hopi was established after 1937 when he began teaching art at Oraibi High School, and a strong tradition at Hopi of painting kachina images on paper dates from that time.

A more abstract alternative tradition inspired by prehistoric and protohistoric Hopi murals was begun in the 1940s, also by Kabotie. Its fuller development since the 1970s as a fusion of ancient Hopi with Euro-American modernist forms has been by a group of younger artists calling themselves "The Artists Hopid." Their work clearly addresses the position of Southwest Indian art within the broad spectrum of international modernist fine-arts movements (Broder 1978; Brody 1979:608).

Formal Qualities of Kachina Images

Formal changes in kachina images parallel the intrusions of expanding alien market forces upon the Hopi. Early images tend to be stiff, frontal, bilaterally symmetrical, and roughly detailed (Plates 34, 40, Figure 13.3). Carved of cottonwood root, they have moderately rough surfaces and are painted with a limited palette of thick, relatively dull and chalky homemade or commercial pigments. They are iconic, even hieratic in character, and often appear to be in suspended animation with bodies leaning slightly forward, knees bent, and arms fused to the body. Legs also may be joined together. Arms and legs may be painted on the wood rather than carved, and gestures are restricted, with forearms held stiffly across the body and more or less parallel to the waist. The proportion of head to body is generally a squat 1:3. The fusion of sculpted and painted details is most clearly stated on flat slab figures, many of which have carved head features but all other details painted on their rectangular body surfaces. In all cases painting and carving are most elaborated on head areas which are generally the locus for diagnostic iconographic details. Very few carvings stand independently, for they were made to be handled, suspended from rafters, or hung against a wall.

By 1900 a trend toward naturalism and away from the iconic is evident. Dolls wholesaled by Volz in about 1900 and presumably carved for him resemble those from Zuni Pueblo which were not so easily acquired. Volz-style dolls are frontal and elongated, with legs bifurcated and fully carved arms held to the side and extending below the waist. As with Zuni carvings, these are sometimes articulated and gesturing. Muscles and body parts such as fingers may be indicated by carved details, and, as at Zuni, scraps of cloth and other materials were attached as costume details (Figure 13.2). The Zuni-like features of articulation and costuming were soon abandoned, but from about 1900 on, head to body proportions were a more

lifelike 4:1, kilts and other costume details were often carved in place, and natural gestures were commonplace. Most of the diagnostic features of so-called "action dolls" had been introduced.

Smoothly finished surfaces, neatly applied thick and slightly lustrous opaque paint used to describe many small details, and use of pedestals characterize most kachina carvings made for the curio and craft-art markets from the 1930s to the present. These two closely related classes of kachina art are distinguished less by relative differences in style, technical skill, or refinement, than by where and how they are sold, and how closely they adhere to an available documentation of "authenticity" such as a published iconographic canon. Gift shops at major national parks or large tourist hotels can be thought of as selling curios to tourists; those in regional museums or calling themselves art galleries sell craft-art to collectors.

Movement away from iconic and hieratic expression and toward naturalism dominated well before 1930, and most twentieth-century carvings seem to represent kachina impersonators rather than the sacred personages themselves, a difference which may not be a distinction (Plate 37).[3] Finely carved and painted details of muscles, hands, fingers, and fingernails are ubiquitous, as though the objective is to render the most realistic possible human body masquerading as a kachina. Added materials such as cloth and yarn are commonly used, and some carvings of the 1980s are masquerade specific, with removable masks placed on realistically detailed human heads. Paint is almost entirely ancillary and descriptive, and from the mid-1980s is sometimes replaced by washes of color and wood stains, which for the first time place emphasis upon the physical qualities of wood and wood-grain (Plate 38; Teiwes 1991). Most carvings stand on pedestals, making it obvious that they are to be looked at rather than handled. Action figures are increasingly realistic and the ordinary head to body ratio is now an elongated 4.5:1 or 5:1. Short-lived revivals of old-style carvings occurred periodically after about 1940, generally with figures more active, lively, and idiosyncratic than those of the nineteenth century (Plate 39). Other eccentricities made after about 1985 include extremely long and sinuous figures with head to body ratios of 10:1 or greater, and use of clay, stone, and other sculptural materials.

Pictorial conventions of the twentieth century follow somewhat different trends. Images published by Fewkes (1903) have similar proportions to contemporaneous carvings, but most are far more active, show many more narrative and realistic details than do most carvings of the time, and more closely resemble the "revival" carvings noted above (compare Plates 35 and 39). The realistic painting tradition developed by Kabotie and Polelonema and practiced by many artists at Hopi since 1937 has obvious similarities to curio/craft-art carvings, and a number of individuals are adept in both media.

The abstract qualities of the alternative painting tradition of the Artists Hopid are not often seen in kachina carvings. However, their paintings and such novelties as stained carvings and extremely elongated ones synthesize native forms with any of several modernist international art styles. As important, they indicate some degree of acceptance of the value given to artistic idiosyncracy by Euro-American society. Such works, whether or not directed toward alien audiences, are the products of decisions by native makers of kachina images to modify both formal rules and philosophical values to bring them closer to an alien art-classification system. In a tangible way they conceptualize changing social relationships between the artists and the intruding world, and they inevitably alter meanings given to kachina images by either group.

Acts of Classification: From Coarse Monstrosities to Fine Art

Except for paintings on paper, which were ordinarily collected as fine art or ethnic art, the vast majority of kachina images in the Euro-American world are carvings originally acquired because of what they represented. Before 1920 formal aesthetic considerations were rarely a primary selective factor leading to acquisition, and aesthetic judgments by early collectors were often decidedly negative. Yet the objects they acquired are the ones most likely today to be classified as "fine art." Conversely, images made after about 1930 were more likely to be referred to in positive aesthetic terms by their original collectors, but are far less likely than earlier ones to be classified today as "fine art." Over time, the aesthetic classification of kachina images changed in a systematic manner along the continuum: "anti-art" to "kind-of-art" to "fine art."

With rare exceptions kachina images collected before World War I were considered either as curiosities or scientific specimens by their collectors. None were collected for art museums, and most that entered museum collections did so as anthropology specimens within natural history or anthropology museums (Plate 40). Carvings that entered private collections as a kind of art often went into "Indian rooms": "Katcinas, or dolls make interesting objects to use in way of decorations for an Indian room, and a collection of twenty or more would be much admired by your friends" (Vroman 1901 in Kenagy 1989:13). So much so in fact, that a group were included in the popular Indian Room lounge of New York's showplace Hotel Astor during the first decade of the twentieth century (Anonymous n.d.).

The attitude about Indian art expressed by Vroman was no more than a local manifestation of worldwide interest in the art of non-urban, non-industrial people that characterized many Arts and Crafts movements from their beginnings in the mid-nineteenth century (Wichmann 1972). Vroman, James, and others in their circle saw positive moral and ethical values in Native American societies and their arts, and they attempted to emulate some of these in their own lives and art. Even so, kachina carvings were "interesting decorations" rather than "fine art" and, as objects of a "primitive" society, were placed in a segregated position somewhere between nature and culture. That placement was, nonetheless, an opening wedge in their transformation to objects of fine art.

Aesthetic judgments were more likely to be negative—Fewkes was among the few to express neutrality on the issue—until well after the beginning of the twentieth century. Alexander Stephens never pretended that the carvings which interested him greatly were anything other than rude images, and even Fewkes's primary aesthetic concern was that the pictures look authentically "native." Amateur ethnologist and professional Indian fighter Lt. John Gregory Bourke most clearly stated the prevailing anti-art sentiment when he wrote of the kachina carvings which he purchased at the First Mesa town of Hano as "nothing but coarse monstrosities painted in high colors," "idols, which in scores and scores adorn or disfigure the living rooms" (1884:131,254).

It seems likely that prevailing Euro-American opinion about the inherent inferiority of native beliefs and religious practices, bolstered by evolutionary social theory, had something to do with these negative aesthetic judgements, and lack of interest in learning about Pueblo aesthetic views may have been a corollary. Enlightened scientists such as Fewkes and missionaries such as Voth may no longer have considered the images so dangerous as to require destruction, but they still classified them as "idols." As such, they physically embodied both an inferior religious philosophy and faulty ways of thinking about the workings of the physical universe. Pueblo religion and world view needed to be replaced if these "children of nature" (Stevenson 1894) were to improve their lot and advance to higher levels of civilization.

Despite the negative values placed on the images by those first collectors, the classification of them seems to parallel that of Pueblo people. Both seem to agree that rather than be considered art objects the images were to be valued as representational icons that belonged in the sacred realm. Kachina objects made and collected in later years as curios, souvenirs, or craft-art were similarly acquired primarily for representational qualities, but with abstractly expressive iconic values replaced by aesthetically desirable realistic ones and parallel associations with the sacred realm much less clear. Rather than be icons, later images are almost uniformly of human impersonators: they are "kachina dancers" first, "art" second, and two steps removed from the sacred. Their iconic and visual qualities are perceived as "authentic" through the filter of the narrow, marginal, and etic boundaries of knowledge that constrained the collectors who may even expressly deny their spiritual utility as icon or idol (Colton 1959:5; Dockstader 1954:10).

Several factors contribute to this disjunction between iconography and perception of spirituality. First, few twentieth-century collectors had the intensity of interest in iconic affect that is a given for those who are either devoted to practices served by any iconographic system or are dedicated students of such a system. Second, changing political and social attitudes of Euro-Americans brought greater tolerance for diversity of ideologies and world-views. Pueblo beliefs and practices could now be perceived of disinterestedly as legitimate, and kachina images, no longer threatening as "idols," could be classed as only another kind of secularized art subject.

Finally, the publications by Fewkes (1903), and most especially Colton (1959), in their multiple reprintings came to be used almost universally by makers, marketers, and buyers of kachina images as arbiters of iconographic explanation and authenticity. Colton, a natural scientist by training, organized his book as a field guide to his perceptions of diagnostic visual and iconographic attributes of kachinas which he was able to reduce to "keys." It often became, like any biological field guide, a checklist to satisfy casual interest in identifying an unfamiliar form, in this case reducing sacred attributes of the objects to quasi-scientific and secular criteria.

This primacy of iconographic authenticity over abstract formal or expressive qualities defines the

qualified nature of the category "craft-art" as applied to kachina carvings. Attributes of form are
ordinarily definitive in an art taxonomy, and iconography is secondary, but not so here, and in
that respect, the craft-art category extends older
native and Anglo-European perspectives that also
considered subject matter primary. But, by definition, a craft-art object must also conform to
a canon of formal and aesthetic attributes. The
craft-art rules for kachina carvings, initially formalized during the 1930s through the mechanisms of regional museums and Indian arts-and-
crafts fairs, parallel aesthetic principles of the
Arts and Crafts movement, especially by emphasizing craft skills and attention to fine detail.
Mary Russell Colton, co-founder with her husband Harold of the Museum of Northern Arizona
and largely responsible for the original articulation of those rules, was herself an artist raised
in and profoundly committed to Arts and Crafts
principles and philosophy (M. R. Colton 1938).

In recent years, specialized "Indian art" galleries in the Southwest and a seemingly endless
flow of publications contribute importantly to an
ever-expanding critical system for this class of art
which defines several levels of artistic status. The
fundamental principles have hardly changed over
the years: levels of status from curio to craft-art
are measured by success in achieving representational illusionism through application of presumably time-consuming, detailed labor so that
"work" ("craftsmanship") and higher status art are
almost coeval. Yet, kachina objects originating
within the curio / craft-art tradition are seldom
elevated to the highest Euro-American category
of "fine art," which is generally reserved for the
rougher and less detailed carvings that pre-date
World War I. This fits, since neither "work" nor
"craftsmanship" have been positive attributes of
most elitist "fine art" during most of this century.

From the perspective of a late-twentieth-
century art historian with conservative modernist tastes, Bourke and other early collectors could

not have been more wrong in their aesthetic judgments. The kachina images they collected are
precisely the ones that come closest to meeting all
major criteria of Euro-American elitist fine art of
our era. Of all known kachina images, they are
the most likely to be seriously discussed by critics,
scholars, and collectors from outside the Southwest as aesthetic, expressive objects, the most
likely to be exhibited in nonregional art museums
as isolated art objects with minimal labeling information, the most likely to be marketed in elegant
art galleries and international art auction houses,
the most costly, and the most likely to be faked or
stolen (Figure 13.3).

Unless we assume that the early collectors suffered from some hitherto undescribed aesthetic-
deficiency disease, their seeming failure to recognize what are now self-evident aesthetic qualities
is understandable only in terms of their own culture history. From that perspective, their judgments merely conformed to prevailing aesthetic
criteria of their social class. Similarly, the failure
of twentieth-century curio / craft-art objects to
become "fine art" even as late-nineteenth-century
"monstrosities" were so transformed is primarily
explicable in terms of rules of aesthetic value
made within the transforming communities.

Negative aesthetic judgments of Hopi kachina
images that were made by scientific ethnographers in the nineteenth century conform nicely to
both the dominant Euro-American art-evaluation
systems of the time and to a scientific world-
view which condemned Pueblo societies as un-
civilized.[4] From the time of the Renaissance until
early in the twentieth century there was great
consistency in the aesthetic rules of high European art, despite many important regional and
temporal variations. These established a hierarchy
of artistic media, with painting and sculpture
always superior, always separate but operating
under similar rules, and each with its own hierarchy of subsets. There was an inverse correlation
between art and utility: the more useful an object
was, the less artistic it could be, thus establish-

ing bases for the concept of "craft-art" and the secularization of ecclesiastical art.

In the nineteenth-century United States, painting was the most highly valued of the fine arts. Its aesthetic rules, indebted to the European Renaissance and deeply rooted in the ancient Mediterranean world, required that a painting be an illusion of three-dimensional real-world space, atmosphere, and actions on a two-dimensional plane surface. The more convincing the illusion, the more skillful the painting; the more moral its message, the higher its social value. In the transcendental and political mood of the time, Arcadian landscapes showing God in nature and His gifts harvested through the labor of the deserving were perhaps the most highly valued (Novak 1980). Sculpture, three-dimensional to begin with and lower on the aesthetic scale, also had to create the illusion of reality. By convention, sculptural art could not be colored, creating a parallel difficulty in illusionism to that of the two-dimensional painting surfaces. In practice, both media relied on mathematical and scientific rules of observation, followed visual conventions of those disciplines, used their pertinent tools, and supported dominant, conventional social values. Thus, by both aesthetic and social criteria, nineteenth-century kachina carvings were the antithesis of any "fine art" in the prevailing Euro-American art-classification system.

Lower-status kinds of painting, such as book and magazine illustration, were equally illusionistic and required the same skills and training. Some artists, such as Winslow Homer, Frederick Remington, and many who came to the Southwest at the turn of the twentieth century, moved easily from one genre to the other. Among pictorial conventions used in their commercial work are vignettes in which perfectly illusionistic three-dimensional figures act or interact within a spatial void that is given dimension by allusive use of perspective drawing or by shadows cast on an otherwise blank surface (Plate 41). There is confluence

FIGURE 13.3. Advertisement in *American Indian Art Magazine* 6, no. 4, (Autumn 1981): 29. Nineteenth-century Hopi kachina doll used to promote Sotheby's art auction house, New York.

here with aboriginal Pueblo modes of handling figure-ground relationships, with the incipient illusionism and perspective-drawing conventions in the Hopi pictures commissioned by Fewkes which have no obvious Pueblo prototypes, and with the later illusionistic paintings of Kabotie, Polelonema, and their followers (compare Plates 35, 36, 41).

Hopi familiarity with Euro-American illustrative artists began late in the nineteenth century, and illustrated books and magazines were available there as early as 1875 (Wade and McChesney 1980:9). California artist-illustrator Jo Mora spent parts of several years at Hopi from 1904 to 1906 painting watercolors which remarkably foreshadow the Hopi kachina-painting tradition while demonstrating its close visual affinity to contemporaneous illustrative art (Stewart 1979; Plate 41). Association in the twentieth century of illustrative art with "commercial art" on one hand, and regional traditions of nostalgic "Western art" on the other, creates a firm position for most Hopi kachina paintings: they are a subset of a popular art that is diametrically opposed to the elite realm of modernist, international "fine art." By extension, curio / craft-art kachina carvings that carry almost identical illustrative values and objectives are also a subset of that same conservative and largely regional art tradition.

The massive industrialization and urbanization of the Western world was a catalyst during the nineteenth century for elaborate reconfigurations of its art systems. A countercultural "avant garde" artistic elite became increasingly powerful, specialized, and alienated from popular audiences. What might be termed its genteel wing led to various national (and sometimes nationalist) Arts and Crafts movements, including the American version that was so strong in California (Clark 1972). Together, these created a new, high status for handcrafted, useful, luxury art objects. A more radical wing, increasingly international and intellectualized, led through Impressionism to Cubism and the modernist tradition

with its extraordinary proliferation of competing fine-art styles and philosophical systems. Most of these systems share aspects of an ideology that collectively replaced that of most earlier Euro-American fine-art institutions during the course of the twentieth century, also spreading throughout the industrialized world. The subject matter of art is now art; its source is ego; the sources of aesthetic form include all sensory experiences and all of the world's art; the purpose of art is to critically examine human conditions and institutions through the agency of personal expression. There are few media restrictions. No status implications are attached to media; idiosyncratic expression is highly valued, but positive values are not ordinarily attached to illusionism, craft skills, or to support of so-called middle-class values.

Kachina images were slow to affect or be affected by modernist art. Adoption of primitivist modes by early modernists was a strategy of social criticism: "the more that bourgeois society prized . . . salon styles, the more certain painters began to value . . . those non-Western arts they called 'savage'" (Rubin 1984:2). It was to express "savage" values that the German Expressionist painter Emil Nolde first used kachina carvings as the subject of two 1911 paintings (Franzke 1981:8,9, figs. 2,3,4). However, kachina images seem to have been largely ignored by most modernists until the 1930s. They were included as "Surrealist Objects" with other decontextualized objects including Marcel Duchamp's famous "Bottle Rack" in Paris and London exhibitions in 1936 (Franzke 1981:12; Maurer 1984:546). Other Surrealists, profoundly concerned with relationships between the individual subconscious and collective humanity, acquired kachina carvings. Max Ernst may have been the first, André Bréton and Paul Masson also collected, and their common friend, structural anthropologist Claude Lévi-Strauss, helped them build their collections (Franzke 1981:11). Kachina carvings were later included as aesthetic objects in the 1940 exhibition "Indian Art in the

United States" at New York's trend-setting Museum of Modern Art (Douglas and d'Harnoncourt 1940) and, in the years since, have been incorporated within fine art collections of major museums across the country. Almost invariably, only carvings that fit the nineteenth-century aesthetic profile are transformed into art.

It is ironic that the ideological transformation of kachina carvings into fine art came first, through being "savaged" by German Expressionism, and later by becoming icons of Surrealism, among the most idiosyncratic and socially alienated of modernist movements. Few objects are made so unambiguously to represent benevolent sacred personages as they participate in intensely integrative social activities. Irony upon irony, later carvings that are considerably less iconic, more illusionistic, far more ambiguous in their expressive intent, and often made to be sold to an alien society cannot presently become fine art. For, within that narrow category, the counterculture of modernism became dominant, and the once-dominant illusionistic tradition is now marginalized as another kind of counterculture.

Lévi-Strauss may well have considered these inversions and appropriations as related, patterned, and providing insights about relationships between the affected societies. In summarizing a discussion of quite another set of artistic appropriations and transformations, masks made by Salish and southern Kwakiutl people of the Northwest Coast of North America, he wrote:

> By means of logical operations that project at a distance, and transform or invert art objects, a story, which unfolded . . . on a time scale of millennia,

has come to overlap another more recent story with a shorter periodicity . . . ideological structures were built up compatible with the inherent constraints of their mental nature and which, in agreement with these constraints, encoded . . . the givens of the environment and of history. These ideological structures incorporate the information with pre-existing paradigms and also generate new ones in the shape of mythic beliefs, ritual practices, and plastic works. Over this immense territory, these beliefs, practices, and works remain mutually congruent when they imitate one another, and even, perhaps above all, when they seem to be contradictory.   (Lévi-Strauss 1982:147–48)

Contradiction is the key. The kind of analysis done here, of art classifications based largely on formal aesthetic qualities, may legitimately be interpreted as a denial of spiritual intent or content of kachina images and apparently opposes traditional native classification of them. Therein lies the contradiction that defines the problem: the term "kachina art" may be an oxymoron, for it appears that no object can simultaneously be valued as both. Yet both the term and the complex of values encompassed within it are in general use by most of those involved in the transactions discussed above. Oxymoron or not, "kachina art" is a social reality that, barring radical social restructuring, cannot be erased and may only be replaced by a linguistic euphemism. The contradiction likewise can be neither dismissed nor ignored for it is itself a critical, crosscultural social strategy, a kind of inversion created to allow both sides of an unequal social encounter to deal better with its consequences.

NOTES

1. I am indebted to Philip K. Bock of the Department of Anthropology, University of New Mexico, for reading an early draft of this paper and providing me with many useful comments. I am, of course, solely responsible for what follows.

2. A considerable debate on these issues within the

museum, anthropology, and fine-arts communities became focused during the 1980s by the 1984 "Primitivism in Twentieth Century Art" exhibition at New York's Museum of Modern Art. Since basic questions were raised about the premises, values, and beliefs of each of those disciplines and their institutions, no consensus view has emerged, and conceivably none will. However, the grounds for debate have shifted from polemics to thoughtful, searching inquires. See *Museum Anthropology* 16(1):7–43.

3. It is important to note that this difference may not even be made, let alone considered significant, by a participant in any group which makes or uses kachina images.

4. I consider "dominance" to be expressed by control over artistic institutions through patronage and other mechanisms by those with access to wealth and political power.

14

Stories of Kachinas and the Dance of Life and Death

DENNIS TEDLOCK

AMONG THE published reports of field research among the Pueblos are the texts of hundreds of narratives that tell of the origins, lives, and varied characters of kachinas. Yet our customary first move as cultural anthropologists, whenever we reconsider a subject such as that of kachinas, is to reread ethnographic accounts in which the voices of the consultants have been reduced to a few brief quotations, most likely responses to interview questions. In effect, we look for information that has already been converted into usable data and then explore the possibility of making new connections, which is what I myself will do at the beginning of the present essay. But when we meanwhile set aside the lengthiest and most connected statements of those whose culture is under study, we leave them in their roles as producers of bits of information while keeping the roles of organizers and interpreters for ourselves. What I will try to do in the main body of the present essay is to break with this pattern by undertaking a close and sustained reading of some Zuni texts that account for the origin and nature of kachinas and kachina impersonation, bringing Zuni narratives into a dialogue with historical documents and with current archaeological and ethnological notions about kachinas.[1]

Elsie Clews Parsons once wrote that "there is a specific kachina ideology which is fuller and clearer at Zuni than anywhere else" (1939:174), but this opinion is at least partly a measure of the high quality of the field dialogues that have taken place at Zuni, above all the dialogues between Ruth L. Bunzel and the Rain priest of the south and his associates in the 1920s. It may also be a measure of the fact that the responsibility for kachina performances at Zuni is almost entirely concentrated in the hands of a single organization, the Kotikyanne or "kachina society,"[2] rather than being dispersed, as it is almost everywhere else, among a number of religious societies of varied character. In any case there is no need to suppose that Zuni lies closer to the original source of kachina ideology than other Pueblos, somehow preserving intact what they have blurred. It may rather be the case that present-day Zuni ideology is a product of a synthesizing effort, carried out in response to a complex cultural history. If so, it was not the kind of effort that obliterates traces of the past, as we shall see.

The high visibility of kachinas among the Hopi and Zuni in our own time is misleading, to say the least. Kachinas were everywhere in the Pueblo world of the seventeenth century, in villages of every language that exists today, without exception, and in the Piro and Tompiro villages that once occupied the southeastern reaches of that world as well. Kachinas are everywhere among the Pueblos of our own day as well, though they may be disguised or hidden from view in many places, a condition that is clearly the direct result of suppression during the Spanish period (C. Schaafsma, this volume). As we move from west to east, anyone may witness a kachina dance at a Hopi village, Hispanics are forbidden to watch kachinas at Zuni, and all non-Indians are excluded everywhere east of there, a gradation of visibility that is a direct measure of past suppression.

In villages of every language, even in the east, outsiders of the present era have been able to witness performances in which line dancers wear turtleshell leg rattles and sing songs with the characteristic five-part structure of kachina music. In the west these dancers might be the Hemis (Jemez) kachinas at the Hopi Niman ceremony, or perhaps the Kokkokshi (Good Kachinas) who dance for many days following the solstices at Zuni. When outsiders are allowed to see such a dance in the east the performers are unmasked, whether they appear with ram's horns on their heads on Christmas Eve at San Felipe (a Keresan village) or they perform the Basket Dance at Santa Clara or the Turtle Dance at San Juan (both Tewa villages). As for Tiwa villages, masked kachina dancing is apparently lacking even in secret ceremonies, but the unmasked Turtle Dance has been witnessed in the north at Taos (Parsons 1939:783–84) and in the south at Isleta (Parsons 1932:332–36). Indeed, a version of the Turtle Dance is done all the way down at Ysleta del Sur near El Paso (settled by Tiwas and Piros at the time of the Pueblo Revolt), complete with a couple of side performers who wear kachina-like masks (Houser 1979:337 and Fig. 6).

Whenever we map out features of kachina culture without regard to the question of whether we are allowed to watch masked dances or not, their distribution always violates the grand east-west dichotomy that has long clouded the thinking of social anthropologists and archaeologists alike. If we want there to be rain-bringing beings known in the local language as *katsina* or some cognate thereof, then it is not only the *katsina* of Hopi and the *k'ats'ina* of the western Keresan villages of Acoma and Laguna that find places on the map, but the *k'ats'ina* of all the eastern Keresans as well,[3] together with the *k'ats'ana* of Towa Jemez (Parsons 1925:61) and the *lhatsina* of Tiwa Taos (Parsons 1939:938). Missing from this same map are Zuni in the west and the Tewa villages in the east. If we want a large group of kachinas (by whatever name) to live in or near a source of water located to the west of human villagers, then Zuni joins the Hopi and Keresan villages, but so does Tiwa Isleta (Parsons 1932:342–44). And if we want one of the names of that western place to be Wenimatse or Wenima or Welima, then Hopi drops out but Isleta stays in.

Trying a different angle, we might want the dead (or at least some of them) to be able to take the form of kachinas. In that case we will find that the Hopi and Zuni are joined by the Towa (Ellis 1964:34) and Tewa (White 1935:198), while the Keresan villages are in disagreement and the Tiwa stay out of the picture. If we want kachina impersonators who perform initiations and exorcisms with yucca whips, then the Towa (Parsons 1925:73) and Tewa (Laski 1958:26, Hill 1982:218) remain within the picture and the Keresan presence becomes unanimous. If we want all the males of a village to receive a kachina initiation—ideally, at least—then the picture stays much the same. But if we want all females to be initiated as well (whether or not they actually don masks), then Zuni and the eastern Keresan villages drop out, leaving Hopi (Eggan, this volume) and Acoma (White 1932*a*:70) in the west and Jemez (Ellis 1964:33) and San Juan (Laski 1958:26) in the east. No matter which way we construct our picture, we will not be able to make a clean separation between east and west unless we appeal to the sheer number and complexity of known kachinas at Hopi and Zuni, which brings us right back to the questions of past suppression and present-day eastern secrecy with which we started.

The way Zunis tell the story that accounts for the great majority of their own kachinas, or *kokko,* it unfolds within the western part of the Pueblo world. It is divided into a long series of episodes that take place not only at distinct times but also at distinct places, laid out along a west-to-east and low-to-high axis in the watershed of the Little Colorado. In effect, the story has a well-defined stratigraphy, albeit a diagonal rather than a vertical one. Whatever problems archaeologists might have with mapping this story onto particular sites and their strata, it displays what we might call an *ideological* lamination or seriation.

Zuni kachinas come into the world within a still larger story called *Chimiky'ana'kowa',* "That Which Was the Beginning." We can enter this story at a point when the Zunis have already come out into the daylight and have settled a short distance from the place where they emerged from the darkness beneath the earth. Already with them are four *uwanam aashiwani* or "rain priests," who pray to rain-bringing beings who live on the shores of the four oceans, and two *aapi'lha aashiwani* or "bow priests," who at this point in the story are none other than the Ahayuuta twins, sons of the Sun Father. The first step in the development of what will become kachina ideology occurs when the first witch appears among the Zuni and offers yellow corn in exchange for the life of a child. The person who responds to the witch's proposition is the rain priest of the direction whose color is yellow, the north; he is the first-ranking priest and is also known as Ky'akwemossi or "House Chief." Andrew Peynetsa's interpretation of this episode (D. Tedlock 1972:261–63) carries a gravity and depth of emotion that are marked by his rendition of certain words and phrases with either a loud voice (shown in bold type in the translation given here) or a soft one (small type), and by his generally slow pace, with brief pauses (line breaks) preceding many of the phrases that contain key words and a longer pause (shown as a space with a dot) after the death of the child:[4]

The House Chief
had a child.
"Go ahead, try this one," he said, and he **gave up his little one.**
When he gave up his little one, this child
was witched.
Having been hurt
the little boy died.

   •

His elders
held him.
On the fourth day
he might return:

preparations were made
so that this might be.

So the first human death is followed by the first attempt to ensure an afterlife. The narrator does not specify what was done, since his audience knows only too well. Prayer sticks must be made for the dead, whose bodies are buried and whose spirits depart for the west after four days of mourning.

Preparations were made

•

and when he had been gone
four days

•

the House Chief said to the two Bow Priests, "You must
    go to the Place of Emergence.
Our child
whose road was ended:
you must find out why it is that this had to be."
So he said. They were **lonely** for him, **lonely** for
    their little one.
The two Bow Priests
went back, it was the second time they had
    gone back.

The first time (coming before the passages quoted here) was when they discovered that the first witch had emerged from the earth.

**When they came to the Place of Emergence, the
    little boy was playing there, playing by himself.**
When they entered upon his road, "What a
    surprise, our
child
so you're living here, not far from us," they
    said. "Yes
this
is how I **live**.
When you return you must tell my elders
that they **must not cry**
for when the time **comes**
then I will enter upon their roads," the little boy
    said. "Perhaps so."
"That is why
this happened to me.
They should not cry," he told them. "Very well."

So there was a time, according to this story, when the dead went westward and then resumed their lives at the place of emergence without becoming kachinas. But it was the Ahayuuta, and not living human beings, who were able to visit the place of the dead, see the boy who had died, and hold a direct conversation with him. To this day Zunis keep a distance from the dead in their character as particular individuals, going to the place where they now live only under the protection of an official kachina society pilgrimage and interpreting a dream of a dead relative as a source of potentially fatal illness (B. Tedlock 1992:157–69, 259, 268–69).

The place of emergence was a watery one, judging from the fact that the people who came out of the earth there did so by climbing up a stalk of cane (D. Tedlock 1972:255–56). Indeed, the people themselves had the character of beings who live in watery places until they migrated eastward, after the beginning of death, to a place that came to be called Moss Lake (D. Tedlock 1972:263):

When they came
to this lake
they were still only **moss people**.
They had tails of moss.
Their hands were webbed.
Their feet were webbed.

The Ahayuuta twins wash the moss off the people in Moss Lake, and they cut the webs out from between their fingers and toes. In Andrew Peynetsa's interpretation,

They made us the kind of people we are now,
    they
completed us.

As for the child who returned so easily to the watery place of emergence, he was an incomplete person to begin with, a moss person, something like an amphibian. Whatever time depth Zuni kachinas may have in archaeological terms, their cultural depth is such that Zunis conceive humans without kachinas as not yet fully human. Their story about these proto-humans is nevertheless translatable into archaeological terms. It tells of a people who settled together in groups, who had rain-bringing ritual specialists, and who planted corn and buried their dead. All of this is in harmony with the established archaeological interpretation of Pueblo life as it was until the late thirteenth or early fourteenth century.

The next episode takes place once again in a world without kachinas, but it sets the stage for their coming in a way that is quite obvious to Zunis, though it may seem rather subtle to the rest of us. As it opens the people have moved eastward again, to a site that will become known as Place Where the People Were Divided (D. Tedlock 1972:265–66):

The Ahayuuta said to them, **Now**
my fathers, my children
now we must

    •

test you," they told them. "Very well."
The twins sat down nearby
and they made
the **crow egg** and
the **parrot egg**.
They carried these back to where the others were.
"**Now**, my **fathers**, my **children**
perhaps you will be **wise**:
you must choose
between these two."
That's what
they told them.
On this side
in the direction where the Middle of the world
    would be
was the **crow egg**, beautiful
spotted with blue.
The parrot egg was not beautiful.

    •

The Zuni term translated as "beautiful" here is *tso'ya*, which carries a sense of "multicolored" or "variegated" (B. Tedlock 1986, 1992:191, 232, 262). As an absolute term it seems to require at least two and preferably three or more saturated

hues, distinct and distant from one another (as in the plumage of a parrot or macaw) rather than shaded or gradated. As a relative term it distinguishes things that are strikingly marked, such as a crow egg or an antelope, from those that are plain or dull, such as a parrot egg or a mule deer.

There
those who were to go in coral's direction
chose the parrot egg

    •

and those who were to come this way chose the
    crow egg.

"Coral's direction" is the south, which is where parrots and macaws now come from. One of the narrator's sons remarked, on hearing this episode, "Zunis always do like something beautiful [*tso'ya*]." The irony of the Zuni choice of the crow egg, beautiful on the outside, is deeper than it might seem, since crow fledglings, in their pinfeathers, give the promise of being multicolored.

In the context of present-day Zuni rituals, the aesthetic expressed in this episode is very much a kachina trademark. Most kachina masks and costumes, with or without the addition of parrot feathers, are themselves *tso'ya*. The feathers of adult crows, whose black has the virtue of being intensely and even brightly so, find their places in the larger scheme of kachina color contrasts. The original irony of the beautiful crow egg is preserved in the Zuni sacred name for this bird, which is *kokko kw'inna*, "black kachina."

When the term *tso'ya* is extended metaphorically from the visual into the auditory domain, the only songs that qualify as "multicolored" are kachina songs, which (whether at Zuni or elsewhere) require as much as a two-octave range, make use of semitone embellishments analogous to Western chromaticism, and juxtapose themes that are highly contrastive (B. Tedlock 1980:14–18).

In its fullest expression, the *tso'ya* aesthetic requires an element of unpredictability. This is doubly encoded in the story, where the dull egg produces the parrot and the beautiful egg produces the crow. In some kachina masks it takes the form of an asymmetry of features, which is to say that the appearance of one half of the face cannot be inferred from the other. The canonical form of kachina songs (whether at Zuni or elsewhere) is itself asymmetrical, with three contrasting themes arranged in the sequence AB AB CB CB AB. The the words of part A often raise a question whose answer is disclosed in part C, which is precisely the part that breaks the symmetry of the overall composition (B. Tedlock 1980:19–20).

When we translate the Zuni story into archaeological terms, the episode that sees the birth of the kachina aesthetic recalls the Pueblo world of the fourteenth century, in which the asymmetrical organization of design fields and the representation of kachina masks both enter the scene. In the east the bulk of the evidence for these developments comes from rock art, while the western evidence comes primarily from painted pottery (see Adams, Hays, and P. Schaafsma in this volume). As for the Zuni notion that the parrot egg was taken away to the south, it would seem to refer to a weakening of Mesoamerica contacts. Perhaps the reference is to the twelfth century, when the Pueblos saw their nearest major source of captive parrots and macaws shift southward from Chaco Canyon to Casas Grandes. Immediately north of Casas Grandes and coming to end at about the same time as the shift was the Mimbres culture, whose ceramic iconography seems to have a Mesoamerican character (Thompson, this volume) and an ancestral relationship to kachina art (P. Schaafsma, this volume). If the Mesoamerican aspects of the culture of kachinas (Young, this volume) were already present in the Mimbres culture, whose Classic phase began three centuries before the full appearance of kachinas among the Pueblos, then it should come as no surprise when direct searches for kachina roots in the distant cultures of Mesoamerica itself turn up broad parallels rather than concrete evidence. The hardest archaeological evidence would be imported Meso-

american artifacts in direct association with early evidence of kachinas, while the hardest ideological evidence would be kachina technical terms or proper names that were demonstrably borrowed from a language spoken in Mesoamerica. As of this writing, neither kind of evidence has turned up.

Returning to the Zuni story, the very next episode after the choice of eggs brings us to the first reference to kokko or "kachinas," which appears in the place name Kolhuwalaaw'a or "Kachina Village" (D. Tedlock 1972:266–67):

When they came to where Kachina Village was
    going to be
the Ahayuuta
coming to the waters there, said:
"Now
my children, you must cross here."
That's what they told them.

                •

They crossed
with their children on their backs.

In Andrew Peynetsa's interpretation of this story, what happens next is so momentous as to warrant a change in voice from a storyteller's almost conversational mode to that of an orator's two-tone chant:

Their ^{chil}dren
turned into ^{wa}ter snakes, ^{tur}tles
and ^{bit} their ^{el}ders, ^{half the} children were
    dropped
and it was not good.

Other versions of the story add frogs to the list of animals (see Bunzel 1932b:596), but the general point is that the children turn into creatures of the kinds that live both in and out of water. In effect, they revert to a state something like that of moss people. The audience knows, without the narrator's having to tell them, that the same thing happens when children die today—unless, that is, a boy has already been initiated into the kachina society, or a girl has already par-

Kachinas and the Dance of Life and Death | 167

ticipated in the affairs of the society by preparing food or costumes for kachina impersonators. Now the Ahayuuta intervene:

"Wait
wait wait, before everyone has gone in,
you must not drop your children when they bite
 you, perhaps it will work out this way."
Half the people had already gone in
and when the Ahayuuta said this

•

the others held their children firmly on their backs.
They bit and scratched, but they did not let them
 go and reached the other side.
Some of the children were left behind there.

With this episode the nature of death changes. The child who died in an earlier episode had his own kind of watery second life, back at the place of emergence, but at that time there was no way for the living to see the dead, or for the dead to "enter upon the roads" of the living. Now, by means of transformation, the dead may appear to the living as water snakes, turtles, and frogs, and to this day Zunis are reminded of dead children when they see these creatures. The turtle is particularly important here, since the shells of turtles from Kachina Village and nearby sources provide the leg rattles worn by kachinas who dance in a line and do their own singing rather than having a chorus on the side. This type of dance, as we found earlier, is universal among the Pueblos, and whether we see and hear it today at Hopi or San Juan or somewhere in between, we may be catching a glimpse and an echo of the deepest reaches of the kachina past.

After the children fell and were last seen as creatures of the water, something further happened when they were out of sight beneath the surface. Andrew Peynetsa says only that the place where they fell became Kachina Village (D. Tedlock 1972:268), but his audience knows that when the dead are inside that village, invisible to the living, they are like the boy who returned to the Place of Emergence, which is to say that

they take the same general form they had before they died. For the story of how the hidden life of Kachina Village was first discovered we must turn to a different version of "That Which Was the Beginning," the one told to Ruth Bunzel (1932b) by a person who learned it from the Rain priest of the south. In that version there is an episode in which the two Bow priests ask the help of two Neweeke, or "Clown People," in finding Itiwan'a or the "Middle Place," which is where the Zunis now live. The twins make their request when the people have already crossed the water but are still settled not far east of there. The clowns protest, quite properly, that they are unreliable, but they are sent off on a search anyway. Sure enough, instead of going eastward, toward the Middle Place, they go in the opposite direction, back to the water (Bunzel 1932b:573–75, translation mine):

"Now, let's go speak to our children there," they said, and the two of them went on. When they entered the water, it was full of dancing kachinas.

So the first time kachinas are ever seen by living human beings, they are already in the act of dancing. And whenever a character in a Zuni hearthside tale enters Kachina Village, the narrator always describes that moment with the same words that are used here, Kokko otin pottiye, "It was full of dancing kachinas." In the present story the two visitors are understood to be dreaming their way into the village; any living human being who tried to enter in the flesh would die and thus become a permanent resident. The dance leaders, noticing the visitors, now speak:

"Hold on now! Be still. Our two fathers have come," they said, and the kachinas stood still. When they had stood still they said this to the two of them:

"Now, our two fathers, this very day you have entered upon our roads. Perhaps there is some word, a word of some importance. You will make this known to us, so that we may think about it as we live," he said.

"Yes, in truth. Tomorrow we shall move the village, that's why we have come to speak with you."

"Well, may it be so. May you go in happiness. You will tell our parents this:

'No, don't worry. We didn't end up stretched out. We stopped here to stay forever. Just one more night remains, and because of this we stopped here.'"

That is to say, the distance between Kachina Village and the Middle Place is a journey of two days, with one overnight stay. The message from the kachinas to the living continues:

"When our world grows old, when the waters are depleted, when the seeds are depleted, you need not return to the Place of Emergence. Instead, when the waters are depleted, when the seeds are depleted, you will send prayer sticks. By means of these we shall speak at the Place of Emergence, we shall root them in the earth so the waters will not become scarce. This is why we have settled nearby," they told them.

From now on, kachinas will stand between the aging, drying world of fully human beings and the fresh, wet world of the moss people of the past or the amphibious animals that still exist today. By becoming kachinas, dead people will be able to return to a wetter world without losing their human form or ceasing to live together in a village. At the same time, kachinas will provide communication between the village of living Zunis and the place of emergence. Wherever that place may have been, from now on it will be too far back in the west, or else too distant in time, for living pilgrims to return there. This circumstance recalls the archaeological evidence for migrations before and during the period when kachinas first appeared (Adams, this volume), and it suggests that kachina ideology, right from the beginning, might have provided uprooted people with the means for reconnecting themselves with their past.

Even at this point the Zuni kachina narrative is not complete, since there is as yet no *impersonation* of kachinas by the living. The beginning of masking is accounted for by a separate story, called

Komoss'ona an Penanne or "Word of the Kachina Chief." The Kachina Chief tells this story to Zuni boys on the occasion of their second and final initiation into the kachina society. As it opens, the Zunis are living on Towayalanne or "Corn Mountain," the high mesa that rises a short distance to the east of the Middle Place. The ruins on that mesa are accountable, by means of Spanish documents, to three different interludes when the Zunis, or some of them, took refuge there (Crampton 1977:32–48). The first period (1632–35) came just three years after the establishment of the first mission church among the Zunis, when they killed two Franciscans and feared a military reprisal. The second (1680–99) coincided with the Pueblo Revolt and its immediate aftermath, and the third (1703–5) followed the killing of three Spanish colonists.

In the 1660s, between the first two flights to Corn Mountain, the Holy Inquisition conducted a direct attack on the masked impersonation of what its records call *catzinas*. It is these records, which tell of a massive revival of kachina dancing throughout the Pueblo world, that provide the first evidence for a connection between kachinas and the dead. This connection seems to be missing in the present-day religious ideology of the Tiwa and some Keresans, as we have seen, but Inquisition testimony from eastern villages seems clear on this point. As one Pueblo official put the matter, speaking of the Tiwa and Tewa who then lived east of the Rio Grande and south of Santa Fe, *catzinas* "come from the other life to speak with them" (C. Schaafsma, this volume). What the Inquisition was dealing with was nothing less than a full-blown nativistic movement, the first North American Ghost Dance.[5] This is not to say that kachinas were never associated with the dead before the seventeenth century, but it should be obvious that if indeed they were, kachina dancing would have provided a ready-made vehicle for a nativistic reaction to Spanish domination. Like the Ghost Dance proper, the kachina dances of the seventeenth century would have opened up communication not merely with the ordinary dead, which is to say people who had lived lives just like those of the dancers, but also with the dead who had enjoyed life in a different but not very distant time when native peoples were more numerous and had the freedom to do what was right in their own eyes.

As for the Zuni case, the archaeological evidence makes it clear enough that kachinas and the kachina aesthetic were present in their part of the Pueblo world by the fourteenth century. But the Zuni story that places the origin of masking on Corn Mountain has its own kind of accuracy, preserving the vital link between kachina dancing and a period in the seventeenth century when Zunis religious values were reasserted in the face of a direct threat. Judging from the early archaeological evidence, kachina dancing had its very origins in an era of massive turmoil, one in which people might well have been preoccupied with recent ancestors who had led very different lives.

Like the period that first gave rise to kachinas, the period of Spanish missionization saw the combination of smaller villages into larger ones, or what archaeologists have been calling "aggregation" (Adams, this volume). In the Zuni case, the final descent from Corn Mountain was also the occasion for the final combination of what had once been six villages into the single town where Zunis live to this day (Crampton 1977:45), and it is probably no coincidence that the Zuni kachina society is divided into six groups that use six separate kivas. The Zuni story of how kachina impersonation began says little about the internal organization of the society, but it does evoke an era of aggregation (Bunzel 1932*b*:604–7, translation mine):

Long ago, when the village was up on Corn Mountain, the ones whose roads are in the forefront had a big meeting. When the meeting was in session, they questioned one another.

"What could there be that we would enjoy? Those who are male are more numerous now, those who are female are more numerous now. It's not apparent how we might enjoy ourselves as we continue living," they were saying.

The Zuni verbs expressing enjoyment here are built on the stem *elu*. By itself, *Elu!* is an exclamation of joy or pleasant surprise that suits the kachina aesthetic and is frequently heard in the lyrics of kachina songs. Appropriately enough, the person who begins to answer the question as to "how we might enjoy ourselves" is the priest whose direction is multicolored, which is to say the zenith. His title is Pekwin, or "Word Priest":

Their Word Priest said,
"It's not apparent?" he said.
"No, it's not apparent."
"All right. It's for nothing that you are men! We had our beginning over there, so it would seem that we should set down bundles of prayer sticks for them, since the ones we brought into the world remain quiet over there," he said.
"So that's it!" they said. They made prayer sticks. When they had made prayer sticks, they sent the prayer sticks to Whispering Waters.

Using the name Hatin Ky'ay'a or "Whispering Waters" is a delicate way of referring to Kachina Village, which is located beneath the waters of that name, near the confluence of the Zuni and Little Colorado rivers. When members of the kachina society go there on a pilgrimage today, they can faintly hear the singing of the dancers below. The story scene now shifts to Kachina Village:

Those who received the prayer sticks shared their thoughts:
"Now, who will count the days for our daylight fathers, our mothers, our children at the Middle Place?" they said to the Kachina Priests.

The counting of days refers to the interval that separates the formal announcement of a kachina performance from its actual occurrence, and the "daylight" fathers and mothers are living human beings. Now comes the answer:

"Well, it should be the one we have as our father," they said. They summoned Kyaklo Priest. When their father came to the meeting place, it was by means of prayer sticks that they persuaded him to be strong. They lived o————————n until it was spring. Around the time of the Moon of the Little Wind, wishing for one another, they alerted one another.

Kyaklo, who is the Word Priest of Kachina Village, comes to Zuni today to herald the first of the two stages of kachina initiation (Bunzel 1932*d*:975–85). Spring is the proper time for this event, the "Moon of the Little Wind" being March. With Kyaklo a new kind of aquatic creature enters the story: he always carries a duck in his hand, and being a bit like a duck himself, he isn't very good at walking:

Kyaklo Priest said,
    "How might I enter upon the roads of the daylight fathers, mothers, and children at the Middle Place?" he said. His grandfathers, Molanhakto Priests, carried him along on their backs. Early in the dawn, just before the sun came out, they came to Corn Mountain. When they came to Corn Mountain they went a————————ll around.

Here, for the first time, kachinas enter the world of the living.[6] Molanhakto is an esoteric name for the kachina clowns (distinct from Neweekwe clowns) who are also known as Koyemshi, "Kachina Husbands (or Lovers),"[7] the so-called Mudheads. Today, at the beginning of the quadrennial kachina initiation, they carry Kyaklo into Zuni from the west. When they cross the Zuni River just before entering the Middle Place itself they drop him into the water, but like the people who held on to their children long ago, they manage to get him to the other side. Then they take him to each of the six kivas, where he chants the longest and most authoritative version of "That Which Was the Beginning." But in the present story, which has Kyaklo appearing before there was any such thing as kachina impersonation by the living, he announces the coming of

two kachinas who will henceforth herald the beginning of an annual kachina dance series that actually occupies the winter months rather than waiting for the spring:

It seems they climbed up on a house. Wherever the people were meeting, he spoke about how they should live:
    "Four days from today, my two children will come. The two of them will count the days for you," he said. Then the people said,
    "Very well." Whatever way they were supposed to live, they carried out the rituals. When he had left, the people lived o————————n, and after four days the two kachinas came. Wherever they had their houses, the two counted their days for them.

The "houses" are kivas, and the two kachinas are of the kind named Muluktakkya (Stevenson 1904:143–44 and Plate lxxiii), meaning something like "Slender Frog." Now these two kachinas speak:

"Four days from now we will come. On the third day you will make everything right and on the fourth day we will come. May you pass a good night until the day comes," they said, and the two of them left. When the sun had come up four times, the women prepared food. At dusk the two came.
    "Make haste!" the two of them went around saying. When the sun went down they left. The kachinas came where they were meeting. They went around dancing. When they were finished others came, then they went around dancing, then others came, then those left, then others came, and when those were finished they left.

This is a good description of what a present-day winter night dance is like when the season is already well under way and several kivas are presenting kachina dances on the same night. One group follows the next as they circulate among all the houses that have been prepared for them.

They continued this way, it seems, and a few days later someone died. A few days after that they came again, and when they left someone died again. Each time they came this way, a person's life was ended.

So the cost of having the dead come to entertain the living in person was that someone among the living would go home with the dead when they left.

> They lived on this way. Even though the villagers enjoyed their life, it wasn't right. Those who had been coming said,
>
> "Now, my children, perhaps it shouldn't be this way. It wouldn't be right for us to continue coming," they said. "Take a good look at us. We are not always like this," they said. Two of them set down their face mask, their helmet mask.

This is the moment of initiation: the masks come off, revealing to the novices that "we are not always like this." But in this first moment, instead of adults initiating children, the dead are initiating the living. The particular point of greatest interest is that kachinas, even the ones from Kachina Village itself, *wear masks*. The dead have not so much *become* kachinas as they have been *representing* themselves as kachinas, and they invite the living to join them in their game of representation. This puts the visual focus of what is and is not a kachina squarely on the mask, in case we had any doubt on that point, and it may help explain why most of the kachinas of painted pottery and rock art are represented solely by their masks.

> The people looked at them. When they were looking at them, "You will look at the two of them so that you can copy them. You will bring them to life, so that when you dance with them, we will still be coming to stand in front of you. This way, perhaps, it will turn out right, because when we end one of your lives each time we come, it isn't right."

Here we have a description, in Zuni terms, of what happens when someone dances in a kachina mask. The two key phrases are *ho"i yaaky'a,* "to bring it to life" or "complete its person (or being)," which is what the living dancer does in the flesh, and *lhuw ehkwiky'a,* "to stand in front," which is what the dead person does in spirit. The presence of the spirit becomes visible in the movement of the mask, but remains separated from the dancer

by the mask. Asked whether a dancer "becomes" a kachina, a member of the kachina society recently answered as follows (B. Tedlock 1992:53):

> You don't, really, become one. You imitate, step into it. You make your mask come alive. . . . Otherwise, a mask is just sitting there, sleeping, till you get in there. The mask doesn't come over to you. No, you have to go in there. Then he'll move. You become part of it, but not *really,* because your body will be the same, but just the head, you know, your thoughts.

It is the relationship between the dancer and the mask that is being described here. The spirit of the dead person, for its part, stays in front of the dancer and does not itself possess the dancer's mind. The mask remains in the wearer's awareness not only as the face of the specific kachina he is bringing to life, but as a physical object as well. Dancers may be heard to remark that a mask presses on the nose, even making it sore. A helmet mask makes it difficult to hear, and when the wearer sings he can only hear his own voice, which leaves him with only visual cues to keep his voice in time with those of the other dancers.[8] As for this notion that dancers "become" kachinas, which is often repeated in both the anthropological and popular literatures, what it actually expresses is not an inside belief but the point of view of an observer. It is a tribute, if an unintentional one, to the skill and hard work that go into moving and sounding like a kachina, making a mask come alive in the imaginations of those who only watch and listen.

Returning one more time to the story of how kachina dancing began, what remains is for the living to follow the instructions the dead have given them:

> When the people had spoken to one another they made them, the frontal mask, the helmet mask. They brought them to life, the villagers danced. They did it correctly, the villagers were pleased with themselves. No one died. They lived on this way. When they danced this way, no one died.

Even so, it still happens now and then that someone dies during a kachina dance, or within a few days of a dance. Usually it is a spectator who dies, and it is most likely to happen when a dance is put on by the kiva group whose direction is the white east, properly known as Oheekwe, "Brain People," but nicknamed Lhaknaakwe, "Slayers." What goes wrong, it seems, is that a person is so attracted by a kachina performance, by its *tso'ya* qualities, as to follow the dancers, or rather the dead who stand in front of them, out of the Middle Place and back to Kachina Village (B. Tedlock 1992:269). It is the person's thoughts that follow the dancers, in a sort of waking dream, but the body then sickens and death follows. Those who are recently bereaved may dream of Kachina Village in their sleep, even seeing someone over there who has no mask on. Again the eventual outcome is death, unless a cure is undertaken. This consists of telling the dream to one of the various kachinas who carries a yucca whip and then, like a person being initiated into the kachina society, submitting to blows. The whipping removes dangerous thoughts and puts dreamers right back in their living bodies. Whether they sense the whipper more as a spirit of the dead standing in front or as an impersonator giving life from behind we cannot know, but in either case the face belongs to the mask.

Once in a great while a dancer may die. This is the only instance in which it might be said, after all, that a dancer "becomes" a kachina, though even here the transformation remains incomplete during the performance itself. The first such death, according to Andrew Peynetsa, happened at the now-abandoned Zuni village of Kechipaaw'a or "Gypsum Place," southwest of the Middle Place. The people there were doing the Yaaya, which is one of the few dances that is sponsored not by the kachina society but by one of the smaller societies, in this case the Shumaakwe or "Helical People." The songs of the Helical People are in Keresan, and although their kachinas have a secondary home in the west, their original home

is in the east (Stevenson 1904:531). The Yaaya begins as a social dance in which ordinary people move in rings around a Douglas fir set up in the plaza, but after a time kachinas arrive and dance within the rings, among them six Shumeekuli whose faces display the colors of the six directions. It was when the White Shumeekuli entered the dance that something began to go wrong at Gypsum Place (D. Tedlock 1972:219–22):

Their White Shumeekuli
kept going around the tree. He danced around it, and for
    some reason
he went crazy.

    •

The people **held on tight,** but somehow he broke
    through their rings and ran away.

    •

He ran and ran
and they ran after him.

    •

They ran after him, but
they couldn't catch him and still they kept after him
    shouting as they went.
He was far ahead, the White Shumeekuli was far ahead
    of them.
They kept on going until

    •

they came near **Shuminnkya.**

This is east of Gypsum Place, so the White Shumeekuli is simultaneously running toward the original home of all the Shumeekuli and heading in the direction whose color he wears on his face. Or, if we step behind the mask, the dancer is following the one who stands in front of him, running away from the life of human society. Eventually a sheepherder hears the shouts of those who are chasing the dancer and then catches sight of him. The herder studies his trajectory and waits for him beside a tree:

Sure enough, just as
he came up

past the **tree**
the herder caught him for them.
There he caught him:
the White Shumeekuli
who had run away from the Yaaya Dance.
The others came to get him
and took him back.

•

Now the narrator moves forward only with great hesitation, reenacting the amazement of the people in the story:

They brought him back, and when they
tried to unmask him
the mask
was stuck
to his face.
He was changing over.

•

When they tried to unmask the young man, some
of his
flesh peeled off.

•

This is what happens when the one who stands in front of a dancer takes over, or when the dancer forgets that it is he who is giving life to the mask. Two faces, one in front and one behind, begin to become one. In the flesh. And what happens after the mask is torn off?

Then, the one who had come as the White
Shumeekuli
lived only four days before he died.

Thus the dancer finally did become a kachina, but he completed the change in the same way anyone else would have to do it, which is by dying. The next time the Yaaya was held the person who chose to come as the White Shumeekuli went crazy again, only now the people dancing in rings held on tight and kept him in the village of the living. The danger remains even today:

Because of the flesh that got inside that mask in
former times

when someone comes into the Yaaya Dance as the
White Shumeekuli
something will inevitably happen to his mind.

Similar stories of masks stuck to faces are told in the west at Hopi and in the east at Jemez and among the Tewa (Parsons 1939:430). Most such incidents, whether at Zuni or elsewhere, are attributed to a violation of the rules of abstinence that apply just before and during a day of kachina impersonation, especially sexual abstinence. The most recent incident at Zuni occurred about thirty years ago during the kachina dance called Hilili, which is also performed at Hopi and Keresan villages. The dance leader, Lhemhokt Ona or "One Who Carries a Board on the Head," wears a mask that happens to resemble Shumeekuli masks (see Wright 1985: Plates 37*d* and 53*a*). On the occasion in question, the mask that had been painted for this role began to smother its wearer, who started swaying in the dance line. A pair of Clown People grabbed the man by the arms before he fell down, but when they got him out of the dance room they found he was already dead. His mask was stuck on tight, and they had to slice it off with a knife. Changing over though he might have been, he had to wait four days to enter Kachina Village, like anyone else. The mask was the man's own and was buried with him rather than being passed to the next generation like the White Shumeekuli mask. Even so, in all the Hilili performances that have been staged since this happened, no one has been willing to costume himself as One Who Carries a Board on the Head. Perhaps it is because that man would be standing in front of anyone who did.

Such are the ultimate dangers of the game of representation played out between the living and the dead. More often there come moments of sadness, the kind of sadness Andrew Peynetsa evoked when he told of the death of a child, all the way back near the Place of Emergence. In the excitement of watching kachinas walk into Zuni from the west to start a new season of dancing after the summer solstice, we outsiders may be surprised, at first, to catch the glint of tears on the faces of people who have too many memories. But when the dancing starts and everything is done cor-rectly, masks stay in their places and spectators enjoy a multicolored spectacle, unfolding to the tunes of multicolored music.

NOTES

1. For more on the development of a dialogical approach to anthropology and the role of textual interpretation in such an approach, see D. Tedlock (1983:part 4).

2. In the Zuni orthography used here, vowels may be pronounced approximately as in Spanish; double vowels should be held a bit longer than single ones, like the long vowels in Greek. Most consonants may be pronounced approximately as in English, but *p* and *t* are unaspirated and *lh* is like *Ll* in Welsh "Lloyd." The glottal stop, written ', is like tt in the Scottish pronunciation of "bottle," and when it follows other consonants it is pronounced simultaneously with them. Double consonants are held a bit longer than single ones, like the double consonants in Italian; *cch* is double *ch*, *llh* is double *lh,* and *ssh* is double *sh.* For comparative purposes, several words from other Pueblo languages have been converted to this same scheme. In Zuni words, stress is on the first syllable.

3. On this and on other points, my Keresan sources are Boas for Laguna (1928:277–79); White for Acoma (1932b:69–73), Zia (1962:236–55), Santa Ana (1942: 210, 221), San Felipe (1932a:21–29), and Santo Domingo (1935:88–113); Lange for Cochiti (1968:286–87, 293–94, 420); and White (1935:198–99) for Keresans in general.

4. The passages quoted here incorporate minor revisions of the previously published translation.

5. Mooney includes a discussion of the Pueblo Revolt (1896:659–60) in the introduction to his study of the Ghost Dance that swept across the Great Basin and Plains at the close of the nineteenth century. Curiously, he makes no mention of the role of kachina dancing just before and during the Revolt, though his source (Bandelier) did make that connection (see C. Schaafsma, this volume).

6. The notion that kachinas once came among the living in person is also present (for example) at Acoma (White 1932a:69), Zia (White 1962:236), and San Felipe (White 1932b:21–22).

7. This name is probably an ironic reference to their origin in the incestuous union of a brother and sister, which takes place in a part of "That Which Was the Beginning" not recounted here (see D. Tedlock 1972:267–68).

8. A similar description of the discomforts of masking has been reported for Santo Domingo (White 1935:101).

REFERENCES CITED

Adams, Eleanor B., and Fray Angelico Chavez
1956   *The Missions of New Mexico, 1776: A Description by Fray Francisco Atonasio Domínguez, with Other Contemporary Documents.* University of New Mexico Press, Albuquerque.

Adams, E. Charles
1989   Homol'ovi III: A Pueblo Hamlet in the Middle Little Colorado River Valley. *Kiva* 54:217–30.
1991   *The Origin and Development of the Pueblo Katsina Cult.* University of Arizona Press, Tucson.

Adams, E. Charles, and Kelley Ann Hays (editors)
1991   *Homol'ovi II: Archaeology of an Ancestral Hopi Village, Arizona.* Anthropological Papers of the University of Arizona No. 55. University of Arizona Press, Tucson.

Adams, E. Charles, Miriam Stark, and Deborah Dosh
1990   Ceramic Distributions and Ceramic Exchange: The Distribution of Jeddito Yellow Ware and Implications for Social Complexity. Ms. on file, Arizona State Museum Library, Tucson.

Anderson, Frank Gibbs
1951   The Kachina Cult of the Pueblo Indians. Unpublished Ph.D. dissertation, Department of Anthropology, University of New Mexico, Albuquerque.
1955   The Pueblo Kachina Cult: A Historical Reconstruction. *Southwestern Journal of Anthropology* 11:404–19.
1956   Early Documentary Material on the Pueblo Kachina Cult. *Anthropological Quarterly* 29:31–44.
1960   Inter-tribal Relations in the Pueblo Kachina Cult. *Fifth International Congress of Anthropological and Ethnological Sciences, Selected Papers,* pp. 377–383.

Anonymous
n.d.   Hotel Astor American Indian Room.
1919   Exhibit by Indian Pupils. *El Palacio* 6(9):142–143.
1966   James S. Kewanwytewa 1899–1966. *Plateau* 39(1):71.

Anton, Ferdinand
1969   *Ancient Mexican Art.* Thames and Hudson, London.

Anyon, Roger, and Steven A. LeBlanc
1984   *The Galaz Ruin: A Prehistoric Mimbres Village in Southwestern New Mexico.* Maxwell Museum of Anthropology and University of New Mexico Press, Albuquerque.

Ayer, Mrs. Edward E.
1916   *The Memorial of Fray Alonso de Benavides, 1630.* Privately printed, Chicago.

Baldwin, Stuart L.
n.d.   Studies in Piro-Tompiro Ethnohistory and Western Tompiro Archaeology. Manuscript.

Bandelier, Adolph F.
1890   *Final Report of Investigations among the Indians of the Southwestern United States.* Papers, Archaeological Institute of America, American Series, Vol. 3.

Barnett, Franklin
1969   *Tonque Pueblo: A Report of Partial Excavation of an Ancient Pueblo IV Indian Ruin in New Mexico.* Albuquerque Archaeological Society, Albuquerque.

Bartlett, Katharine
1936   Hopi History No. 2: The Navajo Wars 1823–
        1870. *Museum of Northern Arizona, Museum Notes*
        8(7):33–37.

Basso, Keith H.
1979   History of Ethnological Research. In *Southwest,*
        edited by Alfonso Ortiz, pp. 587–602. Vol. 9,
        Handbook of North American Indians. Smithsonian
        Institution Press, Washington, D.C.

Beals, Ralph L.
1932   Masks in the Southwest. *American Anthropologist*
        34:166–69.
1943   Relations Between Mesoamerica and the South-
        west, pp. 245–52. In *El Norte de Mexico y el
        Sur de los Estados Unidos.* Sociedad Mexicana de
        Antropología, Mexico City.

Bently, Mark T.
1987   Masked Anthropomorphic Representations and
        Mogollon Cultural Ceremonialism, a Possible
        Pacific Coastal Influence through Exchange. *The
        Artifact* 25(4):61–120.

Berlo, Janet C., and Ruth B. Phillips
1992   "Vitalizing" the Things of the Past: Museum
        Representations of Native North American Art
        in the 1990s. *Museum Anthropology* 16(1):29–43.

Black, Mary E.
1984   Maidens and Metaphors: An Analysis of Hopi
        Corn Metaphors. *Ethnology* 23:279–88.

Bloom, Lansing B.
1933   Fray Estevan de Perea's *Relación. The New Mexico
        Historical Review* 8:211–35.

Bluhm, Elaine A.
1957   The Sawmill Site; a Reserve Phase Village, Pine
        Lawn Valley, Western New Mexico. *Fieldiana:
        Anthropology* 47.

Boas, Franz
1928   *Keresan Texts, Part 1.* Publications of the
        American Ethnological Society 8, New York.

Bol, Marsha
1991   Personal communication.

Bourdieu, Pierre
1977   *Outline of a Theory of Practice.* Cambridge
        University Press, New York.

Bourke, John C.
1884   *The Snake-dance of the Moquis of Arizona . . . with
        an Account of the Tablet Dance of the Pueblo of Santo
        Domingo, New Mexico,* etc. Charles Scribner's
        Sons, N.Y. (Reprinted: Rio Grande Press,
        Glorieta, N.M., 1962).

Boyer, Jeffrey L., James L. Moore, Daisy F. Levine, and
Linda Mick-O'Hara
n.d.   Studying the Taos Frontier: The Pot Creek
        Data Recovery Project. Submitted by Timothy
        Maxwell. *Archaeology Note* 68, Office of Archaeo-
        logical Studies, Museum of New Mexico,
        Santa Fe.

Bradfield, Richard Maitland
1973   *A Natural History of Associations: A Study of the
        Meaning of Community.* 2 vols. International
        Universities Press, New York.

Bradfield, Wesley
1925   The Pithouses of Cameron Creek. *El Palacio*
        19(8):173–77.
1928   Mimbres Excavation in 1928. *El Palacio*
        25(8–11):151–60.
1929   *Cameron Creek Village. A Site in the Mimbres Area
        in Grant County, New Mexico.* School of American
        Research Monograph No. 1, Santa Fe.

Breternitz, David A.
1966   *An Appraisal of Tree-ring Dated Pottery in the South-
        west.* Anthropological Papers of the University
        of Arizona No. 10. University of Arizona Press,
        Tucson.

Brew, J. O.
1943   On the Pueblo IV and on the Katchina-Tlaloc
        Relations, pp. 241–45. In *El Norte de México y el
        Sur de los Estados Unidos.* Sociedad Mexicana de
        Antropología, Mexico City.

Broder, Patricia Janis
1978   *Hopi Paintings: The World of the Hopis.* Brandywine
        Press, New York.

Brody, J. J.
1977a   *Mimbres Painted Pottery.* School of American
        Research and University of New Mexico Press,
        Santa Fe and Albuquerque.
1977b   Mimbres Art: Sidetracked on the Trail of
        a Mexican Connection. *American Indian Art*
        2(4):2–31.
1979   Pueblo Fine Arts. In *Southwest,* edited by Alfonso
        Ortiz, pp. 603–9. Vol. 9, *Handbook of North
        American Indians* Smithsonian Institution Press,
        Washington, D.C.
1983   Mimbres Painting. In *Mimbres Pottery: Ancient*

Art of the American Southwest, edited by J. J. Brody, C. J. Scott, and S. A. LeBlanc, pp. 69–125. Hudson Hills Press, New York.

1991 *Anasazi and Pueblo Painting.* University of New Mexico Press, Albuquerque.

Bunzel, Ruth L.

1932a Introduction to Zuñi Ceremonialism. *Forty-seventh Annual Report of the Bureau of American Ethnology 1929–1930,* pp. 467–544.

1932b Zuñi Origin Myths. *Forty-seventh Annual Report of the Bureau of American Ethnology 1929–1930,* pp. 545–610.

1932c Zuñi Ritual Poetry. *Forty-seventh Annual Report of the Bureau of American Ethnology, 1929–1930,* pp. 611–836.

1932d Zuñi Katcinas. *Forty-seventh Annual Report of the Bureau of American Ethnology, 1929–1930,* pp. 837–1086.

Burton, Jeffrey R.

1990 *Archeological Investigations at Puerco Ruin, Petrified Forest, National Park, Arizona.* Publications in Anthropology No. 54. Western Archeological and Conservation Center, Tucson.

Caperton, Thomas J.

1981 An Archaeological Reconnaissance of the Gran Quivira Area. In *Contributions to Gran Quivira Archaeology, Gran Quivira National Monument, New Mexico,* pp. 3–11. Publications in Archaeology 17, National Park Service, Department of the Interior, Washington, D.C.

Carlson, Roy L.

1970 *White Mountain Redware: A Pottery Tradition of East-Central Arizona and Western New Mexico.* Anthropological Papers of the University of Arizona No. 19. University of Arizona Press, Tucson.

1982a The Mimbres Kachina Cult. In *Mogollon Archaeology: Proceedings of the 1980 Mogollon Conference,* edited by Patrick H. Beckett and Kira Silverbird, pp. 147–57. Acoma Books, Ramona Calif.

1982b The Polychrome Complexes. In *Southwestern Ceramics: A Comparative Review,* edited by Albert H. Schroeder, pp. 201–204. The Arizona Archaeologist No. 15, Arizona Archaeological Society, Phoenix.

Carr, Pat

1979 *Mimbres Mythology.* Southwest Studies Monograph 56, The University of Texas at El Paso.

Caso, Alfonso

1958 *The Aztecs: People of the Sun.* University of Oklahoma Press, Norman.

Clark, Robert Judson

1972 *The Arts and Crafts Movement in America, 1876–1916.* Princeton University Press, Princeton.

Coe, Michael D.

1973 *The Maya Scribe and His World.* The Grolier Club, New York.

1975 *Classic Maya Pottery at Dumbarton Oaks.* Dumbarton Oaks Trustees for Harvard University, Washington, D.C.

1978 *Lords of the Underworld: Masterpieces of Classic Maya Ceramics.* Princeton University Press, Princeton.

1982 *Old Gods and Young Heros: The Pearlman Collection of Maya Ceramics.* The Israel Museum, Jerusalem.

1989 The Hero Twins: Myth and Image. In *The Maya Vase Book: A Corpus of Rollout Photographs of Maya Vases,* edited by Justin Kerr. Volume I, pp. 161–84, Kerr Associates, New York.

Cole, Sally J.

1984 *The Abo Painted Rocks, Documentation and Analysis.* Privately printed, Grand Junction, Colorado.

1989 Katsina Iconography in Homol'ovi Rock Art. *The Kiva* 54(3):313–29.

1990 *Legacy in Stone.* Johnson Books, Boulder.

1991 Kachina Imagery in Colorado Plateau Rock Art. Paper presented at "World View and Ritual: Kachinas in the Pueblo World," Recursos de Santa Fe, Santa Fe.

1992 Katsina Iconography in Homol'ovi Rock Art, Central Little Colorado River Valley, Arizona. *The Arizona Archaeologist* 25, Arizona Archaeological Society, Phoenix.

Colton, Harold S.

1940 Exhibitions of Indian Arts and Crafts. *Plateau* 12:60–65.

1959 *Hopi Kachina Dolls: With a Key to their Identification, Historic Background, Processes, and Methods of Manufacture.* (Revision of 1949 edition.) University of New Mexico Press, Albuquerque.

Colton, Mary Russell
1938　The Arts and Crafts of the Hopi Indians: Their Future and the Work of the Museum for the Maintenance of Hopi Art. *Museum Notes* 11:3–24.

Connelly, John
1979　Hopi Social Organization. In *Southwest,* edited by Alfonso Ortiz, pp. 539–53. Vol. 9, *Handbook of North American Indians.* Smithsonian Institution Press, Washington, D.C.

Cordell, Linda S.
1979　Prehistory: Eastern Anasazi. In *Southwest,* edited by Alfonso Ortiz, pp. 131–51. Vol. 9, *Handbook of North American Indians.* Smithsonian Institution Press, Washington, D.C.

Cortez, Constance
1986　The Principal Bird Deity in Preclassic and Early Classic Maya Art. Unpublished M.A. thesis, Department of Anthropology, the University of Texas at Austin.

Courlander, Harold
1971　*The Fourth World of the Hopi.* Crown Publishers, New York.

Covarrubias, Miguel
1946　El Arte "Olmeca" o de La Venta. *Cuadernos Americanos* 28:153–79.

Crampton, Gregory
1977　*The Zunis of Cibola.* University of Utah Press, Salt Lake City.

Creamer, Winifred and Jonathan Haas
1988　Warfare, Disease and Colonial Contact in the Pueblos of Northern New Mexico. Unpublished manuscript. Laboratory of Anthropology, Santa Fe.
1991　Pueblo: Search for the Ancient Ones, In *1491: America Before Columbus. National Geographic* 180(4):84–99.

Creel, Darrell G.
1989　Anthropomorphic Rock Art Figures in the Middle Mimbres Valley New Mexico. *The Kiva* 55(1):71–86.

Crick, Malcolm
1976　*Explorations in Language and Meaning: Towards a Semantic Anthropology.* John Wiley, New York.

Crotty, Helen K.
1985　Masks Portrayed in Pueblo IV Kiva Murals: New Evidence for the Origins of Pueblo Ceremonialism. Manuscript.

Crown, Patricia
1990　The Chronology of the Taos Area Anasazi. In *Clues to the Past: Papers in Honor of William M. Sundt,* edited by Meliha S. Duran and David T. Kirkpatrick, pp. 63–74. Archaeological Society of New Mexico, Albuquerque.
1991　Evaluating the Construction Sequence and Population of Pot Creek Pueblo, Northern New Mexico. *American Antiquity* 56(2):291–314.

Culler, Jonathan
1977　*Ferdinand de Saussure.* Penguin Books, New York.

Cushing, Frank H.
1896　Outlines of Zuñi Creation Myths. *13th Annual Report of the Bureau of American Ethnology for the Years 1891–1892.*

Dean, Jeffrey S.
1969　*Chronological Analysis of Tsegi Phase Sites in Northeastern Arizona.* Papers of the Laboratory of Tree-ring Research No. 3. University of Arizona Press, Tucson.

Dean, Jeffrey S., Robert C. Euler, George J. Gumerman, Fred Plog, Richard Hevley, and Thor N. V. Karlstrom
1985　Human Behavior, Demography and Paleoenvironment on the Colorado Plateaus. *American Antiquity* 50:537–54.

Dedrick, Philip
1958　An Analysis of the Human Figure Motif on North American Prehistoric Painted Pottery. M.A. thesis, Department of Anthropology, University of New Mexico, Albuquerque.

Di Peso, Charles C., John B. Rinaldo, and Gloria J. Fenner
1974　*Casas Grandes: A Fallen Trading Center of the Gran Chicimeca.* 8 vols. The Amerind Foundation, Inc., Dragoon, and Northland Press, Flagstaff.

Di Peso, Charles C.
1950　Painted Stone Slabs of Point of Pines, Arizona. *American Antiquity* 16:57–65.

Dillingham, Rick, Nancy Fox, Kate Peck Kent, Stewart Peckham, John A. Ware, Andrew Hunter Whiteford
1989　*I Am Here.* Museum of New Mexico Press, Santa Fe.

Dixon, Keith A.
1963   The Interamerican Diffusion of a Cooking
        Technique: The Culinary Shoe-Pot. *American
        Anthropologist* 65:593–619.
1976   Shoe-Pots, Patajos, and the Principal of
        Whimsy. *American Antiquity* 41:386–91.

Dockstader, Frederick F.
1954   *The Kachina and the White Man: The Influences
        of White Culture on the Hopi Kachina Religion.*
        Cranbrook Institute of Science Bulletin 35,
        Bloomfield Hills, Michigan. (1985 second
        edition, revised, University of New Mexico
        Press, Albuquerque.)

Douglas, Frederick H., and Rene d'Harnoncourt
1940   *Indian Art of the United States.* Museum of Modern
        Art, New York.

Dutton, Bertha P.
1963   *Sun Father's Way: the Kiva Murals of Kuaua.*
        University of New Mexico Press, Albuquerque.

Earle, Edwin and Edward A. Kennard
1938   *Hopi Kachinas.* J. J. Augustin, New York.
        (Second revised edition, 1971 Museum of the
        American Indian, Heye Foundation, New York.)

Eastvold, Issac C.
1986   Ethnographic Background for the Rock Art of
        the West Mesa Escarpment. In Las Imagines:
        the Archaeology of Albuquerque's West Mesa
        Escarpment, by Matthew F. Schmader and
        John D. Hays. Ms. prepared for Open Space
        Division, Parks and Recreation Dept., City
        of Albuquerque and the Historic Preservation
        Division of the Office of Cultural Affairs, State of
        New Mexico, Albuquerque and Santa Fe.

Edmonson, Monro S.
1971   *The Book of Counsel: The Popol Vuh of the Quiche
        Maya of Guatemala.* Middle American Research
        Institute Publication 35. Tulane University, New
        Orleans.

Eggan, Fred
1950   *Social Organization of the Western Pueblos.*
        University of Chicago Press, Chicago.
1983   Comparative Social Organization. In *Southwest,*
        edited by Alfonso Ortiz, pp. 723–42. Vol. 10,
        Handbook of North American Indians. Smithsonian
        Institution Press, Washington, D.C.
1986   The Hopi Indians, with Special Reference to

their Cosmology or World View, as Expressed in
        their Traditions, Religious Beliefs, Practices and
        Social Organization. Paper submitted in support
        of the 1934 Navajo Reservation Litigation,
        Brown & Bain, Phoenix.

Elliott, Michael
1982   Large Pueblo Sites near Jemez Springs, New
        Mexico. *Santa Fe National Forest Cultural Resources
        Report* No. 3, Santa Fe.

Ellis, Florence Hawley
1964   *A Reconstruction of the Basic Jemez Pattern of Social
        Organization, with Comparisons to Other Tanoan
        Social Structure.* University of New Mexico
        Publications in Anthropology 11, Albuquerque.
1968   An Interpretation of Prehistoric Death Customs
        in Terms of Modern Southwestern Parallels.
        Papers of the Archaeological Society of New Mexico
        1:57–76.
1976   Datable Ritual Components Proclaiming Mexi-
        can Influence in the Upper Rio Grande of New
        Mexico. *Papers of the Archaeological Society of New
        Mexico* 3:85–105.
1979   Isleta Pueblo. In *Southwest,* edited by Alfonso
        Ortiz, pp. 351–65. Vol. 9, *Handbook of North
        American Indians.* Smithsonian Institution Press,
        Washington, D.C.
1989   *Some Notable Parallels between Pueblo and Mexi-
        can Pantheons and Ceremonies.* Anthropology
        Teaching Museum Research Paper Number 2.
        Theodore R. Frisbie, Series editor. Southern
        Illinois University, Edwardsville.

Ellis, Florence Hawley, and Laurens Hammack
1968   The Inner Sanctum of Feather Cave, A Mogollon
        Sun and Earth Shrine Linking Mexico and the
        Southwest. *American Antiquity* 33(1):25–44.

Erickson, Jon T.
1977   *Kachinas: An Evolving Hopi Art Form?* The Heard
        Museum, Phoenix.

Espinosa, J. Manuel
1988   *The Pueblo Indian Revolt of 1969, and the Franciscan
        Missions in New Mexico: Letters of the Missionaries
        and Related Documents.* University of Oklahoma
        Press, Norman.

Esser, Janet Brody
1988   *Behind the Mask in Mexico.* Museum of Interna-
        tional Folk Art, Museum of New Mexico Press,
        Santa Fe.

Ferg, Alan

1982   14th Century Kachina Depictions on Ceramics.
       In *Collected Papers in Honor of John H. Runyon,*
       edited by Gerald X. Fitzgerald, pp. 13–29.
       Papers of the Archaeological Society of New
       Mexico. No. 7. Archaeological Society of New
       Mexico, Albuquerque.

Fewkes, Jesse Walter

1892a A Few Tusayan Pictographs. *American
       Anthropologist* 5:9–26.

1892b A Few Summer Ceremonials at the Tusayan
       Pueblos. *A Journal of American Ethnology and
       Archaeology* 2:1–160.

1894a Dolls of the Tusayan Indians. *Internationales
       Archiv für Ethnologie* 7:45–74.

1894b The Snake Ceremonials at Walpi. *Journal of
       American Ethnology and Archaeology* 4:106–26.

1897   Tusayan Katcinas. *15th Annual Report of the
       Bureau of American Ethnology, 1893–1894,* pp.
       245–313.

1898   Preliminary Account of an Expedition to the
       Pueblo Ruins Near Winslow, Arizona in 1896.
       *Annual Report of the Smithsonian Institution for
       1896,* pp. 517–40.

1900   A Theatrical Performance at Walpi. *Proceedings of
       the Washington Academy of Sciences* 2:605–29.

1902   Sky-God Personations in Hopi Worship. *Journal
       of American Folklore* 15:14–32.

1903   Hopi Katcinas Drawn by Native Artists.
       Annual Report of the Bureau of American Ethnology
       21:3–126.

1904   Ancient Pueblo and Mexican Water Symbols.
       American Antiquity 6:535–38.

1914   *Archaeology of the Lower Mimbres Valley, New
       Mexico.* Smithsonian Miscellaneous Collections
       63(10). Smithsonian Institution, Washington,
       D.C.

1918   Sun Worship of the Hopi Indians. *Smithsonian
       Annual Report for 1918,* pp. 493–526.

1923   *Designs on Prehistoric Pottery from the Mimbres
       Valley, New Mexico.* Smithsonian Miscellaneous
       Collections 74(6). Smithsonian Institution,
       Washington, D.C.

1973   *Designs on Prehistoric Hopi Pottery.* Dover
       Publications, New York.

Forrestal, Peter P.

1954   *Benavides' Memorial of 1630.* Academy of
       American Franciscan History, Washington, D.C.

Franzke, Andreas

1981   Kachina in der Kunst des 20. Jahrhunderts.
       In *Kachina,* 5–19. Badisches Landesmuseum,
       Karlsruhe, Germany.

Frigout, Arlette

1979   Hopi Ceremonial Organization. In *Southwest,*
       edited by Alfonso Ortiz, pp. 546–76. Vol. 9,
       Handbook of North American Indians. Smithsonian
       Institution Press, Washington.

Ford, Richard I.

1981   Gardening and Farming Before A.D. 1000:
       Patterns of Prehistoric Cultivation North of
       Mexico. *Journal of Ethnobiology* 1:6–27.

Furst, Peter T.

1974   Hallucinogens in Precolumbian Art. In *Art and
       Environment in Native America,* edited by Mary
       Elizabeth King and Idris R. Traylor, pp. 55–101.
       Special Publication No. 7. The Museum, Texas
       Tech University, Lubbock.

Geertz, Armin

1986   A Typology of Hopi Indian Ritual. *Tenemos*
       22:41–56.

Geertz, Armin, and Michael Lomatuwayma

1987   *Children of Cottonwood: Piety and Ceremonialism
       in Hopi Indian Puppetry.* University of Nebraska
       Press, Lincoln.

Geertz, Cifford

1973   *The Interpretation of Cultures.* Basic Books,
       New York.

1983   *Local Knowledge.* Basic Books, New York.

Goldwater, Barry

1969   *The Goldwater Kachina Doll Collection.* The Heard
       Museum, Phoenix.

Griffith, James Seavey

1983   Kachinas and Masking. In *Southwest,* edited by
       Alfonso Ortiz, pp. 764–77. Vol. 10, *Handbook of
       North American Indians.* Smithsonian Institution
       Press, Washington, D.C.

Grove, David C.

1970   *The Olmec Paintings of Oxtotitlan Cave, Guer-
       rero, Mexico.* Studies in Pre-Columbian Art
       and Archaeology No. 6, Dumbarton Oaks,
       Washington, D.C.

Haas, Jonathan, and Winifred Creamer

1992   Demography of the Protohistoric Pueblos of the
       Northern Rio Grande, A.D. 1450–1680. In

Current Research on the Late Prehistory and Early History of New Mexico, edited by Bradley J. Vierra. Special Publication No. 1, pp. 21–28, New Mexico Archaeological Council, Albuquerque.

Habicht Mauche, J. A.
1988 An Analysis of Southwestern-style Utility Ware Ceramics from the Southwestern Plains in the Context of Protohistoric Plains–Pueblo Interaction. Ph.D. dissertation, Department of Anthropology, Harvard University, Cambridge.

Hackett, Charles W. (editor)
1937 *Historical Documents Relating to New Mexico, Nueva Vizcaya and Approaches Thereto, to 1773.* Adolph F.A. Bandelier and Fanny R. Bandelier, colls. Vol. 3. Carnegie Institution of Washington Publication 330(2). Washington.
1942 *Revolt of the Pueblo Indians of New Mexico and Otermín's Attempted Reconquest, 1680–1682.* Charmion Shelby, trans. 2 vols. University of New Mexico Press, Albuquerque.

Hammack, Laurens C.
1974 Effigy Vessels in the Prehistoric American Southwest. *Arizona Highways* 50(2):32–35.

Hammond, George Peter, and Agapito Rey (eds. and translators)
1928 *Obregón's History of 16th Century Explorations in Western America, Entitled: Chronicle, Commentary, or Relation of the Ancient and Modern Discoveries in New Spain New Mexico, and Mexico, 1584.* Wetzel Publishing Co., Los Angeles.
1929 *Expedition into New Mexico made by Antonio de Espejo, 1582–83, as revealed in the journal of Diego Perez de Luxán.* Quivira Society Publications, vol. 1, Albuquerque.
1953 *Don Juan de Oñate, Colonizer of New Mexico, 1595–1628.* Coronado Cuarto Centennial Publications, No. 5 and 6. University of New Mexico Press, Albuquerque.
1966 *The Rediscovery of New Mexico, 1580–1594: The Explorations of Chamuscado, Espejo, Castaño de Sosa, Morlete, and Leyva de Bonilla and Humaña.* Coronado Cuarto Centennial Publications, No. 3. University of New Mexico Press, Albuquerque.

Hargrave, Lyndon L.
1970 *Mexican Macaws: Comparative Osteology and Survey of Remains from the Southwest.* Anthropological

Papers of the University of Arizona No. 20. University of Arizona Press, Tucson.

Harvey, Byron III.
1963 The Fred Harvey Collection, 1899–1963. *Plateau* 36(2):33–53.

Haury, Emil W.
1945 *The Excavation of Los Muertos and Neighboring Ruins in the Salt River Valley, Southern Arizona.* Papers of the Peabody Museum of American Archaeology and Ethnology 24(1). Harvard University, Cambridge.
1958 Evidence at Point of Pines for a Prehistoric Migration from Northern Arizona. In *Migrations in New World Culture History,* edited by Raymond H. Thompson. University of Arizona Bulletin 29:2, Social Science Bulletin 27:1–8, Tucson.

Hayes, Alden C., Jon Nathan Young, and A. Helene Warren
1981 *Excavation of Mound 7, Gran Quivira National Monument, New Mexico.* Publications in Archeology 16. U.S. Department of the Interior, National Park Service, Washington, D.C.

Hays, Kelley Ann
1989 Katsina Depictions on Homol'ovi Ceramics: Toward a Fourteenth-Century Pueblo Iconography. *The Kiva* 54(3):297–312.
1991 Ceramics. In *Homol'ovi II: Archaeology of an Ancestral Hopi Village, Arizona,* edited by E. Charles Adams and Kelley Ann Hays, pp. 23–48. University of Arizona Anthropological Papers No. 55. University of Arizona Press, Tucson.
1992a Anasazi Ceramics as Text and Tool: Toward a Theory of Ceramic Design "Messaging." Unpublished Ph.D. dissertation, Department of Anthropology, University of Arizona, Tucson.
1992b Shalako Depictions on Prehistoric Hopi Pottery. In *Archaeology, Art, and Anthropology: Papers in Honor of J. J. Brody,* edited by Melia Duran and David T. Kirkpatrick, pp. 73–84. Archaeological Society of New Mexico, Albuquerque.

Hedrick, Basil C., J. Charles Kelley, and Carroll L. Riley
1974 The Mesoamerican Southwest, Part 1. In *The Mesoamerican Southwest: Readings in Archaeology, Ethnohistory, and Ethnology,* edited by Basil C. Hedrick, J. Charles Kelley, and Carroll L. Riley. Southern Illinois University Press, Carbondale.

Henderson, John S.
1981   *The World of the Ancient Maya.* Cornell University Press, Ithaca.

Hibben, Frank C.
1955   Excavations at Pottery Mound, New Mexico. *American Antiquity* 21(2):179–80.
1960   Prehispanic Paintings at Pottery Mound. *Archaeology* 13(4):267–74.
1966   A Possible Pyramidal Structure and Other Mexican Influences at Pottery Mound, New Mexico. *American Antiquity* 31(4):522–29.
1967   Mexican Features of Mural Painting at Pottery Mound. *Archaeology* 20(2):84–87.
1975   *Kiva Art of the Anasazi at Pottery Mound.* KC Publications, Las Vegas.

Hieb, Louis A.
1979*a*   Hopi World View. In *Southwest,* edited by Alfonso Ortiz, pp. 577–80. Vol. 9, *Handbook of North American Indians.* Smithsonian Institution Press, Washington.
1979*b*   The Ritual Clown: Humor and Ethics. In *Forms of Play of Native North Americans,* edited by Edward Norbeck and Claire R. Farrer, pp. 171–88. 1977 Proceedings of the American Ethnological Society, St. Paul. West Publishing Company, St. Paul.
1985   The Language of Dance: Communicative Dimensions of Hopi Katsina Dances. *Phoebus: A Journal of Art History* 4:32–42.

Hill, W. W.
1982   *An Ethnography of Santa Clara Pueblo, New Mexico,* edited by Charles H. Lange. University of New Mexico Press, Albuquerque.

Hodge, Frederick Webb, George P. Hammond, and Agapito Rey
1945   *Fray Alonso de Benavides' Revised Memorial of 1634.* Coronado Cuarto Centennial Publications, No. 4. University of New Mexico Press, Albuquerque.

Hopi Hearings
1953   July 15–30, p. 111. Manuscript, United States Department of the Interior, Bureau of Indian Affairs, Phoenix Area Office, Hopi Agency, Keams Canyon, Arizona.

Houser, Nicholas P.
1979   Tigua Pueblo. In *Southwest,* edited by Alfonso Ortiz, pp. 336–42. Vol. 9, *Handbook of North American Indians.* Smithsonian Institution Press, Washington, D.C.

Hu-DeHart, Evelyn
1981   *Missionaries, Miners & Indians.* The University of Arizona Press, Tucson.

Ivey, James E.
1988   *In the Midst of a Loneliness: the Architectural History of the Salinas Missions.* Southwest Cultural Resources Center, Professional Papers No. 15. National Park Service, Santa Fe.

James, Harry C.
1974   *Pages from Hopi History.* University of Arizona Press, Tucson.

Jenks, Albert E.
1928   The Institute's Expedition to the Mimbres Valley. *Bulletin of the Minneapolis Institute of Art* 17(20):98–100.

Jett, Stephen C., and Peter B. Moyle
1986   The Exotic Origins of Fishes Depicted on Prehistoric Pottery from New Mexico. *American Antiquity* 51(4):688–720.

Johnson, Gregory
1989   Dynamics of Southwestern Prehistory: Far Outside—Looking In. In *Dynamics of Southwestern Prehistory,* edited by Linda S. Cordell and George J. Gumerman, pp. 371–389. Smithsonian Institution Press, Washington, D.C.

Joralemon, Peter David
1976   The Olmec Dragon: A Study in Pre-Columbian Iconography. In *Origins of Religious Art and Iconography in Preclassic Mesoamerica,* edited by Henry B. Nicholson, pp. 27–71. UCLA Latin American Series No. 31. UCLA Latin American Center Publications, Los Angeles.

Judd, Neil M.
1954   *The Material Culture of Pueblo Bonito.* Smithsonian Miscellaneous Collections 124, Washington, D.C.

Kaboti, Fred
1982   *Designs From the Ancient Mimbreños with a Hopi Interpretation.* Northland Press, Flagstaff.

Kabotie, Fred (with Bill Belknap)
1971   *Fred Kabotie: Hopi Indian Artist.* Northland Press, Flagstaff.

Kaemlein, Wilma
1967   *An Inventory of Southwestern American Indian Specimens in European Museums.* Arizona State Museum, Tucson.

Kelley, J. Charles
1966   Mesoamerica and the Southwestern United States. In *Handbook of Middle American Indians* vol. 4, edited by Robert Wauchope, pp. 95–110. University of Texas Press, Austin.

Kelley, Jane Holden
1984   *The Archaeology of the Sierra Blanca Region of Southwestern New Mexico.* Museum of Anthropology, University of Michigan, Ann Arbor.

Kenaghy, Suzanne G.
1986   Ritual Pueblo Ceramics: Symbolic Stylistic Behavior as a Medium of Information Exchange. Ph.D. dissertation, Department of Art History, University of New Mexico, Albuquerque.
1989   The A. C. Vroman Collection of Southwest Artifacts at the Southwest Museum. *Masterkey* 63(1):12–23. Southwest Museum, Los Angeles.

Kidder, Alfred V.
1932   *The Artifacts of Pecos.* Papers of the Southwestern Expedition 6. Published for Phillips Academy by Yale University Press, New Haven.
1936   *The Pottery of Pecos.* 2 vols. Papers of the Southwestern Expedition 7. Published for Phillips Academy by Yale University Press, New Haven.

Kintigh, Keith W.
1985   *Settlement, Subsistence and Society in Late Zuni Prehistory.* Anthropological Papers of the University of Arizona No. 44. University of Arizona Press, Tucson.

Kornstein, Charlotte
1985   The Southwest and the Arts and Crafts Movement. *West Coast Peddler* 16(188):1,16–19. Whittier, Calif.

LeBlanc, Steven A.
1983   *The Mimbres People: Ancient Pueblo Painters of the Southwest.* Thames and Hudson, New York.

Lambert, Marjorie F.
1954   *Paa-ko, Archaeological Chronicle of an Indian Village in North Central New Mexico.* Monographs of the School of American Research No. 19, Santa Fe.

Lange, Charles H.
1990   *Cochiti: A New Mexico Pueblo, Past and Present.* University of New Mexico Press, Albuquerque.

Laski, Vera
1958   *Seeking Life.* Memoirs of the American Folklore Society 50.

Lebel, Robert
1959   *Marcel Duchamp.* Paragraphic Books, New York.

Lévi-Strauss, Claude
1950   Introduction. In *Sociologie et anthropologie,* edited by Marcel Mauss, pp. ix–lii. Presses Universitaires de France, Paris.
1982   *The Way of the Mask.* University of Washington Press, Seattle.

Lister, Robert, and Florence Lister
1978   *Anasazi Pottery.* University of New Mexico Press, Albuquerque.

Loftin, John D.
1986   Supplication and Participation: The Distance and Relation of the Sacred in Hopi Prayer Rites. *Anthropos* 81:177–201.
1991   *Religion and Hopi Life in the Twentieth Century.* Indiana University Press, Bloomington.

Longacre, William A.
1964   A Synthesis of Upper Little Colorado Prehistory, Eastern Arizona. In Chapters in the Prehistory of Arizona, II, assembled by Paul S. Martin, pp. 201–215. *Fieldiana: Anthropology* 55.

Madsen, John H., and Kelley Ann Hays
1991   Architecture. In *Homol'ovi II: Archaeology of an Ancestral Hopi Village, Arizona,* edited by E. Charles Adams and Kelley Ann Hays, pp. 10–22. University of Arizona Anthropological Papers No. 55. University of Arizona Press, Tucson.

Malotki, Ekkehart
n.d.   *Hopiikwa Panggawuu.* "Say It in Hopi": Language as a Key to Cultural Understanding. Ms. on file, Department of Anthropology, University of Arizona, Tucson.

Martin, Paul S., John B. Rinado, Elaine A. Bluhm, Hugh C. Cutler, and Roger Grange, Jr.
1952   Mogollon Cultural Continuity and Change: The Stratigraphic Analysis of Tularosa and Cordova Caves. *Fieldiana: Anthropology* 40.

Martin, Paul S., John B. Rinaldo, and William A. Longacre
1961   Mineral Creek Site and Hooper Ranch Pueblo, Eastern Arizona. *Fieldiana: Anthropology* 52.

Martin, Paul S., John B. Rinaldo, William A. Longacre, Constance Cronin, Leslie G. Freeman, Jr., James A. Brown, Richard H. Hevly, and M. E. Cooley
1962   Chapters in the Prehistory of Eastern Arizona I. *Fieldiana: Anthropology* 53.

Martin, Paul S., and John B. Rinaldo
1960   Table Rock Pueblo, Arizona. *Fieldiana: Anthropology* 51(2), Chicago.

Martin, Paul S., and Elizabeth S. Willis
1940   *Anasazi Painted Pottery in the Field Museum of Natural History.* Field Museum of Natural History Anthropology Memoirs 5, Chicago.

Marshall, Michael P.
1987   Qualaqu: Archeological Investigation of a Piro Pueblo. U.S. Fish and Wildlife Service, University of New Mexico Office of Contract Archaeology, Albuquerque.

Marshall, Michael P., and Henry J. Walt
1984   *Rio Abajo, Prehistory and History of a Rio Grande Province.* New Mexico Historic Preservation Division, Santa Fe.
1985   *Rio Medio District Survey.* New Mexico Historic Preservation Division, Santa Fe.

Mathews, Washington
1902   Myths of Gestation and Parturition. *American Anthropologist* 4(4): 737–42.

Maurer, Evan
1984   Dada and Surrealism. In *Primitivism in 20th Century Art.* Vol. II:534–93, edited by William Rubin. Museum of Modern Art, New York.

McGuire, Randall H.
1980   The Mesoamerican Connection in the Southwest. *The Kiva* 46:3–38.

McKusick, Charmion R.
1974   The Casas Grandes Avian Report. In *Casas Grandes: A Fallen Trading Center of the Gran Chichimeca,* by C. C. Di Peso, J. B. Rinado and G. J. Fenner, Vol. 8:273–84. The Amerind Foundation, Inc., Dragoon, Ariz.

Mera, H. P.
1934   *A Survey of the Biscuit Ware Area in Northern New Mexico.* Laboratory of Anthropology Technical Series Bulletin no. 6, Santa Fe.
1940   *Population Changes in the Rio Grande Glaze-Paint Area.* Technical Series, Bulletin No. 9, Laboratory of Anthropology, Santa Fe.

Mooney, James
1896   The Ghost Dance Religion and the Sioux Outbreak of 1890. In *Fourteenth Annual Report of the Bureau of American Ethnology,* pp. 641–1136.

Moulard, Barbara L.
1984   *Within the Underword Sky: Mimbres Ceramic Art in Context.* Twelvetree Press, Pasadena, Calif.

Museum Anthropology
1992   Volume 16, Number 1, February.

Nagata, Shuichi
1970   *Modern Transformations of Moenkopi Pueblo.* Illinois Studies in Anthropology 6, Urbana.

Nelson, N. C.
1914   *Pueblo Ruins of the Galisteo Basin, New Mexico.* Anthropological Papers of the American Museum of Natural History Vol. XV, part I, New York.

Nicholson, Henry B.
1976   Preclassic Mesoamerican Iconography from the Perspective of the Postclassic: Problems in Interpretational Analysis. In *Origins of Religious Art and Iconography in Preclassic Mesoamerica,* edited by Henry B. Nicholson, pp. 157–75. UCLA Latin American Studies Series 31. UCLA Latin American Center Publications, Los Angeles.

Norman, V. Garth
1976   *Izapa Sculpture.* Part 2. Papers of the New World Archaeological Foundation 33. Brigham Young University, Provo.

Novak, Barbara
1980   *Nature and Culture: American Landscape and Painting, 1825–1875.* Oxford University Press, New York.

Ortiz, Alfonso
1969   *The Tewa World: Space, Time, Being and Becoming in a Pueblo Society.* University of Chicago Press, Chicago.

Owens, J. G.
1892   Natal Ceremonies of the Hopi Indians. *Journal of American Ethnology and Archaeology* 2:163–75.

Paddock, John
1966   Oaxaca in Ancient Mesoamerica. In *Ancient Oaxaca,* edited by John Paddock, pp. 83–240. Stanford University Press, Stanford.

Parsons, Elsie Clews
1917   *Notes on Zuñi.* Part 1. Memoirs of the

American Anthropological Association, 4(3), Menasha, Wisc.

1924　*The Scalp Ceremonial of Zuni.* Memoirs of the American Anthropological Association 31, Menasha, Wisc.

1925　*The Pueblo of Jemez.* Yale University Press, New Haven.

1930　Spanish elements in the Kachina Cult of the Pueblos. pp. 582–603 in *Proceedings of the 23d International Congress of Americanists.* New York, 1928.

1932　Isleta, New Mexico. *Forty-seventh Annual Report of the Bureau of American Ethnology,* pp. 193–466.

1933　Some Aztec and Pueblo Parallels. *American Anthropologist* 35:611–31.

1939　*Pueblo Indian Religion,* 2 vols. University of Chicago Press, Chicago.

1940　*Taos Tales.* American Folklore Society, J. J. Augustin Publisher, New York.

Peckham, Stewart

1990　*From this Earth: The Ancient Art of Pueblo Pottery.* Museum of New Mexico Press, Santa Fe.

Peterson, Frederick

1961　*Ancient Mexico.* George Allen and Unwin Ltd, London.

Pilles, Peter J., Jr.

1975　Petroglyphs of the Little Colorado River Valley, Arizona. *American Indian Rock Art,* edited by Shari T. Grove, vol. 1:1–27. San Juan County Museum Association, Farmington, New Mexico.

Pond, Gordon

1966　A Painted Kiva near Winslow, Arizona. *American Antiquity* 31:555–58.

Price, Sally

1989　*Primitive Art in Civilized Places.* University of Chicago Press, Chicago.

Quinn, William W., Jr.

1983　Something Old, Something True: A Hopi Example of the Need for Cosmology. *South Dakota Review* 21(2):20–55.

Ravesloot, John C.

1988　*Mortuary Practices and Social Differentiation at Casas Grandes, Chihuahua, Mexico.* Archaeological Papers of the University of Arizona No. 49. University of Arizona Press, Tucson.

Recinos, Adrián D.

1950　*Popul Vuh: The Sacred Book of the Quiché Maya.* Translated by Delia Goetz and Sylvanus G. Morley. University of Oklahoma Press, Norman.

Reed, Erik K.

1948　The Western Pueblo Archaeological Complex. *El Palacio* 55(1):9–15.

Rice, Glen E., and Charles L. Redman

1992　Power in the Past. *Native Peoples* 5(4):18–25.

Rubin, William

1984　Modernist Primitivism: An Introduction. *Primitivism in 20th Century Art,* edited by William Rubin, Vol. I:1081. Museum of Modern Art, New York.

Sahagún, Fray Bernadino de

1953　*General History of the Things of New Spain.* Translated by Arthur J. O. Anderson and Charles E. Dibble, Book VII. School of American Research, Santa Fe.

1976　*A History of Ancient Mexico: 1547–1577.* Translated by A. F. Bandelier. Originally published in 1932. The Rio Grande Press, Inc. Glorieta, N.M.

Sahlins, Marshall

1976　Colors and Cultures. *Semiotica* 16:1–22.

Saussure, Ferdinand de

1966　*Course in General Linguistics.* McGraw-Hill, New York.

Schaafsma, Curtis F.

1987　The Tiguex Province Revisited: the Río Medio Survey. In *Secrets of a City: Papers on Albuquerque Area Archaeology, in Honor of Richard A. Bice,* edited by Anne V. Poore and John Montgomery, pp. 6–13. Papers of the Archaeological Society of New Mexico No. 13. Ancient City Press, Santa Fe.

Schaafsma, Polly

1968　The Los Lunas Petroglyphs. *El Palacio* 75(2):13–24.

1972　*Rock Art in New Mexico.* State Planning Office, Santa Fe.

1975　Rock Art and Ideology of the Mimbres and Jornada Mogollon. *The Artifact* 13:2–14.

1980　*Indian Rock Art of the Southwest.* School of American Research, Santa Fe, and University of New Mexico Press, Albuquerque.

1981   Kachinas in Rock Art. *Journal of New World
        Archaeology* 4(2):24–31.

1990   "The Pine Tree Site: A Galisteo Basin Pueblo IV
        Shrine," *In Clues to the Past: Papers in Honor of
        William M. Sundt,* edited by Meliha S. Duran
        and David T. Kirkpatrick, pp. 239–58. The
        Archaeological Society of New Mexico No. 16,
        Albuquerque.

1992a   War Imagery and Magic: Petroglyphs at
        Comanche Gap, Galisteo Basin, New Mexico. In
        *Archaeology, Art, and Anthropology: Papers in Honor
        of J. J. Brody.* The Archaeological Society of New
        Mexico No. 18, edited by Meliha S. Duran and
        David T. Kirkpatrick, pp. 157–74. Albuquerque
        Archaeological Society, Albuquerque.

1992b   *Rock Art in New Mexico.* Museum of New Mexico
        Press, Santa Fe.

Schaafsma, Polly, and Curtis F. Schaafsma

1974   Evidence for the Origins of the Pueblo Kachina
        Cult as Suggested by Southwestern Rock Art.
        American Antiquity 39(4):535–45.

Schaafsma, Polly, and Regge N. Wiseman

1992   Serpents in the Prehistoric Pecos Valley of
        Southeastern New Mexico. In *Archaeology,
        Art, and Anthropology: Papers in Honor of J. J.
        Brody.* The Archaeological Society of New
        Mexico No. 18, edited by Meliha S. Duran and
        David T. Kirkpatrick, pp. 175–83. Albuquerque
        Archaeological Society, Albuquerque.

Schele, Linda

1977   Palenque: The House of the Dying Sun. In *Native
        American Astronomy,* edited by Anthony F. Aveni,
        pp. 42–56. University of Texas Press, Austin.

Schele, Linda, and Jeffery H. Miller

1983   *The Mirror, the Rabbit, and the Bundle: Accession
        Expressions from the Classic Maya Inscriptions.*
        Studies in Pre-Columbian Art and Archaeology
        25. Dumbarton Oaks, Washington, D.C.

Schmader, Matthew F. and John D. Hays.

1986   *Las Imagines: The Archaeology of Albuquerque's
        West Mesa Escarpment.* Parks and Recreation
        Department, Albuquerque.

Schneider, David M.

1972   What is Kinship All About? In *Kinship Studies
        in the Morgan Centennial Year,* edited by Priscilla
        Reining, pp. 32–63. The Anthropological
        Society of Washington, Washington.

1976a   Notes Toward a Theory of Culture. In *Meaning
        in Anthropology,* edited by Keith H. Basso and
        Henry A. Selby, pp. 197–220. University of
        New Mexico Press, Albuquerque.

1976b   The Meaning of Incest. *Journal of the Polynesian
        Society* 85:149–69.

Scholes, France V. and Lansing B. Bloom

1944   Friar Personnel and Mission Chronology,
        1598–1629. *New Mexico Historical Review.*
        19(4):319–26.

1945   Friar Personnel and Mission Chronology,
        1598–1629. *New Mexico Historical Review.*
        20(1):58–82.

Schwartz, Douglas W. and R. W. Lang

1973   *Archaeological Investigations at the Arroyo Hondo
        Site.* Third Field Report—1972. School of
        American Research, Santa Fe.

Sebastien, Lynne and Frances Levine

1989   The Protohistoric and Spanish Colonial Periods.
        In *Living on the Land: 11,000 Years of Human
        Adaptation In New Mexico,* edited by Lynne
        Sebastian and Signa Larralde, pp. 93–104.
        Cultural Resources Series, No. 6, Bureau of
        Land Management.

Sekaquaptewa, Emory

1976   Hopi Indian Ceremonies. In *Seeing with a Native
        Eye: Essays on Native American Religions,* edited by
        Walter H. Capps, pp. 35–43. Harper and Row,
        New York.

Seller, Eduard

1963   *Códice Borgia.* Facsimile edition. Spanish
        translation, Mariana Frenk. Fondo de Cultura
        Económico, México.

Seymour, Tryntje Van Ness

1988   *When the Rainbow Touches Down.* The Heard
        Museum, Phoenix.

Shepard, Anna O.

1956   *Ceramics for the Archaeologist.* Carnegie Institution
        of Washington Publication 609.

Shore, Bradd

1991   Twice-Born, Once Conceived: Meaning Con-
        struction and Cultural Cognition. *American
        Anthropologist* 93:9–27.

Sims, Agnes C.

1963   Rock Carvings, a Record of Folk History. In *Sun
        Father's Way* by Bertha P. Dutton. The University

of New Mexico Press, School of American Research and the Museum of New Mexico.

Smith, Watson

1952 *Kiva Mural Decorations at Awatovi and Kawaika-a.* Papers of the Peabody Museum of Archaeology and Ethnology No. 37, Harvard University, Cambridge.

1971 *Painted Ceramics of the Western Mound at Awatovi.* Papers of the Peabody Museum of American Archaeology and Ethnology No. 38, Harvard University, Cambridge.

Smith, Watson, Richard Woodbury, and Natalie Woodbury

1966 *Excavations at Hawikuh by Frederick Webb Hodge: Report of the Hendricks-Hodge Expedition, 1917–1923.* Contributions from the Museum of the American Indian, Heye Foundation No. 20, New York.

Smithsonian Institution

1979 *The Year of the Hopi: Paintings and Photographs by Joseph Mora, 1904–1906.* Washington, D.C.

Snow, David

1976 *Archaeological Excavations at Pueblo del Encierro, LA 70, Cochiti Dam Salvage Project, Cochiti, New Mexico, Final Report: 1964–1965 Field Seasons.* Laboratory of Anthropology Notes 78. Museum of New Mexico, Santa Fe.

1990 Tener Comal y Metate: Protohistoric Rio Grande Maize Use and Diet. In *Perspectives on Southwest Prehistory,* edited by Paul E. Minnis and Charles L. Redman, pp. 289–300. Westview Press, Boulder.

Snow, David and A. Helene Warren

1976 *Archaeological Excavations at Pueblo del Encierro, LA 70, Cochiti Dam Salvage Project, Cochiti, New Mexico.* Laboratory of Anthropology Notes No. 78b–e, Museum of New Mexico, Santa Fe.

Spence, Lewis

1912 *The Civilization of Ancient Mexico.* G. P. Putnam's Sons, New York.

Spicer, Edward H.

1962 *Cycles of Conquest: The Impact of Spain, Mexico, and the United States on the Indians of the Southwest, 1533–1960.* University of Arizona Press, Tucson.

Stanislawski, Michael B.

1979 Hopi-Tewa. In *Southwest,* edited by Alfonso

Ortiz, pp. 587–602. Vol. 9, *Handbook of North American Indians.* Smithsonian Institution Press, Washington, D.C.

Stephen, Alexander M.

1898 Pigments in Ceremonials of the Hopi. *Archives of the International Folk-Lore Association* 1:260–65.

1929 Hopi Tales. *Journal of American Folklore* 42:1–72.

1936 *Hopi Journal of Alexander M. Stephen.* Edited by E. C. Parsons, Columbia University Contributions to Anthropology 23 (2 vols.). Columbia University Press, New York.

1939– Hopi Indians of Arizona. *The Masterkey* 13:197–
1940 204; 14:20–27, 102–9, 143–49, 170–79, 207–15.

1940 Hopi Indians of Arizona. *Southwest Museum Leaflet* No. 14, Los Angeles.

Stevenson, James

1883 Illustrated Catalogue of the Collections Obtained from the Indians of New Mexico and Arizona. (Extract from the *2nd Annual Report of the Bureau of American Ethnology*). Washington, D.C.

Stevenson, Matilda Coxe

1894 The Sia. *11th Annual Report of the Bureau of American Ethnology for the Years 1889–1890,* pp. 3–157.

1904 The Zuñi Indians: Their Mythology, Esoteric Fraternities, and Ceremonies. *Twenty-third Annual Report of the Bureau of American Ethnology,* pp. 3–634.

Steward, Julian

1938 *Basin-Plateau Aboriginal Sociopolitical Groups.* Bureau of American Ethnology Bulletin 120. U. S. Government Printing Office, Washington, D.C.

Stewart, Tyrone

1979 The Hopi and Jo Mora. In *The Year of the Hopi: Paintings and Photographs by Joseph Mora, 1904–06,* 3–5. Smithsonian Institution Press, Washington, D.C.

Stirling, Matthew W.

1942 *Origin Myth of Acoma and Other Records.* Bureau of American Ethnology Bulletin 135. Smithsonian Institution, Washington, D.C.

Stuart, David E., and Rory P. Gauthier

1981 *Prehistoric New Mexico: Background for Survey.* State Historic Preservation Bureau, Santa Fe.

Stubbs, Stanley A., and W. S. Stallings, Jr.

1953   *The Excavation of Pindi Pueblo, New Mexico.*
        Monographs of the School of American Research
        18, Santa Fe.

Sundt, William M.

1987   Pottery of Central New Mexico and Its Role
        as Key to both time and Space. In *Secrets of a
        City: Papers on Albuquerque Area Archaeology in
        Honor of Richard A. Bice,* edited by Anne V.
        Poore and John Montgomery pp. 116–147. The
        Archaeological Society of New Mexico, Ancient
        City Press, Santa Fe.

Switzer, Ronald R.

n.d.   *The Origin and Significance of Snake-Lightning Cults
        in the Pueblo Southwest.* Special Report No. 2, El
        Paso Archaeological Society. El Paso.

Talayesva, Don

1942   *Sun Chief, The Autobiography of a Hopi Indian,*
        edited by Leo W. Simmons. Yale University
        Press, New Haven and London.

Taube, Karl A.

1986   The Teotihuacan Cave of Origin: The iconog-
        raphy and architecture of emergence mythology
        in Mesoamerica and the American South-
        west. *RES: Anthropology and Aesthetics* No. 12
        (Autumn): 51–82.

Tedlock, Barbara

1980   Songs of the Zuni Kachina Society: Composition,
        Rehearsal, and Performance. In *Southwestern
        Indian Ritual Drama,* edited by Charlotte J.
        Frisbie, pp. 7–35. A School of American
        Research Book. University of New Mexico Press,
        Albuquerque.

1986   Crossing Sensory Domains. In *Explorations
        in Ethnomusicology,* edited by Charlotte J.
        Frisbie, pp. 187–98. Detroit Monographs
        in Musicology 9. Information Coordinators,
        Detroit.

1992   *The Beautiful and the Dangerous: Encounters with the
        Zuni Indians.* Viking Press, New York.

Tedlock, Dennis

1972   *Finding the Center: Narrative Poetry of the Zuni
        Indians.* Dial Press, New York. (Reprinted 1978,
        University of Nebraska Press, Lincoln.)

1975   An American Indian View of Death. In *Teachings
        From the American Earth,* edited by Dennis

Tedlock and Barbara Tedlock, pp. 248–71.
        Liveright, New York.

1979   Zuni Religion and World View. In *Southwest,*
        edited by A. Ortiz, pp. 499–508. Vol. 9,
        Handbook of North American Indians. Smithsonian
        Institution Press, Washington, D.C.

1983   *The Spoken Word and the Work of Interpretation.*
        University of Pennsylvania Publications in
        Conduct and Communication. University of
        Pennsylvania Press, Philadelphia.

1985   *Popol Vuh: The Definitive Edition of the Mayan Book
        of the Dawn and the Glories of Gods and Kings.*
        Simon and Schuster, New York.

Teiwes, Helga

1991   Contemporary Developments in Hopi Kachina
        Doll Carving. *American Indian Art Magazine*
        14(4):40–51. Scottsdale.

Titiev, Mischa

1937   A Hopi Salt Expedition. *American Anthropologist*
        39(2):244–58.

1944   Old Oraibi, a study of the Hopi Indians of
        Third Mesa. *Papers of the Peabody Museum of
        American Archaelogy and Ethnology* 22(1), Harvard
        University, Cambridge, Mass.

Thompson, J. Eric S.

1930   *Ethnology of the Mayas of Southern and Central
        British Honduras.* Field Museum of Natural
        History, Anthropology Series 17(2).

1939   *The Moon Goddess in Middle America with Notes on
        Related Deities.* Carnegie Institution Publication
        No. 509, Washington, D.C.

Tonkin, Elizabeth

1979   Masks and Powers. *Man* 14:237–48.

Torgovnick, Marianna

1990   *Gone Primitive: Savage Intellects, Modern Lives.*
        University of Chicago Press, Chicago.

Turner, Victor

1968   Religious Specialists. In *International Encyclopedia
        of the Social Sciences* edited by David L. Sills,
        13:437–44. Macmillan / Free Press, New York.

Tyler, Hamilton A.

1964   *Pueblo Gods and Myths.* University of Oklahoma
        Press, Norman.

Vierra, Bradley J.

1987   The Tiguex Province: A Tale of Two Cities.
        In *Secrets of a City: Papers on Albuquerque Area*

Archaeology in Honor of Richard A. Bice, edited by Anne V. Poore and John Montgomery. The Archaeological Society of New Mexico 13:70–86. Ancient City Press, Santa Fe.

Vivian, Patricia B.

1961 Kachina: The Study of Pueblo Animism and Anthropomorphism with the Ceremonial Wall Paintings of Pottery Mound and the Jeddito. M.A. thesis, University of Iowa, Ames.

Voll, Charles

1961 The Glaze Paint Ceramics of Pottery Mound. M.A. thesis. University of New Mexico.

von Winning, Hasso

1976 Late and Terminal Preclassic: The Emergence of Teotihuacán. In *Origins of Religious Art and Iconography in Preclassic Mesoamerica,* edited by Henry B. Nicholson, pp. 141–56. UCLA Latin American Studies Series 31, UCLA Latin American Center Publications, Los Angeles.

Voth, H. R.

1901 *The Oraibi Powamu Ceremony.* Field Columbian Museum Publication No. 61; Anthropological Series No. 3(2). Field Columbian Museum, Chicago.

1905 *The Traditions of the Hopi.* Field Columbian Museum Publication No. 96; Anthropological Series No. 8. Field Columbian Museum, Chicago.

1912 *The Oraibi Marau Ceremony.* Field Museum of Natural History Publication No. 156; Anthropological Series No. 9(1). Field Museum of Natural History, Chicago.

Wade, Edwin L., and Lea S. McChesney

1981 *Historic Hopi Ceramics: The Thomas V. Keam Collection of The Peabody Museum of Archaeology and Ethnology, Harvard University.* Peabody Museum Press, Cambridge.

1980 *American's Great Lost Expedition: The Thomas V. Keam Collection of Hopi Pottery from the Second Hemenway Expedition, 1890–1894.* The Heard Museum, Phoenix.

Wagner, Roy

1975 *The Invention of Culture.* Prentice-Hall, Englewood Cliffs, N.J.

Washburn, Dorothy K., editor

1980 *Hopi Kachina, Spirit of Life.* California Academy of Science, San Francisco.

Wendorf, Fred, and Eric K. Reed

1955 An Alternative Reconstruction of Northern Rio Grande Prehistory. *El Palacio* 62:131–73.

Wetherington, Ronald K.

1968 *Pot Creek Pueblo.* Fort Burgwin Research Center, No. 6, Taos.

White, Leslie A.

1932a The Acoma Indians. *Forty-seventh Annual Report of the Bureau of American Ethnology, 1929–1930,* pp. 17–192.

1932b *The Pueblo of San Felipe, New Mexico.* Memoirs of the American Anthropological Association 38.

1934 Masks in the Southwest. *American Anthropologist* 36:626–28.

1935 *The Pueblo of Santo Domingo, New Mexico.* Memoirs of the American Anthropological Association 43.

1942 *The Pueblo of Santa Ana, New Mexico.* Memoirs of the American Anthropological Association 60.

1962 *The Pueblo of Sia, New Mexico.* Bureau of American Ethnology Bulletin 184.

Whiteley, Peter

1988 *Deliberate Acts: Changing Hopi Culture through the Oraibi Split.* University of Arizona Press, Tucson.

Wichmann, Siegfried, ed.

1972 *World Cultures and Modern Art.* Bruchmann Publishers, Munich.

Wilcox, David R.

1981 Changing Perspectives on the Protohistoric Pueblos. In *The Protohistoric Period in the North American Southwest, A.D. 1450–1700,* edited by David R. Wilcox and W. Bruce Masse, pp. 378–409. Arizona State University Anthropological Research Papers 24, Tempe.

Winship, George P.

1896 The Coronado Expedition of 1540–1542. In *14th Annual Report of the Bureau of American Ethnology for the years 1892–1893.*

Wiseman, Regge

1983 Rhodes Canyon Ceramics. In *The Prehistory of Rhodes Canyon, New Mexico,* edited by Peter L. Eidenbach. Human Systems Research, Inc., Tularosa.

Withers, Arnold

1976 Some Pictographs from Northwestern Chihuahua. In *Collected Papers in honor of Marjorie Ferguson Lambert. Papers of the Archaeological Society of New Mexico* 3, pp. 109–112. Albuquerque Archaeological Society Press.

Wright, Barton

1965   *This is a Hopi Kachina.* The Museum of Northern Arizona, Flagstaff.

1973   *Kachinas: A Hopi Artist's Documentary.* Illustrations by Cliff Bahnimptewa. Northland Press, Flagstaff.

1977   *Hopi Kachinas: the Complete Guide to Collecting Kachina Dolls.* Northland Press, Flagstaff.

1984   The Shalako. School of American Research, unpublished ms.

1985   *Kachinas of the Zuni.* Original paintings by Duane Dishta. Northland Press in cooperation with the Southwest Museum, Flagstaff.

Young, M. Jane

1985   Images of Power and the Power of Images: The Significance of Rock Art of Contemporary Zunis. *Journal of American Folklore* 98:3–48.

1986   Humor and Anti-Humor in Western Puebloan Puppetry Performances. In *Humor and Comedy in Puppeting,* edited by Dina Sherzer and Joel Sherzer, pp. 127–50. The Popular Press, Bowling Green, Ohio.

1988   *Signs from the Ancestors.* University of New Mexico Press, Albuquerque.

1989   The Southwest Connection: Similarities between Western Puebloan and Mesoamerican Cosmology. In *World Archaeoastronomy,* edited by Anthony Aveni, pp. 167–79. Cambridge University Press, Cambridge.

1991   Morning Star, Evening Star: Zuni Traditional Stories. In *Earth and Sky: Visions of the Cosmos in Native American Folklore,* edited by Ray A. Williamson and Claire R. Farrer. University of New Mexico Press, Albuquerque.

in   Astronomy in Pueblo and Navajo World Views.
press   In *Songs from the Sky: Indigenous Astronomical and Cosmological Traditions of the World,* edited by Von del Chamerlain, M. Jane Young, and John B. Carlson. Center for Archaeoastronomy, College Park, MD.

Young, M. Jane, and Ray A. Williamson

1981   Ethnoastronomy: The Zuni Case. In *Archaeoastronomy in the Americas,* edited by Ray A. Williamson, pp. 183–91. Ballena Press, Los Altos, Calif.

Index

Boldface indicates a figure or caption.